KLUWER EUROPEAN LAW COLLECTION – 5

THE RIGHT TO DAMAGES IN EUROPEAN LAW

Kluwer European Law Collection

GENERAL EDITIOR

Andrea Biondi

LIST OF PUBLICATIONS IN THIS SERIES

1. E. Guild: *The Legal Elements of European Identity: EU Citizenship and Migration Law*. 2004. ISBN: 9041123040
2. E. Spaventa: *Free Movement of Persons in the European Union: Barriers to Movement in their Constitutional Context*. 2007. ISBN: 9789041124708
3. M. van Empel: *Financial Services in Europe: An Introductory Overview*. 2007. ISBN: 9789041127013
4. A. F. Tatham: *Enlargement of the European Union*. 2009. ISBN: 9789041124630
5. A. Biondi and M. Farley: *The Right to Damages in European Law*. 2009. ISBN: 9789041124760

Kluwer Law International

KLUWER EUROPEAN LAW COLLECTION – 5

THE RIGHT TO DAMAGES IN EUROPEAN LAW

By

Andrea Biondi
Martin Farley

Wolters Kluwer
Law & Business

AUSTIN BOSTON CHICAGO NEW YORK THE NETHERLANDS

Published by:
Kluwer Law International
PO Box 316
2400 AH Alphen aan den Rijn
The Netherlands
Website: www.kluwerlaw.com

Sold and distributed in North, Central and South America by:
Aspen Publishers, Inc.
7201 McKinney Circle
Frederick, MD 21704
United States of America
Email: customer.care@aspenpubl.com

Sold and distributed in all other countries by:
Turpin Distribution Services Ltd.
Stratton Business Park
Pegasus Drive, Biggleswade
Bedfordshire SG18 8TQ
United Kingdom
Email: kluwerlaw@turpin-distribution.com

ISBN 978-90-411-2476-0

Summary of Contents

Table of Contents

About the Authors

Andrea Biondi is Professor of European Union Law and Co-Director of the Centre of European Law at King's College London, Visiting Professor at the College of Europe and Georgetown University and Academic Member of Francis Taylor Building Chambers.

Martin Farley graduated from King's College London (LL.B.) and the College of Europe, Bruges (LL.M.) and is a trainee solicitor at Lovells LLP and visiting tutor at King's College London.

Table of Cases (Numerical Order)

29, 31, 36, 39 to 47, 50 and 51/63 *Société anonyme des laminoirs, hauts fourneaux, forges, fonderies et usines de la Providence and others v High Authority of the ECSC* [1965] ECR 911 — 103, 156

Court of First Instance (Numerical Order)

National Cases (Chronological Order)

Table of Legislation

EC and EU Treaties

Community Secondary Legislation

Second Council Directive (EEC) 79/32 on taxes other than turnover taxes which affect the consumption of manufactured tobacco [1979] OJ L10/8	50
Council Directive (EEC) 80/987 on the approximation of the laws of the Member States relating to the protection of employees in the event of the insolvency of their employer [1980] OJ L283/23	13, 14, 17, 54, 81, 83
Council Directive (EEC) 83/189 laying down a procedure for the provision of information in the field of technical standards and regulations [1983] OJ L109/8	38
Second Council Directive (EEC) 84/5 on the approximation of the laws of the Member States relating to insurance against civil liability in respect of the use of motor vehicles [1984] OJ L8/17	45
Council Directive (EEC) 90/314 on package travel, package holidays and package tours [1990] OJ L158/59	32, 59
Council Directive (EEC) 90/531 on the procurement procedures of entities operating in the water, energy, transport and telecommunications sectors [1990] OJ L297/1	48
Directive (EC) 94/19 of the European Parliament and of the Council on deposit-guarantee schemes [1994] OJ L135/5	36
Directive (EC) 98/37 of the European Parliament and of the Council on the approximation of the laws of the Member States relating to machinery [1998] OJ L 207/1	47
Council Directive (EC) 2000/78 establishing a general framework for equal treatment in employment and occupation [2002] OJ L303/16	39
Council Regulation (EC, Euratom) 1605/2002 on the Financial Regulation applicable to the general budget of the European Communities [2002] OJ 2002 L248/1	110

Official Documents

House of Lords, Hansard Debates, 8 February 2001	57
Information Notice on references from national courts for a preliminary ruling, 2005 C 143/01	57
European Commission, *Green Paper – Damages actions for breach of the EC antitrust rules*, COM (2005) 672 Final	74
European Commission, *Annex to the Green Paper: Damages actions for breach of the EC antitrust rules* (Commission Staff Working Paper), SEC (2005) 1732	74

Introduction

Anyone who suffers damage should be entitled to some form of compensation. This is one of the most basic tenets of western legal tradition. There may be many functions, rules, priorities, and cases, all of which diverge in one way or another, but the right to ask for redress in tort is a type of action common to all legal systems. Despite various attempts to come up with more sophisticated forms of affording a more satisfactory form of protection, financial compensation still provides an important remedy to guarantee the protection of individual rights and an orderly societal coexistence.

The EU legal system is no exception. The present text aims at providing a straightforward account of how an action for damages works in the EU context. Whilst there are certainly many works on the general theme of the enforcement of rights and remedies, fewer works, however, have dedicated extensive amounts of ink to an in-depth discussion of the issue of the right of individuals to receive damages in respect of breaches of EU law committed by Member States and Community institutions. EU law provides for a variety of enforcement procedures to be used by individuals to protect their rights. Article 230 EC, for example, sets down judicial review procedures that allow an individual to challenge the legality of a measure enacted by the Community. Equally, under Article 232 EC, an individual can challenge the Community's failure to act when it was under a duty to do so. More generally, an individual can protect his or her Community rights indirectly through the preliminary reference procedure provided for in Article 234 EC. While most forms of actions, including those noted above, have the important effect of ensuring that the Community institutions and national authorities perform their obligations and duties under the EC Treaty and thereby enable the efficient and effective running of the Community, generally, they do little to make good the loss that the individual may already have suffered as a result of the Community having introduced the illegal measure in the first place, or the incorrect application of EC law by Member States. It is in this context that Community liability under Article 288 EC and State liability have a significant role to play in the enforcement of EU law.

The present text does not pretend to present a complete treatise of the right to damages under EU law. Rather, and in the spirit of the aims of the Kluwer European Law Collection, it seeks to raise and consider the key issues facing students and practitioners when confronted with an issue concerning either State or Community liability.

The gradual convergence between the two actions of Community and State liability has been actively promoted by the case law of the Court of Justice and in theory it is possible to speak of a unitary 'test' for EU damages actions. Such a test is structured around three conditions laid down by the European Court of Justice (ECJ) in the celebrated *Brasserie du Pêcheur* and *Factortame* case of 1996, namely that the rule of law infringed must be intended to confer rights on individuals; the breach must be sufficiently serious; and there must be a direct causal link between the breach of the obligation resting on the State and the damage sustained by the injured parties. Later, in the *Bergaderm* judgment of 2000, the Court clarified that an action in damages against the Community should be governed by the same conditions. In practice, however, there remain numerous, important differences between the two forms of actions, and separate treatment is still necessary. In seeking to tackle the different actions for damages under EU law therefore, the authors first focus on the question of State liability, and then chart the evolution of the ECJ's case law and the development of the principle of State liability – a concept that is not provided for within the text of the EU Treaty. After having set the contextual scene of State liability, the second chapter addresses the substantive and procedural criteria that need to be satisfied in order for an individual to succeed in a claim for damages against the State. The analysis then focuses on the Court of Justice's case law in relation to non-contractual liability of the Community under Article 288(2) EC, and the procedural and substantive conditions that need to be satisfied in order to bring a claim for damages against the Community institutions. The final chapter concentrates on the relative jurisdictions of national courts and the Court of Justice in relation to actions for damages. Many otherwise meritorious claims have been struck out by the ECJ on the basis that the applicant should have brought an action against the Member State rather than the Community institutions, and, as such, the ECJ (and now the Court of First Instance) was not competent to deal with the case. This chapter therefore examines which claims may be brought directly before the ECJ and which are dependant upon the applicant having first exhausted all national remedies before being able to bring a claim before the Court of First Instance under Article 288(2) EC.

This book was completed in August 2008, at a time when the future of the Lisbon Treaty was still very much uncertain. In previous drafts the authors had, rather hopefully, included the article numbers of the new Treaty and fully embraced the one pillar European Union terminology. It appears that this may have been a little too much, too soon. Thus, the Treaty of Nice numbers have been retained, and the reader is asked for forgiveness for some hopping between the terms 'European Community' and 'European Union'.

As even the most casual of readers will quickly realize, this text is built almost exclusively around the case law of the European Courts. This is for the very obvious reason that the main developments in this area are advanced by judges. It also reflects, however, the slight obsession with judges and courts, shared by the authors, both of whom – one by birth and one by adoption – are common law enthusiasts.

Finally, we would like to thank Katherine Kennell for her help, and everybody at Kluwer Law International, in particular Karel van der Linde, for their support and unfailing patience.

Andrea Biondi, Martin Farley
London, August 2008

Chapter 1

The Foundations of State Liability in European Law

INTRODUCTION

The relationship between rights and remedies in law is tightly woven – without a remedy any right granted to individuals becomes worthless. In fact, it could be argued that rather than the remedy following the right, it is the remedy that defines the right by giving substance to an otherwise abstract guarantee.

This is as true for European law as for any other body of law. The development of remedies has not only been crucial in protecting the rights guaranteed for individuals, but has also been essential for the very definition and impact of those rights. In this context, the remedy of State liability can be seen as one of the lynchpins of the European Union legal order, provoking emotional responses, from being saluted as 'the most important aspect of the principle of effectiveness'[1] to being considered, more controversially, as 'the most drastic example of the intrusion of EC law into national remedies'.[2]

The idea of a State being liable for its wrongs is well grounded in national law. The basic principle of most of the civil law rules on non-contractual liability is *neminem laedere*,[3] as variously interpreted and limited, under which everyone is bound to make good loss or damage arising as a result of his conduct in breach of a legal duty. This principle is the foundation for various rules, the majority of which have been developed by the courts, governing liability on the part of

1. T. Tridimas, *The General Principles of EU Law*, 2nd edn (Oxford: OUP, 2006), at 313.
2. S. Douglas Scott, *Constitutional Law of the European Union* (Harlow: Pearson Longman, 2002).
3. See AG Tesauro's Opinion in Joined Cases C-46/93 and C-48/93 *Brasserie du Pêcheur and Factortame* [1996] ECR I-1029, para. 12.

public authorities – although this particular form of liability tends to have special features given the types of activities for which Member States could be held responsible.[4]

As has often been opined, the role of the European Court of Justice (ECJ) in the development of Community law has been crucial. In the absence of explicit or effective Treaty provisions, it has been the Court of Justice's role to ensure the viability of the legal system framed by the Treaties. To ensure the effectiveness of the legal system, the Court has been charged with elucidating the framework put in place by the Treaty. It has done so by creating mechanisms that would, on the one hand, ensure full compliance by Member States of their obligations under EU law, and, on the other hand, guarantee remedies for individuals whose rights may be infringed. The principle of State liability is one of the many examples of the purposive and strident approach of the ECJ (not the political institutions) to ensure the efficacy of European law throughout the European Union. State liability in a nutshell is the principle by which Member States will be liable in damages for breaches of EU law attributable to them. This definition leaves a lot of questions unanswered, including: What is the basis for this liability? Which acts are attributable to Member States? And what are the parameters and conditions for liability? Before attempting to provide answers to these and other questions, it is first necessary to provide an overview of the state of play of remedies available to enforce EU rights.

1. THE ENFORCEMENT OF EU RIGHTS

The Treaty itself provides for two main procedures for the exercise of direct control by the ECJ over the actions or inactions of Member States. Under Article 226 EC, the European Commission can initiate an action against a Member State that has breached its Community obligations, and under Article 227 EC a Member State can bring the same action. In practice, the latter method has proved totally ineffective, as political considerations militated against direct confrontation between Member States themselves. It became apparent, however, as noted by some,[5] that even Article 226's judgments were not being complied with by Member States, particularly in the case of a failure by a Member State to implement a directive. The inertia of the Member States was to some extent exacerbated by the limited powers available to the ECJ to enforce its judgments. Member States were required to take all 'necessary measures to comply with a judgment of the Court of Justice', but it was only after Maastricht, with the insertion of a specific new article (Article 228

4. For an essential understanding of the relevant rules in the various Member States, see F. Schockweiler, G. Wivenes and J.M. Godart, *Le regime de la responsabilité extra-contractuelle du fait d'actes juridiques dans la Communauté européenne* (1990) Revue Trimestrielle de Droit Européen, 26.
5. D. Curtin, 'Directives: The Effectiveness of Judicial Protection of Individual Rights', *CMLRev.* 27 (1990): 709.

EC), that the Court was empowered to sanction a Member State financially for a subsequent failure to follow a judgment.[6]

Apart from those Treaty provisions, the enforcement of EU rights relies instead on national legal systems. The ECJ itself has always emphasized the role played by national law, and has consistently ruled that the Treaty was not intended to create new remedies in the national courts to ensure the observance of EU law other than those already laid down by national law:

> [I]n the absence of Community rules governing the matter, it is for the domestic legal system of each Member State to designate the courts and tribunals having jurisdiction and to lay down the detailed procedural rules governing actions for safeguarding rights which individuals derive from Community law.[7]

Nonetheless, the Court itself has developed certain principles and tools capable of providing for alternatives to the perceived lack of efficient supranational enforcement mechanisms. The following paragraphs will attempt to summarize the main features of the system of judicial protection in EU law.

1.1. Direct Effect, Supremacy and Indirect Effect: Court Developed Principles

Even in the absence of effective Treaty mechanisms, the development of the principles of supremacy and direct effect in the Court's early case law[8] became integral to the functioning of the European legal order. The principle of direct effect meant that individuals had the right to invoke Community law in their national courts to challenge or evade the application of inconsistent national law. The principle of supremacy addressed the ensuing conflict, and represents what may be termed as a 'legal revolution' in some Member States' domestic law – where there was a conflict, European law would prevail, even where the national constitution was involved.[9]

The case law on supremacy and direct effect speaks in the language of rights. As is all too well known, the Court famously held in *Van Gend en Loos* that

> [t]he Community constitutes a new legal order of international law for the benefit of which the states have limited their sovereign rights, albeit within limited fields, and the subjects of which comprise not only Member States but

6. For a discussion on the relationship between liability and the penalty procedure see Ch. 2 below.
7. Case 158/80 *Rewe-Handelsgesellschaft Nord mbH v. Hauptzollamt Kiel* [1981] ECR 1805, para. 44.
8. Case 26/62 *NV Algemene Transport- en Expeditie Onderneming van Gend & Loos v Netherlands Inland Revenue Administration* [1963] ECR 3.
9. Case 11/70 *Internationale Handelsgesellschaft mbH v. Einfuhr- und Vorratssttelle für Getreide und Futtermittel* [1970] ECR 1125.

> also their nationals. Independently of the legislation of Member States, Community law therefore not only imposes obligations on individuals but is also intended to confer upon them rights that become part of their legal heritage. These rights arise not only where they are expressly granted by the Treaty, but also by reason of obligations which the Treaty imposes in a clearly defined way upon individuals as well as upon the Member States and upon the Institutions of the Community.[10]

The Court of Justice's reasoning, however, not only placed the rights of individuals centre stage, but, by assuming that the Treaty had to be considered as 'something' different from a standard international agreement creating mutual obligations between the contracting parties, allowed direct effect to be *presumed as the rule and not the exception.*[11] It is arguable that the Court simply used a clever circular form of reasoning (it is a new legal order because it produced direct effect and it produces direct effect because it is a new legal order), but the fact remains that the interpretation given by the Court is firmly based on the assumption that all of the Treaty provisions are capable of producing direct effect, although it may still be possible to demonstrate that certain provisions are not. In other words, the Court had established the direct effect concept '*as a general operational principle of the Community system*'.[12]

Therefore, the question of the mechanisms that have to be adopted to make a Treaty provision fully operational is central. The Court's quest for the effective application of the Treaty is clear from the reply it gave in *Van Gend en Loos* to the argument presented by Member States that the allegations of a possible breach of European law had to be brought by the Commission under the specific procedure of Article 169 EEC (now Article 226 EC) and not by individuals. The Court replied:

> The fact that under this Article it is the Member States who are made the subject of the negative obligation does not imply that their nationals cannot benefit from this obligation. In addition the argument based on articles 169 and 170 of the Treaty put forward by the three governments which have submitted observations to the Court in their statements of case is misconceived. The fact that these articles of the Treaty enable the Commission and the Member States to bring before the Court a State which has not fulfilled its obligations does not mean that individuals cannot plead these obligations, should the occasion arise, before a national court, any more than the fact that the Treaty places at the disposal of the Commission ways of ensuring that obligations imposed upon those subject to the Treaty are observed, precludes the possibility, in actions between individuals before a national court,

10. Case 26/62 *van Gend & Loos* [1963] ECR 3, at p. 12.
11. B. de Witte, 'Direct Effect, Supremacy and the Nature of the Legal Order', in *The Evolution of EU Law*, eds P Craig & G de Búrca (Oxford: OUP, 1999), 177.
12. E. Stein, 'Lawyers, Judges and the Making of a Transnational Constitution', *American Journal of International Law* 75, no. 1 (1981): 10.

> of pleading infringements of these obligations. A restriction of the guarantees against an infringement of article 12 by Member States to the procedures under article 169 and 170 would remove all direct legal protection of the individual rights of their nationals. There is the risk that recourse to the procedure under these articles would be ineffective if it were to occur after the implementation of a national decision taken contrary to the provisions of the Treaty. The vigilance of individuals concerned to protect their rights amounts to an effective supervision in addition to the supervision entrusted by articles 169 and 170 to the diligence of the Commission and of the Member States.[13]

This idea of supplementary supervision that can be exercised by individuals reflects the very pragmatic approach adopted by the Court. The principle of direct effect has then to be considered as an unwritten principle which has been necessarily implied by the Treaty and is functionally indispensable for the very existence of the Community and for the achievement of the objectives laid down by the Member States in the Treaty.[14] The same argument applies of course to supremacy. As De Witte writes 'the only decisive argument for supremacy is the effet util argument – if states accept legal duties at the international level they should be prepared to allow for the translation of those international duties into daily practice, by means of judicial and other instruments'.[15]

Another dimension of the direct effect/supremacy evolution is also of note. Although the focus of both doctrines is the right of the individual, coupled with the idea of effective enforcement, those doctrines also involve the imposition of specific obligations placed on national courts. In particular, in the *Simmenthal* case, the ECJ explained that there are specific and detailed consequences of according precedence to EU law:

> Every national court must, in a case within its jurisdiction, apply Community law in its entirety and protect rights which the latter confers on individuals and must accordingly set aside any provision of national law which may conflict with it, whether prior or subsequent to the Community rule. Accordingly any provision of a national legal system and any legislative, administrative or judicial practice which might impair the effectiveness of Community law by withholding from the national court having jurisdiction to apply such law the power to do everything necessary at the moment of its application to set aside national legislative provisions which might prevent Community rules from having full force and effect are incompatible with those requirements which are the very essence of Community law.[16]

---

13. Case 26/62 *van Gend & Loos* [1963] ECR 3, at p. 13.
14. E Stein, 'Toward Supremacy of Treaty-Constitution by Judicial Fiat: On the Margin of the Costa Case', *Michigan Law Review* 63 (1965): 491, 511.
15. B. de Witte, 'Direct Effect, Supremacy and the Nature of the Legal Order', in *The Evolution of EU Law*, eds P Craig & G de Búrca (OUP, Oxford, 1999), 183.
16. Case C-92/78 *Simmenthal SpA v. Commission* [1979] ECR 777, para. 21-22.

Furthermore, in *Factortame I*,[17] when faced with national procedural rules barring the provision of interim relief, the ECJ commented that

> [i]n accordance with the case-law of the Court, it is for the national courts, in application of the principle of cooperation laid down in Article 5 of the EEC Treaty (now Article 10EC), to ensure the legal protection which persons derive from the direct effect of provisions of Community law.[18]

Although the principles of direct effect and supremacy were accepted in the main by national courts,[19] they also proved insufficient to secure the full enforcement of Community law in all cases. The conditions for direct effect as further elaborated by the ECJ were that the Community provisions be clear, precise and unconditional. Where these conditions were not satisfied, the provision could not be relied on by individuals in front of their national courts. The concept, although crucial to the Community legal system as we know it today, fell short in a number of respects. First, the conditions for direct effect could not be fulfilled in all circumstances, and even where those conditions were fulfilled, the shortcomings of the national law would still remain, leaving litigants in a state of uncertainty. Second, there was the problem of directives. These were deemed by the Treaty to be '*binding, as to the result to be achieved, upon each Member State to which it is addressed, but shall leave to the national authorities the choice of form and methods*'.[20] The Court, using arguments based on the nature of directives, the obligation for Member States set out in Article 10 EC and in the logic of *effet util*, found a basis for the vertical direct effect of directives.[21] They could therefore be enforced against public bodies. The Court did not, however, succeed in ensuring horizontal direct effect of directives.[22] An anomaly was thus created between the protection individuals received, depending on whether they were claiming a right against a public or private body. Although the Court aimed to construe the concept of a public body as widely as possible,[23] in cases involving two private parties the Court confirmed again and again that individuals could not rely on the provisions of a directive.[24] This deficiency was tempered by the introduction of the principle of indirect effect developed in *Von Colson*[25] and expanded in *Marleasing*,[26] whereby

17. Case C-213/89 *R. v. Secretary of State for Transport Ex p. Factortame Ltd* [1990] ECR I-2433.
18. Ibid., para. 19-20.
19. *R. v Secretary of State for Transport Ex p. Factortame Ltd (No.2)*, House of Lords, [1990] 3 C.M.L.R. 375.
20. Art 249 EC.
21. Case C-41/74 *Van Duyn v. Home Office* [1974] ECR 1337.
22. Case C-152/84 *Marshall v. Southampton and South-West Hampshire Area Health Authority* [1986] ECR 723.
23. Case 103/88 *Fratelli Costanzo SpA v. Comune di Milano* [1989] ECR 1839.
24. See Case C-91/92 *Paola Faccini Dori v. Recreb Srl.* [1994] ECR I-3325; and Case C-316/93 *Vaneetveld v. Le Foyer* [1994] ECR I-763.
25. Case C-14/83 *Von Colson and Kamann v. Land Nordrhein-Westfalen* [1984] ECR 1891.
26. Case C-106/89 *Marleasing SA v. La Commercial Internacional de Alimentacion SA* [1992] ECR I-4135.

national courts are under an obligation to interpret national law in such a way as to achieve the results required by the directive, even though it does not have direct effect. After several judgments where the Court itself struggled with very improbable constructions,[27] the ECJ seems now to have fully embraced the principle of consistent interpretation as the panacea for any problems it has with the full enforcement of directives where two private parties are involved. Such a judicial preference has gradually emerged through judgments such as *Carbonari, Ocean Grupo Editorial* and *Centrosteel*[28] where the Court, confronted with rather complicated preliminary references, not only reaffirmed the old *Van Colson* and *Marleasing* principle,[29] but also added new strength to the principle by insisting that the concept of 'consistent interpretation' requires all national authorities, and in particular national courts, to fully enforce the obligations imposed by a directive upon Member States. In other words, according to the Court, the duty of the national court is to do everything possible to interpret national law according to the wording of the directive and in the light of its aim. This duty is just one manifestation of the general principle of effectiveness of EU law and should now be considered a constitutional principle.[30] The reaffirmation of the centrality of this doctrine is further clarified in the *Pfeiffer* judgment.[31] The whole case revolved around the interpretation of the forty-eight-hour working time limit imposed by Article 6 of Directive 93/104 and its implementation in German law. The Court found that the conditions of unconditionality and precision were satisfied. Furthermore, as for the possible horizontal effect produced by such a finding, the Court reiterated that, especially when a directive lays down clear individual rights, it is the responsibility of the national courts to interpret such a Directive so as to provide the legal protection which individuals derive from the rules of Community law and to ensure that those rules are fully effective. The duty of the national courts is to take into account national law as a whole in order to assess the extent to which it may be applied, so as not to produce a result contrary to that sought by the directive. In particular,

> [i]f the application of interpretative methods recognised by national law enables, in certain circumstances, a provision of domestic law to be construed in such a way as to avoid conflict with another rule of domestic law or the scope of that provision to be restricted to that end by applying it only in so far

---

27. See Case C-194/94 *CIA Security International v. Signalson and Securitel* [1996] ECR I-2201; and Case C-443/98 *Unilever v. Central Food* [2000] ECR I-7535.
28. Case C-131/97 *Carbonari and Others* [1999] ECR I-1103; Case C-244/98 *Océano Grupo Editorial and Salvat Editores* [2000] ECR I-4941 and Case C-456/98 *Centrosteel* [2000] ECR I-6007.
29. Case C-14/83 *Von Colson and Kamann v. Land Nordrhein-Westfalen* [1984] ECR 1891; Case C-106/89 *Marleasing SA v. La Commercial Internacional de Alimentacion SA* [1992] ECR I-4135.
30. The ECJ held that such a principle should be considered as 'inherent' in the Treaty in Case C-160/01 *Karin Mau v. Bundesanstalt für Arbeit* [2003] ECR I-4791, para. 34.
31. Joined Cases C-397-403/01 *Bernhard Pfeiffer and Others v. Deutsches Rotes Kreuz, Kreisverband Waldshute* [2004] ECR I-8835.

> as it is compatible with the rule concerned, the national court is bound to use those methods in order to achieve the result sought by the directive.[32]

Pfeiffer once again confirmed that effectiveness, or dare we say the primacy of EU law over national law, applies not only in cases of direct conflict but also as far as 'interpretation' is concerned. The difference is of course that the primacy of EU law, when the doctrine of consistent interpretation is invoked, is 'filtered' through an application of national law and not directly based on EU law.[33] This concept still proved, however, to be insufficient to guarantee full protection of individual rights. Some provisions simply cannot be read so as to be consistent with Community law.[34] Furthermore, such a concept also introduced yet more uncertainty for litigants. In respect of civil matters, where these doctrines have reached their limit, State liability has stepped in, giving individuals the option of bringing proceedings in damages against the State for a failure to fulfil a Community obligation. Intriguing questions arise, however, as a result of the Court's further expansion of the application of the principles of consistent interpretation into the realm of second and third pillar EU measures, in particular with reference to framework decisions.[35] It remains to be seen whether a State liability claim can also be brought against a Member State for a breach of a Union framework decision. As these measures deal mainly with the approximation of criminal law, the mere transplantation of the substantive and procedural conditions elaborated on by the Court for non-contractual liability actions seems somewhat problematic.

1.2. The Development of the General Principle of Effective Judicial Protection

Despite the *Rewe/Comet* assumption that EU law did not intend to create new remedies apart from direct effect and supremacy, the ECJ developed another technique aimed at ensuring the full effective application of EU law before national jurisdictions. In the *Johnston* case, the Court was faced with a question on the interpretation of Article 6 of Directive 76/207 on sex equality, which provides that all persons who consider themselves wronged by discrimination must be able to pursue their claims by judicial process. The Court took the opportunity to declare that the requirement of judicial control stipulated by that article reflected a general principle of law of effective judicial protection. As for any other general principles of European law, the need to ensure an effective judicial control was found in two sources: the 'constitutional traditions common to the Member States', and Articles 6

32. Ibid., para. 116.
33. See in general S. Drake, 'Twenty Years after Von Colson: The Impact of 'Indirect Effect' on the Protection of the Individual's Community Rights' ELR 30 (2005): 329 and M.G. Ross, 'Effectiveness in the European Legal Order(s): Beyond Supremacy to Constitutional Proportionality?', *ELRev.* 31 (2006): 474.
34. As notably illustrated by the case of *Webb v. EMO Air Cargo (UK) Ltd*, Court of Appeal (Civil Division), [1992] 1 C.M.L.R. 793.
35. See Case C-105/03 *Pupino* [2005] ECR I-5285.

and 13 of the European Convention for the Protection of Human Rights and Fundamental Freedoms.[36] This now well established line of case law,[37] strictly speaking, concerned the interpretation of EC measures in the light of the general principle of judicial protection. It creates an inevitable tension, however, between, on the one hand, the claim that no new remedies are needed, apart from those provided by national law, and, on the other hand, the obligation placed upon Member States to ensure the effective protection of EU rights. Such a tension is clearly evident in the case law related to the application of the *Rewe/Comet* principle as well. After paying respect to the autonomy of national procedural remedies, the ECJ added that such autonomy needed to be understood as meaning that the national procedural conditions could 'not be less favourable than those relating to similar actions of a domestic nature nor render virtually impossible or excessively difficult the exercise of rights conferred by Community law'.[38]

Despite paying deference to the role of national procedural autonomy, the Court's ruling serves to limit such autonomy by introducing the two conditions of equivalence and effectiveness. Such a balancing exercise between preserving national competence and respecting the principles of equivalence and effectiveness has given rise to some of the Court's most complicated and erratic case law.[39] Without wishing to reopen the whole debate, it suffices to outline the main aspects of the Court's reasoning in this context. In particular, as far as the principle of equivalence is concerned, the Court explained that to establish the comparability of the two systems – National and Community law – the specific features as well as the essential characteristics of the domestic system of reference should be examined.[40] The specific steps that such a comparison should entail were spelled out by Advocate General Cosmas in the *Palmisani* case:

> First, the claims in respect of which judicial satisfaction is sought must be similar; secondly, the procedural rules on which the comparison is based must not be considered in isolation, but in their procedural context; and thirdly, those procedures must not be chosen at random but must be of a similar kind.[41]

36. Case C-222/84 *Johnston v. Chief Constable of the Royal Ulster Constabulary* [1986] ECR 1651; Case C-222/86 *Unectef v. Heylens* [1987] ECR 4097.
37. Case C-14/83 *Von Colson and Kamann v. Land Nordrhein-Westfalen* [1984] ECR 1891; Case C-152/84 *Marshall v. Southampton and South-West Hampshire Area Health Authority* [1986] ECR 723; Case C-185/97 *Coote v. Granada Hospitality Ltd* [1998] ECR I-5199 and Case C-432/05 *Unibet* [2007] ECR I-2271.
38. Case C-33/76 *Rewe v. Landwirtschaftskammer für das Saarland* [1976] ECR 1989 and Case C-45/76 *Comet v. Produktschap voor Siergewassen* [1976] ECR 2043; Case C-312/93 *Peterbroeck v. Belgian State* [1995] ECR I-4599; Joined Cases C-430-431/93 *Van Schijndel and Others v. Stichting Pensioenfonds voor Fysiotherapeuten* [1995] ECR I-4705.
39. See T. Tridimas, *The General Principles of EU Law*, 2nd edn (Oxford: OUP, 2006), 313 with extensive bibliography.
40. Case C-261/95 *Palmisani v. INPS* [1997] ECR I-4025. See also Case C-180/95 *Draehmpaehel v. Urania Immoblienservice* [1997] ECR I-2195.
41. AG Cosmas's Opinion in Case C-261/95 *Palmisani v. INPS* [1997] ECR I-4025, para. 26.

In short, this means that national procedural rules should not treat Community claims 'less favourably', although this does not oblige a Member State to extend its most favourable rules to applicants relying on principles of EU law.[42] As for the principle of effectiveness, the test devised by the ECJ is contained in the cases of *Peterbroek* and *Van Schijndel.*[43] In these two decisions, the Court held that compliance with the principles of effectiveness should be analyzed in the light of the role of national procedural rules and the basic tenets of the domestic legal system, such as the rights of defence or the principle of legal certainty.[44] In other words, in reaching a decision, the national court has to weigh the nature of the Community right and of the Community rule from which it is derived, the nature and the gravity of the breach and the seriousness of the injury caused, against the nature and the aim of the domestic law provision under scrutiny in the light of fundamental principles such as due process, legal certainty, the right of defence and so on.[45] Although the contours of the application of such a principle are far from being defined, to borrow the words of Advocate General Maduro, the principle of effectiveness does require '*that parties be given a genuine opportunity*' to raise their EU claim before a national court.[46] The application of these two conditions to the State liability principle will be analyzed in due course, but in this context it is sufficient to establish that before *Francovich* the majority of protection afforded to individuals stemmed essentially from the national judicial system, although Community law influenced the parameters of any remedy granted. As Advocate General Tesauro later remarked in *Factortame III*, however,

> far from being a moment of eccentricity in the case law of the Court, *Francovich* was completely consistent with and a logical extension of a value which has been upheld on several occasions without question in Luxembourg: effectiveness of Community provisions and hence complete judicial protection.[47]

---

42. Case C-231/96 *Edilizia Industriale Siderurgica Srl (Edis) v. Ministero delle Finanze* [1998] ECR I-4951.
43. Case C-312/93 *Peterbroeck v. Belgian State* [1995] ECR I-4599; Joined Cases C-430-431/93 *Van Schijndel and Others v. Stichting Pensioenfonds voor Fysiotherapeuten* [1995] ECR I-4705.
44. See in general F. Jacobs, 'Enforcing Community Rights and obligations in National Courts: Striking the Balance', in *Remedies for Breach of EC Law*, eds J. Lonbay & A. Biondi (Chichester: Wiley's, 1997); M. Hoskins, 'Tilting the Balance: Supremacy and National Procedural Rules', 21 *ELRev.* (1996): 365; S. Prechal, 'Community Law in National Courts: The Lessons from Van Schijndel', *CMLRev.* 35 (1998): 681; and A. Biondi, 'The European Court of Justice and Certain National Procedural Limitations: Not Such a Tough Relationship', *CMLRev.* 36 (1999): 1271.
45. W. Van Gerven, 'Of Rights, Remedies and Procedures', *CMLRev.* 37 (2000): 501.
46. AG Poiares Maduro's Opinion in Joined Cases C-222-225/05 *Van der Weerd and Others v. Minister van Landbouw, Natuur en Voedselkwaliteit* [2007] ECR I-4233, para. 29.
47. AG Tesauro's Opinion in Joined Cases C-46/93 and C-48/93 *Brasserie du Pêcheur and Factortame* [1996] ECR I-1029, para. 32.

2. LIABILITY BEFORE *FRANCOVICH*

The state of affairs before *Francovich* was that there was arguable authority that non-contractual liability of Member States could be based in Community law. However, the conditions of liability were to be provided by national law subject to requirements that the protection be 'direct and immediate'[48] and 'effective'.[49] The idea that Member States should be accountable for any violations of EU law provisions attributable to them had been on the agenda for several years. From the very early days of the European Economic Community, the Court of Justice seemed to hint several times at such a possible judicial development. Such a reference is found in a very early case decided under the Coal and Steel Community Treaty. The Court stated in *Humblet* that

> [i]f the Court rules in a judgment that a legislative or administrative measure adopted by the authorities of a Member State is contrary to Community law, that Member State is obliged, by virtue of Article 86 of ECSC Treaty,[50] to rescind the measure in question and to make reparation for any unlawful consequences which may have ensued. This obligation is evident from the Treaty and from the Protocol which have the force of law in the Member States following their ratification and which take precedence over national law.[51]

Another classic reference is usually taken from a case decided some fifteen years later. In the *Russo* judgment,[52] the Italian government was found to have taken actions incompatible with the common organization of the market in cereals by purchasing durum wheat on the world market and subsequently reselling it on the Community market at a price lower than the target price. The Italian producers of durum wheat claiming to be affected by these actions sought damages from the state agency concerned. Upon a preliminary reference, the ECJ pronounced that

> [i]t is for the national court to decide on the basis of the facts of each case whether an individual producer has suffered such damage. If such damage has been caused through an infringement of Community law the State is liable to the injured party for the consequences, in the context of the provisions of national law on the liability of the State.[53]

Other tentative references are also to be found in cases on the application of the enforcement action provided by Article 226 EC. The Court has often suggested that Member States have to take appropriate measures once an infringement of EU law

48. Case 13/68 *Salgoil v. Italian Ministry of Foreign Trade* [1968] ECR 453.
49. Case 179/84 *Bozzetti v. Invernizzi* [1985] ECR 2301.
50. Art. 86 ECSC, Treaty establishing the European Coal and Steel Community. 1951.
51. Case 6/60 *Jean-E. Humblet v Belgian State* [1960] ECR 559.
52. Case 60/75 *Russo (Carmine Antonio) v. Azienda di Stato per GLI Interventi sul Mercato, Agricolo (AIMA)* [1976] ECR 45.
53. Ibid., paras 8-9.

has been established, including reparation to the individuals affected.[54] As Prechal rightly pointed out, as the Article 226 EC procedure is intended to eliminate any kind of infringement both related to the future and to the past, in cases where retroactive compliance might prove to be difficult, financial reparation could be useful.[55] Furthermore, in discussing the nature of the European Commission interest in pursuing a certain breach, the Court has repeatedly made it clear that a judgment of the Court could be useful to establish not only the responsibility of certain Member States towards the Community and other Member States, but to private parties as well.[56]

All these rulings are, of course, rather laconic and thus susceptible to different interpretations. The general consensus seemed to be that the Court was merely referring to the possibility that an action for reparation could have been brought as a matter of national law.[57] However, it is arguable that the reference to national law meant that, whilst there was a general principle of liability, its procedural condition had to be left to national systems.[58] Given the possibility of multiple interpretations of the case law, the stage appeared to be set for a case to settle the debate one way or the other.[59]

54. See for example Case 39/72 *Commission v, Italy* [1973] ECR 101, Joined Cases 24 and 97/80 *Commission v, France* [1980] ECR 1319.
55. S. Prechal, *Directives in EC Law*, 2nd edn (Oxford: OUP, 2006), 273.
56. See for instance Case 39/72 *Commission v. Italy* [1973] ECR 101.
57. N. Green & A. Barav, 'Damages in the National Courts for Breach of Community Law', *YEL* (1986): 55.
58. AG Mischo's Opinion in Joined Cases C-6 and C-9/90, *Francovich and Others v. Italy* [1991] ECR I-5357 para. 44.
59. That times were more than ripe for a fuller judicial development is also shown by several attempts made by national courts to address the same problem. See the overview provided by Schockweiler, G. Wivenes and J.M. Godart, *Le regime de la responsabilité extra-contractuelle du fait d'actes juridiques dans la Communauté européenne* (1990) Revue Trimestrielle de Droit Européen, 26. The English case of *Bourgoin SA v. Ministry of Agriculture, Fisheries and Food* [1986] 3 All ER 585 CA (Civ Div) is also often quoted. The Court of Appeal held that damages for breach of statutory duty were not available for administrative acts, legislative or quasi-legislative acts. Although the article of the Treaty in contention was held to have direct effect so as to create individual rights, it was found by the English Court that the Treaty laid down no procedures for remedies and that national law must therefore govern such procedures. An individual aggrieved by a similar breach of a UK law would be entitled merely to the right to seek judicial review of the *ultra vires* exercise of a power and not to seek damages. The Court of Appeal also held that to confine the plaintiffs in this case to such a remedy would not deprive them of an 'effective' means of enforcing the rights given to them under the Treaty. However, the now celebrated dissenting opinion of one of the judges, Oliver LJ, contained a pressing case for establishing a new cause of action where an individual right under the Treaty had been breached. He argued that when a breach of a public duty inflicts loss or damage on the individual he has, as an individual, a cause of complaint. If the law gives him no remedy for that damage then he would not ordinarily be said to have any individual right. See further J. Convery, 'State Liability in the United Kingdom after "*Brasserie du Pêcheur*"', *CML Rev.* 34 (1997): 603.

3. THE PRINCIPLE OF STATE LIABILITY

Despite the early indications that a remedy in damages might be available against Member States where they breached EC law, it was only in 1991, in its judgment in *Francovich*, that the Court formulated a resolute conclusion. As Waelbroeck has noted, 'One must inevitably wonder why it took more than thirty years for the Court to come to a conclusion which seems to be so inherent to the whole legal system of the Community, and in particular to the system of direct applicability and primacy of Community law.'[60] An attempt will be made to explain the principle of State liability within the evolution of the Court's case law on judicial remedies. For the time being, as far as dates are concerned, the timing might not have been entirely accidental. The drive towards harmonization, with the deadline of 31 December 1992 set for the completion of the internal market, not only brought about the adoption of a considerable number of more sophisticated measures, but also made their application to Member States more complicated, rendering even more troublesome the constant problem of effective and timely monitoring and the enforcement of national implementation of the new legislation coming from the Community.[61]

Whatever the reasons for such a 'delay', and although it is always good to strive for originality, it might be useful, in order to attempt a reconstruction of EU law on liability, to start from the beginning: the *Francovich*[62] and *Brassiere du Pêcheur/Factortame*[63] judgments, where the Court first laid down the constitutional foundations, and the procedural conditions of the principle of State liability. In this chapter, these two judgments are once again revisited and their fundamental features highlighted so as to provide a basis for further discussion and analysis.

3.1. *Mr Andrea Francovich v. the Italian State*

As is often the case in EU law, the spark that caused the forest fire developed from a very concrete and specific individual action. Mr Francovich's action centred on Directive 80/987,[64] which provided for the protection of employees in the event of

60. D. Waelbroeck, 'Treaty Violations and Liability of Member States: The Effect of the Francovich Case Law', in *The Action for Damages in Community Law*, eds T. Heukels & A. McDonnell (Dordrecht: Kluwer, 1997), 311.
61. S. Douglas Scott, *Constitutional Law of the European Union* (Harlow: Pearson Longman, 2002), 323.
62. AG Mischo's Opinion in Joined Cases C-6 and C-9/90, *Francovich and Others v. Italy* [1991] ECR I-5357 para. 44.
63. AG Tesauro's Opinion in Joined Cases C-46/93 and C-48/93 *Brasserie du Pêcheur and Factortame* [1996] ECR I-1029, para. 12.
64. Council Directive 80/987/EEC of 20 Oct. 1980 on the approximation of the laws of the Member States relating to the protection of employees in the event of the insolvency of their employer [1980] OJ L283/23.

redundancy. In particular, it provided for specific guarantees of payment of unpaid wage claims. Under Article 11 of the Directive, Member States were required to implement the Directive before 23 October 1983 and set up or designate a guarantee institution to ensure payment of outstanding employee claims in the event of their employer's insolvency. The Italian Republic failed to fulfil that obligation, and its default was in fact sanctioned by the Court on 2 February 1989.[65] Two workers, Andrea Francovich and Daniela Bonifaci, sought to rely on the rights provided for them by that directive. Andrea Francovich had worked for CDN Elettronica Snc. in Vicenza but had only received sporadic wage payments. He brought proceedings ordering the defendant to pay approximately LIT 6 million in the local courts. Unfortunately, the money was not forthcoming, so Mr Francovich then claimed that the Italian State was obliged to honour the guarantees provided for in Directive 80/987 or alternatively pay him compensation. Daniela Bonifaci and others had worked for Gaia Confezioni Srl., which had become insolvent on 5 April 1985. They were owed wages which were unlikely to be funded through the insolvency process, and they therefore brought proceedings against the Italian Republic based on its obligation to implement Directive 80/987. Andrea Francovich and Daniela Bonifaci's case reached the ECJ by way of reference for a preliminary ruling. Advocate General Mischo commented rather dramatically at the start of his Opinion in the case that '[r]arely has the Court been called upon to decide a case in which the adverse consequences for the individuals concerned of failure to implement a directive were as shocking as in the case now before us'.[66]

3.2. State Liability as an '*Inherent Principle*' of European Law

The first question referred by the national court to the ECJ was whether Mr Francovich and the other parties could rely directly on the Directive. Both the Court and the Advocate General came to the conclusion that the relevant provisions of the Directive did not have direct effect, as they were not sufficiently precise and unconditional as to give rise to rights which individuals could enforce in the courts, or to make the State directly liable as a guarantor. Where the Court and Advocate General differed in terms of the direct effect point, however, is in their views on how this answer then framed the terms of the second, straightforward and concise question, posed by the national court, of whether in any event, the individual was entitled to claim reparation of the loss and damage sustained as a result of the failure on the part of the Italian State to implement the

65. Case 22/87 *Commission v. Italy* [1989] ECR 143.
66. Joined Cases C-6 and C-9/90, *Francovich and Others v. Italy* [1991] ECR I-5357 para. 1.

Directive. Advocate General Mischo, in a very elaborate Opinion, inserted liability into the standard effectiveness/equivalence test:

> As Community law now stands, an action for damages brought against the Member State before the national court is subject to the rules of national law as regards other aspects, in particular the assessment of the harm suffered and the procedure, subject to the dual reservation that those rules may not be less favourable than those relating to similar claims of an internal nature and may not be so framed as to make it virtually impossible to obtain reparation for the loss and damage suffered. That means at least that the most appropriate remedies existing in the national legal system must be interpreted in such a manner as to comply with those requirements, and even that an appropriate remedy must be created if it does not exist.[67]

The Court's discussion of the existence of State liability as a matter of principle is rooted firmly in the teleological language and drive initiated in *Van Gend en Loos*.[68] The Court first recalled that the EU legal order is defined by its attitude of creating and protecting individual rights. Secondly that the national courts are vested with a specific task of giving full effect to European law and must protect the rights which they confer on individuals.

Thus the Court held that

> [t]he full effectiveness of Community rules would be impaired and the protection of the rights which they grant would be weakened if individuals were unable to obtain redress when their rights are infringed by a breach of Community law for which a Member State can be held responsible.
>
> It follows that the principle whereby the State must be liable for loss and damage caused to individuals as a result of breaches of Community law for which the State can be held responsible is inherent in the system of the Treaty.
>
> A further basis for the obligation of Member States to make good such loss and damage is to be found in Article 5 of the Treaty [now Article 10 EC], under which the Member States are required to take all appropriate measures, whether general or particular, to ensure fulfilment of their obligations under Community law. Among these is the obligation to nullify the unlawful consequences of breach of Community law.[69]

---

67. Ibid., para. 33. Still the Advocate General did not refrain from providing an indication on how an effective remedy for compensation should entail drawing parallels with the Court's case law on interim relief and Community liability.
68. Case 26/62 *van Gend & Loos* [1963] ECR 3.
69. Joined Cases C-6 and C-9/90, *Francovich and Others v. Italy* [1991] ECR I-5357 para. 31.

These poignantly drafted paragraphs contain at least four subplots: the first two are essentially a review of previous episodes, whilst the second two contain new material.

In an otherwise very rare collective appearance, the Court deploys its most constitutionally relevant precedents: First, the Court drew direct inspiration from some of its earliest, and arguably most fundamental, case law on direct effect and supremacy (*Van Gend en Loos* and *Costa v. ENEL*) by emphasizing that the European Community created rights and obligations not only for Member States, but also for individuals. These rights arise not only from the text of the Treaty, but also as a consequence of the obligations placed on individuals, Member States and the Community Institutions by the Treaty. Second, the Court, by relying on two of the most celebrated cases of its consolidated case law on effective judicial protection, *Simmenthal and Factortame I*, reiterated the obligation placed on national courts to protect those rights and ensure their full effect.[70] On such a basis, the Court moved to the 'innovative' part of the judgment by highlighting the fact that those rights would be weakened – and the full effectiveness of Community law impaired – if individuals were unable to obtain redress when their rights were infringed as a consequence of a failure attributable to a Member State. This conclusion is strengthened when read in light of the obligation placed on Member States by Article 10 EC (fourth plot) to take all appropriate measures, whether general or particular, to ensure fulfilment of their obligations under EU law. In this context the Court drew on its earlier jurisprudence to support the notion that such a duty includes the obligation to 'nullify the unlawful consequences of a breach of Community law'.[71]

3.3. Conditions of State Liability

As for the conditions of State liability, the Court tersely commented that they 'depend on the nature of the breach of Community law giving rise to the loss and damage'.[72] The Court limited its discussion in *Francovich* to the situation in which a Member State fails to fulfil its obligation under the third paragraph of Article 249 EC – to take all the measures necessary to achieve the result prescribed by a directive. In this situation, three conditions would need to be fulfilled to ensure the effectiveness of the rights to be protected: the result prescribed by the directive should entail the granting of rights to individuals; the content of those rights should be identifiable; and there must be a causal link between the breach of the State's obligation and the loss and damage suffered by the injured parties.[73] Although the

70. *Amministrazione delle Finanze dello Stato v. Simmenthal, cit.* 16, para. 16, and *Factortame I cit.* 17, para. 19.
71. Case 6/60 *Jean-E. Humblet v Belgian State* [1960] ECR 559.
72. Joined Cases C-6 and C-9/90, *Francovich and Others v. Italy* [1991] ECR I-5357 para. 38.
73. Ibid., paras 39-40.

action for damages would be dealt with in the context of national law, the conditions set were subject to the proviso that they must not be less favourable than those relating to similar domestic claims and must not be framed so as to make it virtually impossible or excessively difficult to obtain reparation.[74] National law would then designate the competent courts and lay down the detailed procedural rules for legal proceedings. On the facts of the case, the Court found that the conditions in relation to the breach of individual rights had been met and the case was sent back to the Italian court to determine causality and the level of damages.

3.4. The Limits of *Francovich*

Contrary to previous *dicta* of the Court, *Francovich*, in a wider sense, strengthened the argument already developed,[75] that EU law could in fact impose a duty on a Member State to construct a remedy, either where similar remedies did not exist at a national level, or where the national remedy would not normally be available to an applicant on the same sort of conditions.[76] The Court also made it clear that this remedy did not depend on the provision in question having a direct effect. Some saw this as the breakthrough of *Francovich*.[77] It is of note, however, that there was some ambiguity left by the judgment as to whether this remedy would only be of use when a provision did not have direct effect. The Advocate General specifically framed the question of State liability in terms of a situation in which there is no direct effect, by opining that:

> in the second place, the situation where the relevant provisions of Directive 80/987 are not sufficiently precise and unconditional to be relied upon directly before the national courts; the question is whether, in that event, an individual harmed by the failure of a Member State to implement the directive may claim compensation for the loss which he may have suffered as a result.[78]

The Court, however, did not limit its ruling in this way and held more generally that in the second part of the first question the national court sought to determine whether a Member State is obliged to make good loss and damage suffered by individuals as a result of the failure to transpose Directive 80/987.[79] This difference has led some to question whether the remedy of State liability would apply in cases where provisions did have direct effect. Furthermore, it remained unclear in the

74. Ibid., para. 43.
75. As commented by P. Oliver, '*Brasserie du Pecheur/Factortame* Case Note', *CMLRev.* 34(3) (1997): 675.
76. For further discussion see P. Craig, Francovich, Remedies and the Scope of Damages Liability [1993] L.Q.R. 1993, 595.
77. J. Steiner, 'From Direct Effects to Francovich: Shifting Means of enforcement of Community Law', *ELRev.* 18(1) (1993): 3.
78. Joined Cases C-6 and C-9/90, *Francovich and Others v. Italy* [1991] ECR I-5357 para. 32.
79. Ibid., para. 28.

judgment how far this remedy would extend. The Advocate General commented that the principle 'is capable of being extended to cover any failure of Member States to observe Community law . . . whether the failure is in breach of the Treaty, Regulations or Directives, whether they have direct effect or not'.[80]

Once again, the Court's formulation is far broader, where it rules that a Member State is 'liable to make good damage to individuals caused by a breach of Community law for which it is responsible'.[81] Did the remedy only apply where there was a total failure to implement a directive or could damages be sought for other types of breaches, such as where implementation measures have been adopted, but they are faulty or inadequate? There may also be different actors responsible for the breach – legislative, executive, or even judicial. It was also far from clear whether the breach of an EU norm needs to have been established by the Court under Articles 226, 227 or 234 EC procedures – which was the case in *Francovich* – or whether liability could be established without such a pronouncement. The Court limits itself to a discussion of the broad conditions applicable, but only in the case where a directive is not implemented. No specific conditions on how an action of damages should be governed were mentioned. Presumably those conditions had to be left to national law, provided that the claimants were not placed in a disadvantageous position compared to similar claims which might arise in a purely national context, or that this did not render compensation practically impossible or excessively difficult to obtain. This still leaves an enormous amount of room for manoeuvre. While there are similarities between the Member States' domestic laws relating to non-contractual State liability, there are also important differences. *Francovich* left a series of unanswered questions in this regard – if the imposition of State liability is in the name of the effective enforcement of individual rights, some degree of uniformity would seem to be required. The principles guiding such application of State liability, it is argued, should surely reflect the special nature of Community law:

> Member States obligations to implement Community law are not the same as public authorities duties under national law; nor are they analogous to those of Community institutions. In implementing Community obligations Member States are carrying out a unique function, in a unique institutional context. These factors must therefore shape the appropriate rules.[82]

There was also doubt concerning the relevance of rules relating to Community non-contractual liability set out in Article 288 EC. Advocate General Mischo argued in particular that in general, Member States should not be liable except on the same

80. AG Mischo's Opinion in Joined Cases C-6 and C 9/90 *Francovich and others v. Italy* [1991] ECR I-5357, para. 85.
81. Ibid., para. 37.
82. See J Steiner, 'From Direct Effects to Francovich: Shifting Means of enforcement of Community Law', *ELRev.* 18(1) (1993): 3 at 7.

conditions as the Community itself would be liable under Article 288 EC. The Court, however, did not give any support in its judgment to the suggestion that State liability for breaches of EU law should be aligned with the Community's non-contractual liability under the second paragraph of Article 288 EC.[83]

4. THE CLARIFICATION OF THE STATE LIABILITY PRINCIPLE IN *BRASSERIE DU PÊCHEUR/FACTORTAME*

Most of the above questions were answered, or at least partly answered, in the case of *Brasserie du Pêcheur/Factortame*.[84]

4.1. Facts

4.1.1. The *Factortame* Affair

The Merchant Shipping Act 1988 provided for the establishment of a new register in which all British fishing vessels were to be registered, including those which were already registered in the old general register maintained under the Merchant Shipping Act 1894. Only fishing vessels fulfilling the conditions laid down in Section 14 of the 1988 Act could, however, be registered in the new register. Paragraph 1 of that section provided that a fishing vessel was only eligible to be registered in the new register if the vessel was British-owned. According to Section 14(2), a fishing vessel was deemed to be British-owned if the legal title to the vessel was vested wholly in one or more qualified persons or companies, and if the vessel was beneficially owned by one or more qualified companies or, as to not less than 75%, by one or more qualified persons. According to Section 14(7), 'qualified person' meant a person who was a British citizen and resident domiciled in the United Kingdom, and 'qualified company' meant a company incorporated in the United Kingdom and having its principal place of business there, with at least 75% of its shares being owned by one or more qualified persons or companies, and at least 75% of its directors being qualified persons.

In *Factortame* the applicant, a Spanish company, together with other owners and operators of fishing vessels which were registered in the UK prior to the enactment of the 1988 Act, but which were originally registered in Spain and flew the Spanish flag, and therefore did not satisfy Section 14(2) of the 1988 Act, contended that these conditions, relating to nationality, residence and domicile of the owners of the vessels, were contrary to EU law and therefore invalid. On 10 March 1989, the English High Court decided to stay the proceedings and to make a reference for a preliminary ruling on whether the provisions of the

83. See below Ch. 3.
84. AG Tesauro's Opinion in Joined Cases C-46/93 and C-48/93 *Brasserie du Pêcheur and Factortame* [1996] ECR I-1029, para. 12.

Merchant Shipping Act 1988 were compatible with Community law. The High Court also ordered, by way of interim relief, that the application of Part II of the 1988 Act should be suspended as regards the applicants.

On 13 March 1989, the Secretary of State for Transport appealed against the High Court's order granting interim relief and by judgment of 22 March 1989, the Court of Appeal quashed the interim injunction. Following this decision, the applicant fishermen appealed to the House of Lords, which referred a second question to the Court of Justice, namely whether it was obliged to grant an interim injunction in the circumstances. This action conflicted with national precedent on two counts. First, there was an old common-law rule that injunctive relief could not be given against the Crown, and second, there was also a presumption that an Act of Parliament was in conformity with Community law until such a time as a decision on its compatibility with that law had been given.

In reply to the questions asked in *Factortame I*, the Court of Justice ruled that the English precedent prohibiting interim injunctions against the Crown must be set aside.[85] As to the High Court's question concerning the validity of the Merchant Shipping Act 1988 (*Factortame II*[86]), the Court ruled that the provisions of the Merchant Shipping Act were indeed contrary to Community law. Thus, Section 14 constituted a violation of the freedom of establishment provisions set out in Article 52 EEC (now Article 43 EC) with regard to vessels that were pursuing an economic activity through a fixed establishment in the UK. Following this second ruling, the applicants brought a further action (*Factortame III*[87]) claiming damages against the UK government for the financial loss they had incurred during the period of enforcement of the Merchant Shipping Act 1988 – some GBP 30 million were claimed for the fishing vessels prevented from registering between 1988 and 1991.

4.1.2. *The Brasserie du Pêcheur* Affair

The action for damages arising out of the *Factortame III* litigation was addressed, together with a similar action for damages arising from the German courts. In the case of *Brasserie du Pêcheur*, a French brewer sought compensation from Germany for having been prevented from selling beer on the German market due to restrictions in the German legislation on beer purity. Previously, the Commission had taken proceedings against Germany under Article 226 EC alleging that both the prohibition on imports and also the prohibition on the marketing of such beer under the designation 'Bier' were contrary to Article 28 EC. On that occasion,

85. *Factortame I, cit.* 17.
86. Case C-221/89 *R v. Secretary of State for Transport, ex parte Factortame Ltd and others (Factortame II)* [1991] ECR I-03905.
87. AG Tesauro's Opinion in Joined Cases C-46/93 and C-48/93 *Brasserie du Pêcheur and Factortame* [1996] ECR I-1029, para. 12.

the ECJ upheld both complaints.[88] It ruled that the prohibition on the designation 'Bier' was in breach of Article 28 EC and was not justified by reference to the mandatory requirement of consumer protection, since appropriate labelling would have been sufficient to protect consumers. Further, the prohibition on imports was also in breach of Article 28 EC and could not be justified by reference to the need to protect public health provided in Article 30 EC. Rather, the presumption of mutual recognition, according to which goods lawfully produced and marketed in one Member State could be lawfully introduced into another,[89] had not been rebutted since there was no scientific evidence justifying the ban on certain additives, and indeed under German law, some of these banned additives were allowed in other products. Following this ruling, and since under German law there was no possibility of redress, *Brasserie du Pêcheur* brought a claim for damages under EU law.

4.2. The Damages Claims

In contrast to *Francovich* therefore, where the basis of the claim for damages lay in Italy's failure to implement a directive, the claims in *Brasserie du Pêcheur/Factortame* arose out of national legislation which was in direct contravention to Treaty provisions. In *Brasserie du Pêcheur* the damage was caused by the failure of the legislature to amend a provision contrary to Community law, and in *Factortame* the damage was caused by the passage of a statute that was inconsistent with Community law. In both cases, there was no possibility of seeking damages under the relevant national provisions. The judgments are complex to read but are mainly divided into two parts: a defensive part, where the Court was strongly challenged by Germany and the UK, and a constructive part, where the Court proceeded to spell out specific criteria for the determination of liability. It is interesting then, to summarize the principal arguments against the inclusion of State liability in the list of the constitutional principles of EU law.

4.2.1. The 'Defensive' Part

The most extreme argument was presented by Germany to the effect that there was no principle of liability of the State, and that because of its constitutional implication such a principle, if it was to be created, should have been introduced by legislation and not via litigation before the ECJ. The Court staunchly reiterated its general statement in *Francovich* that State liability for damages is inherent in the

88. Case 178/84 *Commission v. Germany* [1987] ECR 1227.
89. Case 120/78 *Rewe-Zentrale AG v. Bundesmonopolverwaltung fur Branntwein (Cassis de Dijon)* [1979] ECR 649.

Treaty system.[90] Since there was no express provision for State liability in the Treaty,

> [i]t is for the Court, in pursuance of the task conferred on it by Article 164 [now Article 220 EC] of the Treaty of ensuring that in the interpretation and application of the Treaty the law is observed, to rule on such a question in accordance with generally accepted methods of interpretation, in particular by reference to the fundamental principles of the Community legal system and, where necessary, general principles common to the legal systems of the Member States.[91]

The Court also felt that it was necessary to back up this claim with specific arguments. It continued therefore:

> Account should be taken of the principles inherent in the Community legal order which form the basis of State liability, namely, first, the full effectiveness of Community rules and the effective protection of the rights which they confer and, second, the obligation to cooperate imposed on Member States by Article 5 of the Treaty *[now Article 10 EC].* In addition, as the Commission and several governments which submitted observations have emphasized, it is pertinent to refer to the Court's case law on non-contractual liability on the part of the Community.
>
> First, the second paragraph of Article 215 of the Treaty [now Article 288 EC] refers, as regards the non-contractual liability of the Community, to the general principles common to the laws of the Member States, from which, in the absence of written rules, the Court also draws inspiration in other areas of Community law.
>
> Second, the conditions under which the State may incur liability for damage caused to individuals by a breach of Community law cannot, in the absence of particular justification, differ from those governing the liability of the Community in like circumstances. The protection of the rights which individuals derive from Community law cannot vary depending on whether a national authority or a Community authority is responsible for the damage.[92]

The sources for liability identified by the Court are first, the principle of full effectiveness of Community rules and the effective protection of the rights which they confer; second, the obligation to cooperate imposed on Member States by Article 10 EC; and third, the only specific textual reference to liability that was present in the Treaty – the second paragraph of Article 288 EC dealing with non-contractual liability of the Community. The Court makes it clear that it was relevant to refer to its case law on Article 288(2) EC, in particular, as this provision refers explicitly to the general principles common to the laws of the Member States.

---

90. AG Tesauro's Opinion in Joined Cases C-46/93 and C-48/93 *Brasserie du Pêcheur and Factortame* [1996] ECR I-1029, para. 31.
91. Joined Cases C-46/93 and C-48/93 Brasserie du Pêcheur and Factortame [1996] ECR I-1029, para. 27.
92. Ibid., paras 39-42.

Furthermore, the Court highlights that in the absence of any particular justification, the rules relating to State liability should not differ from those governing the liability of the Community in like circumstances. To do otherwise would mean that the protection individuals received would vary depending on whether a national authority or a Community authority was responsible for the damage.[93] The Court regarded such a position as untenable in EU law. These remarks follow the general line of reasoning developed by Advocate General Tesauro in the case, who also urged that Article 288(2) EC case law was a useful point of reference.[94] The Court underlines the fact that the system of rules developed under Article 288(2) EC takes account of the wide discretion possessed by the Community institutions in implementing Community policies. In the context of Community liability, this led to the principle that where legislative action was concerned, the Community could not incur liability unless a Community institution had manifestly and gravely disregarded the limits on the exercise of its powers. Although Member States do not always possess such a wide discretion,[95] where a Member State acted in an area in which it did have a wide discretion, comparable to that of the Community institutions when implementing Community policies, the conditions for liability in damages must be the same as those applicable to the Community itself.[96] In the context of the case, in both *Factortame* and in *Brasserie du Pêcheur*, the national legislatures had a wide discretion in the relevant areas. They were therefore faced with situations which involved choices comparable to those made by the Community institutions when the latter adopted legislative measures pursuant to a Community policy and the conditions applied to both the Community institutions and the national authorities should therefore be the same.

A second string of arguments made by several of the Member States who submitted arguments to the Court, was instead aimed at restricting the field of application of State liability to very limited circumstances making *Francovich* a one-off decision. Two alternatives were presented to the Court. One was to confine the application of *Francovich* to breaches committed by the 'administration' as opposed to the national legislature,[97] and the other was to make the right of reparation dependent on the lack of direct enforceability of the European norm at issue.[98] Both attempts were unsuccessful. On the first point the Court declared that, because of the constitutional status of State liability,

> [i]t follows that that principle holds good for any case in which a Member State breaches Community law, whatever be the organ of the State whose act or omission was responsible for the breach.[99]

93. Ibid., paras 41-42.
94. Ibid., AG Tesauro's Opinion, at para. 61.
95. As illustrated by the facts in Joined Cases C-6 and C-9/90, *Francovich and Others v. Italy* [1991] ECR I-5357 para. 44.
96. *Brasserie du Pêcheur/Factortame, cit.* 47, para. 47.
97. Ibid., para. 24.
98. Ibid., para. 18.
99. Ibid., para. 32.

Since all State authorities, including the legislature, are bound to perform their tasks in compliance with the rules laid down by Community law, each should be liable. In this way a uniform application of Community law is observed. The damage suffered by the applicants in *Brasserie du Pêcheur* was caused by the failure of the legislature to amend a law that was contrary to EC law; while in *Factortame* it was caused by the passage of a statute that was inconsistent with Community law. In both cases, the national courts were prevented by their own national law from awarding damages. Despite this, the ECJ held that the State was nevertheless liable. National rules on the division of power between constitutional authorities and rules barring such compensation cannot be allowed to inhibit the protection of the rights of individuals and the remedies flowing from them.[100]

The second way in which Member State representatives sought to limit the application of *Francovich* was put forward by the German, Dutch and Irish governments,[101] which argued that the aim of the *Francovich* judgment was to fill a lacuna where direct effect did not apply and therefore, in the present case, which concerned provisions having direct effect, the applicants should rely on that protection instead. The Court rejected that argument and found that State liability is not to be limited to situations where direct effect could not be used as a remedy. Direct effect was to be seen as a minimum source of protection for individuals.[102] Direct effect could not on its own ensure that individuals did not suffer damage as a consequence of a breach of Community law and furthermore, as Advocate General Tesauro comments,

> The Court deliberately specified that the principle of liability is an inherent principle of Community law by a general affirmation of principle which holds good for any situation in which Community law is infringed and not merely where there has been a failure to implement a directive.[103]

---

100. Ibid., paras 34-36.
101. Ibid., para. 18. As Advocate General Tesauro comments in his Opinion in *Brasserie du Pêcheur/Factortame*, para. 24,

    The German, Netherlands and Irish Governments have argued to that effect in these proceedings. They reason that the Community legislature did not intend to establish a general system of Member State liability for infringements of Community law. This, they maintain, is borne out in particular by the fact that the Member States did not incorporate any provision on this matter in the Maastricht Treaty. The German Government has further argued that it would not be compatible with the system of division of powers between the Community institutions and the Member States as laid down by the Treaty or with the principle of institutional balance for the case law to flesh out Community law above and beyond cases in which this is justified by a lacuna in the legislation.

102. AG Tesauro's Opinion in Joined Cases C-46/93 and C-48/93 *Brasserie du Pêcheur and Factortame* [1996] ECR I-1029, para. 20 – see further, in particular Case 168/85 *Commission v. Italy* [1986] ECR 2945 para. 11; Case C-120/88 *Commission v. Italy* [1991] ECR I-621 para. 10; and C-119/89 *Commission v. Spain* [1991] ECR I-641 para. 9.
103. AG Tesauro's Opinion in Joined Cases C-46/93 and C-48/93 *Brasserie du Pêcheur and Factortame* [1996] ECR I-1029, para. 25.

Moreover, the Court had already stated that as far as failure to implement a directive was concerned, the right to redress is 'particularly indispensable' and not solely limited to that context. As the Advocate General notes,

> [t]he – now uncontested – affirmation of the State's obligation to compensate the individual in cases of failure to implement a directive, hence in cases in which the infringement of the State's obligation (infringement of Articles 189 and 5 of the Treaty) [now Articles 249 and 10 EC] can be linked only indirectly to a breach of a correlative right of the individual, implies – a fortiori – that the same protection should be available where provisions are directly infringed which guarantee the individual a legal position appertaining to himself and can therefore be relied on directly before the national courts.[104]

4.2.2. The 'Constructive' Part

The second part of the judgment is devoted to the definition of the conditions of liability. As Advocate General Tesauro highlighted in *Factortame III*, it was vital that the Community set out substantive, as opposed to procedural, conditions to ensure the full and effective protection of individuals' rights. The Advocate General points out that the mere reference to national law would create the risk of endorsing a discriminatory system that would provide differential treatment to citizens according to the Member State in which they resided, and thereby undermine the aim of harmonization and integration. In the case of *Francovich*, the Court restricted itself to laying out the conditions that must be fulfilled in the particular circumstance of a Member State failing to implement a directive: The result prescribed by the directive should entail the grant of rights to individuals; it should be possible to identify the content of those rights on the basis of the provisions of the directive; and there must be a causal link between the breach of the State's obligation and the loss and damage suffered by the injured parties. These conditions exemplify a principle of strict liability[105] and differ markedly from those applied in the context of Article 288 EC on the liability of Community institutions, which are more restrictive. As the Court explains in *Brasserie/Factortame*,[106] the more restrictive approach illustrated in the context of Community liability is due to two considerations. First, the legislative function should not be hindered by the prospect of actions for damages whenever the general interest of the Community requires legislative measures to be adopted which may adversely affect individual interests. Second, in the context of legislative activity, the Community institutions have a wide discretion, which is essential for implementing a Community policy, and the Community should not incur liability unless the

104. Ibid., para. 33.
105. J. Convery, 'State Liability in the United Kingdom after "*Brasserie du Pêcheur*"', *CMLRev.* 34 (1997): 603.
106. AG Tesauro's Opinion in Joined Cases C-46/93 and C-48/93 *Brasserie du Pêcheur and Factortame* [1996] ECR I-1029, para. 45.

institution concerned has manifestly and gravely disregarded the limits on the exercise of its powers. By drawing on those standards, the ECJ formulated three conditions for any action for State liability in European law:

The rule of law infringed must be intended to confer rights on individuals; the breach must be sufficiently serious; and there must be a direct causal link between the breach of the obligation resting on the State and the damage sustained by the injured parties.[107]

5. A FINAL COMMENT ON THE FOUNDATIONS OF THE PRINCIPLE OF STATE LIABILITY

There has been, and there still remains, a lively academic debate on the justificatory foundation of the principle of State liability. Most of the initial reactions welcomed the Court's stance emphasizing its usefulness as both a sanctionary instrument against recalcitrant Member States[108] and a way of enhancing the catalogue of individual rights.[109] Certain commentators immediately identified *Francovich* as a turning point in the development of the European legal system. In particular Van Gerven, anticipating some of the later developments, classified the action of State liability as a true new remedy in EU law, sensing its potential to become a uniform action in tort against public authorities in Europe.[110] Nonetheless, one of the main criticisms moved against the *Francovich* case law has been that such case law lacked a coherent theoretical basis. Commentators pointed out that the judgments are ambiguous and not well substantiated, and that they constitute a rather dangerous intrusion into national law.[111] In particular, Harlow identifies *Francovich* as an expression of an old-fashioned sanction theory of tort law, 'in which liability is seen as a substitute for the more intrusive mandatory or punitive remedies not at the time in possession of the ECJ'.[112] Thus, the case law could be simply explained in terms of judicial assertion of power, or even as an act

107. Ibid., para. 51.
108. J. Steiner, 'From Direct Effects to Francovich: Shifting Means of enforcement of Community Law', *ELRev.* 18(1) (1993): 3.
109. E. Szyszczak, 'Making Europe More Relevant to Its Citizens', *ELRev.* 21 (1996): 35.
110. W. Van Gerven, 'Non-contractual Liability of Member States, Community Institutions and Individuals for Breaches of Community Law with a View to a Common Law for Europe', *M.J.* 1 (1994): 6; W. Van Gerven, 'Bridging the Unbridgeable: Community and National Tort Laws after Francovich and Brasserie', *I.C.L.Q.* 45 (1996): 507. See also by the same author, '*Torts: Scope of Protection, is Commune Casebook for the Common Law of Europe* (Oxford: Hart, 1998).
111. C. Harlow, 'Francovich and the Problem of the Disobedient State', *ELJ* 2 (1996): 199; and C. Harlow, *A Common European Law of Remedies*, in C. Kilpatrick, T. Novitz & P. Skidmore, *The Future of Remedies in Europe* (Oxford: Hart, 2000), 69. See also S. Douglas Scott, *Constitutional Law of the European Union* (Harlow: Pearson Longman, 2002), and R. Caranta, 'Governmental Liability after Francovich', *Camb. L.J.* 52 (1993): 272.
112. C. Harlow, *State Liability: Tort Law and Beyond* (Oxford: OUP, 2004), 57.

of defiance by the ECJ.[113] There are certainly many criticisms that can be levelled at the *Francovich* principle, but not that it lacks 'judicial philosophy'.[114] On the contrary, such a philosophy is clearly spelt out in the two judgments discussed above. It is common to refer to the dictum of Advocate General Leger in a later case that 'there are no general principles which are truly common to the Member States'.[115] While this may be true and the issue of State culpability may have been addressed with varying degrees of sophistication, most of the European legal systems provide for some form of compensation for acts of the State. It is curious to note that *Francovich* is sometimes considered as the odd one out in a legal environment where the accepted rules in national administrative law seem to be linked to the fifteenth century conception of absolute privilege, whereby the 'king can do no wrong'. In reality, the different systems of judicial review of administrative actions in most Member States have been through several important changes to make them more responsive towards citizens' demands and less deferential towards national administrations. For the Court, it would therefore have been sufficient to refer to national law, or more correctly to the general principles common to the legal systems of the Member States, to justify the imposition of liability. This is an interpretative technique often employed by the Court, which consists of trying to identify a minimum denominator between the common, but possibly divergent, European legal systems, and adapt it to the specificity of the European legal system. As is well documented, the main function of the general principles of law is certainly that of filling possible lacunae within the system. At the same time, as has been shown by decades of *acquis communitaire*, they eventually became legal sources on their own with their specific norms and facets. In practice, the Court has seldom made reference to a specific national legal system and prefers to simply express the principle in general terms. An often-quoted passage from an early case is illuminating. In *Hoogovens*, Advocate General Lagrange explained that the Court, when referring to national law, '[c]hooses from each of the Member States those solutions which having regard to the objects of the Treaty appear to be the best or, if one may use the expression, the most progressive'.[116]

It came to be accepted that the EU general principles are constitutional values that can be used by the Court to shape the contours of the EU legal system. State liability is no exception. As highlighted above, the Court, when faced with a challenge to its legitimacy, replied by referring explicitly to the general principles common to the legal systems of Member States and in particular to Article 220 EC

113. Ibid., at 58.
114. There have even been some attempts to provide for a philosophical explanation of the European State liability principles. However, these attempts simply re-use several theoretical or economic models which can be applied to any questions dealing with liability, or in general of the question of tort law. See for instance I.B. Lee, *In Search of a Theory of State Liability in the European Union*, Jean Monnet Working Paper no. 9/99, <http://www.jeanmonnetprogram.org/papers/papers99.html>
115. Case C-5/94 *Hedley Lomas* [1996] ECR I-2553, para. 100.
116. AG Lagrange's Opinion in Case 14/61 *Koninklijke Nederlandsche Hoogovens en Staalfabrieken N.V. v. High Authority* [1962] ECR English special edition 253, para. 284.

and the necessity for the Court to ensure that the law is observed. Of course, Article 220 EC takes for granted that there is a system based on the rule of law that has to be guaranteed. However as Tridimas has noted, such emptiness 'mandates the Court to have recourse to the legal traditions of Member States and extrapolate principles of law found therein with a view to developing a notion of the rule of law appropriate to the Community'.[117]

Despite the different approaches at the domestic level, it would perhaps have been sufficient to use the 'general principles of law' technique to justify the elaboration of State liability. The Court felt that it was also necessary to reinforce the foundation of State liability by referring to the rules on liability of the Community itself. Compensation for losses caused by Community action is governed by Article 288 EC, which provides that

> [i]n the case of non-contractual liability, the Community shall, in accordance with the general principles common to the laws of the Member States, make good any damage caused by its institutions or by its servants in the performance of their duties.

The Community is then liable for both '*fautes de service*' – wrongful acts attributable to its institutions – and '*fautes personelles*' – wrongful acts on the part of its servants. The provision leaves much room for manoeuvre regarding the conditions that must be fulfilled for such Community liability to apply. The elements of non-contractual liability can be summarized as follows:

> By virtue of the second paragraph of Article 215 [now Article 28 EC] and the general principles to which this provision refers, the liability of the community presupposes the existence of a set of circumstances comprising actual damage, a causal link between the damage caused and the conduct alleged against the institution, and the legality of such conduct.[118]

How these concepts might have influenced the shaping of the notion of State liability will be analyzed below. Suffice it to note here that although Article 288(2) EC is particularly laconic on the content of the right of reparation, crucially it refers to the general principles common to the laws of the Member States. Thus, not only is the reference to Article 288(2) EC significant, as it enabled the Court to point out that just as the Community can be held liable, so can its Member States, but it also allowed the Court to fall back on the constitutional context of the general principles of law.

However persuasive the reference to general principles might be, there is no hiding from the fact that the true foundation of *Francovich* and *Brasserie du Pêcheur/Factortame* is based on the early case law of the Court. The constitutional foundations of European law, the need to ensure, on the one hand, the effective application of the newborn legal system, and on the other hand, an efficient

117. T. Tridimas, *The General Principles of EU Law*, 2nd edn (Oxford:OUP, 2006), at 313.

118. See Case 4/69 *Lattice v. Commission* [1971] ECR 325, para. 10; Case T-575/93 *Koelman v. Commission* [1996] ECR II-1, para. 89.

guarantee for individuals' rights, have been the two primary concerns of the European Court's case law. If this construction is accepted, the *Francovich* doctrine is easy to explain. *Francovich* is clearly a facet of the quasi-federal system on which the EU is based. To borrow an expression from American scholars, liability can become a way to enforce federalism.[119] Far from an intrusion into national law, a remedy in liability is simply a way of ensuring respect for the European rule of law. After all, the rule of law has traditionally required western legal traditions to develop a remedial mechanism for instances where legal norms have not been complied with. It has been rightly observed that the case law on the principle of State liability represents the 'high point in the evolution of the principle of supremacy from a general principle of constitutional law to a specific obligation on a national court to provide full and effective remedies for the protection of Community rights'.[120] It should also be added that the distinctiveness of *Francovich* in such an evolution is the link between deterrence and reaffirmation of the centrality of individual rights.[121] This is clearly expressed by Advocate General Tesauro in his Opinion in *Brasserie du Pêcheur/Factortame*:

> What was contemplated, therefore, was the means made available in order to reinforce the effectiveness of Community provisions through the effectiveness of the judicial supervision of the legal interests created by those provisions and likewise in order not to leave Member States' failures to fulfil obligations without – inter alia, tangible – consequences. Consequently, it is precisely in the light of those objectives that the position of the individual has been used and given its proper importance. The State's financial liability vis-à-vis individuals for loss or damage caused by legislative inaction has been created by the Court in the final analysis as an instrument for securing protection for individuals and thereby also the proper implementation of Community law. From this point of view, it has remote roots, both in terms of specific precedents for the liability and obligation to compensate of the Member States and in the more general setting of the effective protection of rights asserted by individuals under Community provisions.[122]

119. See inter alia, C. Vasquez, 'What Is Eleventh Amendment Immunity?', *Yale Law Journal* 106 (1996-1997): 1683.
120. T. Tridimas, *The General Principles of EU Law*, 2nd edn (Oxford: OUP, 2006), at 323.
121. See further A. Biondi, 'Francovich, Fifteen Years Later', in *The Past and Future of EU Law, the Classics of EU law Revisited on the 50th Anniversary of the Rome Treaty*, ed. M Poiares Maduro (Oxford: Hart, 2009).
122. See AG Tesauro's Opinion in Joined Cases C-46/93 and C-48/93 *Brasserie du Pêcheur and Factortame* [1996] ECR I-1029, para. 17.

Chapter 2

Substantive Elements of State Liability: Conditions of State Liability

INTRODUCTION

The conditions which must be satisfied for a Member State to be liable in damages are three-fold: the rule of law infringed must be intended to confer rights on individuals; the breach must be sufficiently serious; and there must be a direct causal link between the breach of the obligation resting on the State and the damage sustained by the injured parties. These three requirements have now to be considered the uniform procedural conditions to successfully establish the liability of the State, and the Court of Justice invariably refers to them in all cases dealing with the issue. It should be noted immediately, however, that the Court itself clarified that there is nothing to prevent national law from imposing less stringent requirements.[1] The following section will examine each of these criteria in detail.

1. CONFERRAL OF INDIVIDUAL RIGHTS

The first condition, that the rule infringed must be intended to confer rights on individuals, is the only criterion that is solely determined with reference to EU law, and thus falls squarely within the scope of the Court of Justice's competence.[2] The cases dealing with consumer protection are a good illustration of the assessment that the Court undertakes as regards the grant of rights to individuals. In

1. Case 46/93 *Brasserie du Pêcheur v. Bundesrepublik Deutschland and The Queen v. Secretary of State for Transport, ex parte Factortame and others* [1996] ECR I-1029, para. 66.
2. C-127/95 *Norbrook Laboratories Ltd v. Ministry of Agriculture, Fisheries and Food* [1998] ECR I-1531.

Dillenkofer,[3] the question was whether the result prescribed by Article 7 of Directive 90/314 on Package Travel, which established that the organizer and/or retailer who is party to the contract is to provide sufficient evidence of security for the refund of money paid over by the consumer and for his repatriation, entailed the grant of rights to individuals.[4] The Directive provided that Member States must bring the necessary measures into force by 31 December 1992. Germany, however, did not adopt any legislation implementing the Directive until June 1994. Mr Dillenkofer and others bought package holidays abroad from two operators, who subsequently went insolvent. While some of the claimants never managed to leave the country, others were faced with funding their return journeys home. Each sought reimbursement of the price paid, or alternatively, reimbursement of expenses incurred due to the insolvency. Their claim against the companies failed. The individuals involved therefore sought compensation from the German government, since they would have been protected had the Package Travel Directive been transposed into national law. The German court referred questions to the European Court of Justice (ECJ) under the preliminary reference procedure concerning the implications of the *Francovich* judgment, in particular whether the content of the rights was sufficiently identified by the Directive. In its reasoning, the Court looked at the wording of Article 7, the purpose of the provisions – the protection of consumers against the financial risks arising from the insolvency of package travel organizers – and the result to be achieved. This was then set in the context of the preamble to the Directive, according to which both the consumer and the package travel industry would benefit if organizers were placed under an obligation to provide sufficient evidence of security in the event of insolvency. The Court stated specifically that the fact that the Directive was intended to ensure the attainment of other objectives could not preclude its provisions from also having the aim of protecting consumers. Furthermore, the fact that the provision did not explicitly indicate that such a result is, in actual fact, a right conferred on individuals, does not preclude it from being such a right. In true Court of Justice tradition, the Court concentrated on the substance and purpose of the provision in question, rather than on its form or on strictly interpreting the text. The Court continued by examining whether the content of the rights in question was sufficiently identifiable, and whether the persons having such rights were also sufficiently identifiable. The Court concluded:

> As to the first condition . . . the result prescribed by Article 7 of the Directive entails the grant to package travellers of rights guaranteeing the refund of money that they have paid over and their repatriation in the event of the organiser's insolvency . . . The persons having rights under Article 7 are sufficiently identified as consumers, as defined by Article 2 of the Directive, and that the same holds true of the content of those rights which consists in a

3. Joined Cases C-178-179/94, C-188-190/94 *Dillenkofer and Others v. Bundesrepublik Deutschland* [1996] ECR I-4845.
4. Directive 90/314/EEC, OJ 1990, L 158/59.

> guarantee that money paid over by purchasers of package travel will be refunded and that they will be repatriated in the event of the insolvency of the organiser... The purpose of Article 7 of the Directive must be to grant individuals rights whose content is determinable with sufficient precision.[5]

It is interesting to note how the Court 'used' liability to confirm indirectly consumer access to a fair and transparent market. Through the interpretation of the first liability condition the Court was able to spell out certain basic rights that tourists should be entitled to.[6] This facet of the Court's reasoning was further illustrated in the case of *Rechberger, Geindl and Others v. Austria.*[7] The plaintiffs before the national court in Austria were all subscribers to an Austrian daily newspaper, the *Neue Kronenzeitung*, which had decided to offer subscribers, as a reward for their loyalty, a holiday under an arrangement with the travel agency Arena-Club-Reisen. The holiday consisted of four- or seven-day stays in foreign tourist resorts, including flights with on-board refreshments, airport-hotel-airport transfers, overnight accommodation with breakfast in a double or single room (the latter on payment of a supplement) and a tour in the company of a German-speaking tour guide. The offer was, unsurprisingly, very popular, as subscribers were only asked to pay Austrian airport tax, Greek airport tax and a single-person supplement. The plaintiffs in the case booked their trips between 19 November 1994 and 12 April 1995, with the holidays taking place between 10 April and 23 July 1995. The organizer encountered serious operational problems which lead to financial difficulties culminating in insolvency proceedings, which left the subscribers and their companions with no holiday and suffering financial loss. In order to implement Article 7 of the Package Travel Directive properly, Austria should have adopted all measures necessary to provide purchasers of package travel with a guarantee that, as from that date, they would be refunded any money paid and repatriated in the event of the organizer's insolvency. The Austrian legislation in force only applied, however, to travellers who booked packages after 1 January 1995 and who were due to travel on 1 May 1995 or later. Since the subscribers could not recover their costs against the insolvent organizer, they brought an action against Austria, claiming that their loss was attributable to the State's failure to implement the Package Travel Directive correctly. In addressing the question whether Rechberger and the others could be protected by Article 7, Austria attempted to argue first that the issue did not concern a package holiday, as, in this case, the people travelling were only

5. Joined Cases C-178-179/94, C-188-190/94 *Dillenkofer and Others v. Bundesrepublik Deutschland* [1996] ECR I-4845, paras 42-44.
6. S. Weatherill, 'Addressing Problems of Imbalanced Implementation in EC law', in *The Future of Remedies in Europe* eds C. Kilpatrick, T. Novitz & P. Skidmore (Oxford: Hart, 2000), 87. See also Case C-168/00 *Leitner* [2002] ECR I-2631 where the Court also interpreted the Package holiday directive as entailing compensation for non-material damage arising from the loss of enjoyment of the holiday. In the words of AG Tizzano, 'even in Community law, enjoyment of a holiday is treated as an asset worth protecting and damage arising out of the failure to enjoy it amounts to, in the context of a package contract, a specific loss which justifies compensation' at para. 44.
7. Case C-140/97 *Rechberger and Geindl v. Austria* [1999] ECR I-3499.

required to pay a single-room supplement instead of a global price for a trip that was essentially offered free of charge, and second, that the Directive did not apply to trips which are neither sold nor offered for sale on the market to an unlimited number of potential customers, but are instead offered as a gift to only a predetermined class of persons. The Court was unfazed by these attempts to limit the application of the Directive. Instead, it reaffirmed that the very purpose of the Directive was to protect consumers against any risks arising from the insolvency of the organizer of the package holiday. In the *Rechberger* case, the people who travelled incurred exactly those risks. The Court rejected any sophisticated interpretation of the Directive, and focused instead on the individual dimension of the Community measure. Two comments seem appropriate. The first is that the above cases show that the definition of 'rule intended to confer individual rights' is entirely left to the discretion of the ECJ. In its case law on the interpretation of the Package Travel Directive, the Court clearly uses the procedural conditions of liability as another instrument to provide Community measures with an 'authentic' interpretation, so as to better define their field of application. There is no doubt that *Dillenkofer* and *Rechberger* had the effect of sensibly broadening the scope for individuals to rely upon the provisions of the Package Travel Directive. Second, it is tempting to equate the meaning of 'rules intended to confer individual rights' with the conditions which are applicable to determine whether a certain rule is capable of being directly effective. It is of course true that when a certain rule has been declared capable of being directly effective, the fulfilment of the first liability condition will be easily satisfied. Thus, in *Brasserie du Pêcheur/Factortame*, where the EU provisions at stake were fundamental principles of free movement of goods, establishment and the prohibition of discrimination on the grounds of nationality, all previously declared as directly effective, it was automatic for the Court to conclude, relying on precedents establishing the direct effect of those provisions, that the first condition had to be considered as having been satisfied.[8] However, the opposite is not always true. Prechal has vigorously argued that the creation of rights and direct effect should not be considered synonymous. She opined that directly effective provisions do not always and necessarily confer rights. As such, the principle of direct effect refers more to the possibility for an individual to invoke provisions of EU law in order to protect his or her interest, or in other words, a procedural right to invoke EU law before national courts as a way of ensuring a specific right. As to liability, she suggested that, in common with the domestic solutions of certain Member States, such as Germany, the first condition has been introduced by the Court as a form of 'relative unlawfulness' that is 'only a breach of a rule creating rights for individuals concerned or intended to create or at least protecting their interests can give right to reparation'.[9] Thus, in reality, the imposition of the first requirement can be considered, on the one hand,

8. Respectively, Case 74/76 *Iannelli & Volpi v. Meroni* [1977] ECR 557 and Case 2/74 *Reyners v. Belgium* [1974] ECR 631.
9. S. Prechal, *Directives in EC Law*, 2nd edn (Oxford: OUP, 2006), at 99 and 284.

as a further empowerment for individual claims, and, on the other hand, a procedural barrier against excessive litigation and excessively distant damages.

The controversy surrounding the possible liability arising from the interpretation of several banking directives seems to confirm the possible restrictive use of the first liability condition. It is useful first to refer to a case decided by the English courts. In *Three Rivers District Council v. Bank of England*, the House of Lords held that no liability could be established against the Bank of England for failure to properly exercise its supervisory role over an insolvent bank. The main issue was whether the purpose of the First Banking Directive[10] was to protect depositors, and whether it conferred rights on those individuals that were enforceable before the national courts. Closely linked to this was the question of whether compensation could be paid to depositors because of the central bank's failure to exercise its supervisory powers properly. In the leading opinion, Lord Hope likened the issue of the possible direct effect of the Directive to the question of damages. His reply was that the Directive merely intended to coordinate a process of supervision for credit institutions. Thus, the only obligations imposed by European law related to those of collaboration between the Community and the Member States. It was not possible to trace any enforceable individual rights. He therefore also excluded the possibility that specific individual rights could have been bestowed upon depositors, and therefore the first condition under *Francovich* was deemed not to have been satisfied.[11]

The Court of Justice came to the same conclusion in the case of *Peter Paul.*[12] The situation arose out of proceedings before the German courts. Paul and others were customers of the BVH Bank für Vermögensanlagen und Handel AG (the BVH Bank). In 1987, the BVH Bank obtained authorization from the Bundesaufsichtsamt für das Kreditwesen (the German Federal Banking Supervisory Authority) to engage in banking transactions, subject to the condition that it deal in deposit business only if it was a member of a guarantee scheme of an association of credit institutions, and, as long as that was not the case, that it inform customers that there was no guarantee scheme. From 1987 to 1992 the bank applied unsuccessfully for admission to the deposit-guarantee fund, after which it withdrew from the admission procedure due to its not fulfilling the conditions for admission. The bank's difficult financial situation prompted the Bundesaufsichtsamt to carry out various investigations of the bank's affairs, and, in November 1997, it filed a bankruptcy petition and withdrew the bank's authorization to engage in banking transactions. Mr Paul and others held term accounts with the bank totalling approximately DM 300,000. They brought proceedings against the Bundesrepublik Deutschland for compensation in respect of the loss of their deposits. They claimed

10. Directive 73/183/EEC of 28 Jun. 1973 on the abolition of restrictions on freedom of establishment and freedom to provide services in respect of self-employed activities of banks and other financial institutions (OJ 1973, L 194, p. 1).
11. Lord Hope in *Three Rivers DC v. Bank of England (No. 3)* [2003] QB 1556. See further A. Andenas, 'Liability for Supervisors and Depositors Rights: The BCCI and the Bank of England in the House of Lords', *Comp. Law* 22(8) (2001): 226.
12. C-222/02 *Peter Paul v. Bundesrepublik Deutschland* [2004] ECR I-9425.

that they would not have lost those deposits if Directive 94/19 EC had been transposed before 1 July 1995 – the period prescribed for implementation of the Directive.[13] Directive 94/19 EC on deposit-guarantee schemes provided that, in the event of deposits being unavailable, the aggregate deposits of a depositor had to be covered up to 20,000 euros (EUR). Had the Directive been implemented, the Bundesaufsichtsamt would then have been required to take supervisory measures vis-à-vis the BVH Bank before the applicants made payments to that bank. Instead, however, Directive 94/19 EC was only transposed on 16 July 1998, and did not enter into force until 1 August 1998. The Landgericht Bonn awarded each of the claimants the sum of EUR 20,000 because of the late implementation of the Directive. The claimants sought further compensation from the German government, however, in respect of their loss exceeding that sum, on the ground that the Bundesaufsichtsamt had not discharged its banking supervision obligation properly. The national court, before which the case was then brought, asked the ECJ to decide whether depositors were conferred the right by Directive 94/19 EC, or other directives concerning banking law, to demand that the banking supervisory body take appropriate supervisory measures. It also asked whether this situation was within the scope of the principle of State liability for losses caused to individuals by infringements of Community law that were attributable to the State.

The ECJ held that the Directive did not grant depositors a right to have the competent authorities adopt supervisory measures in their interest. Directive 94/19 EC could not, therefore, be interpreted as precluding a national rule to the effect that the functions of the national authority responsible for supervising credit institutions were to be fulfilled only in the public interest, which, under national law, prevented individuals from claiming compensation for damage resulting from defective supervision on the part of that authority. This conclusion was supported by the 24th recital in the preamble, which stated that the Directive may not result in the Member States or their competent authorities being made liable in respect of depositors if they have ensured the compensation or protection of depositors under the conditions prescribed in the Directive. As regards the other directives on banking law, although they had as one of their objectives the protection of depositors, and imposed on the national authorities a number of supervisory obligations vis-à-vis credit institutions, they did not seek to confer rights on depositors in the event that their deposits were unavailable as a result of defective supervision on the part of the competent national authorities. The Court highlighted the fact that rules relating to supervisory obligations are based on considerations relating to the complexity of banking supervision, in the context of which the authorities were under an obligation to protect a plurality of interests, including, more specifically, the stability of the financial system. Those directives could not be interpreted therefore as conferring on individuals the right to require the banking supervisory body to adopt appropriate supervisory measures, or to claim that that body or the State concerned was liable in the event of defective supervision.

13. Directive 94/19, OJ 1994, L 135/5.

This decision has been fiercely criticized, and probably quite rightly so. The *Peter Paul* reading of the 'individual rights' requirement is certainly much more restrictive than in previous cases. As correctly observed by Tison, the Court – contrary to its own *acquis* – read 'direct effect' and 'liability' as synonyms. As the conclusion of the judgment was that since the aim of the Directives in question was only the promotion of a process of harmonization, and thus no enforceable rights could be derived from their provisions, those rules could not be considered as 'intended to create individual rights'.[14] However, in this case it could simply have been argued that the banking directives were aimed

> at protecting the interests of depositors, in the sense that prudential authorities when exercising supervisions should pursue that protected interest. Depositors under this approach do not necessarily have a legally enforceable right [. . .] but the lack of adequately taking into account the depositors interests could post factum open a right to compensation.[15]

Such a conclusion would have been consistent not only with previous cases on liability, but also with the ECJ's case law on banking supervision.[16]

A possible explanation for such a restrictive reading can be found in the reluctance of the Court to expose supervisory authorities in such a delicate area to too many challenges, with the result of making the State pay for the bank's collapse. A correlated worry could have been the possible risk of excessive litigation. It is true that the Court seems to be resolute in its avoidance of transforming liability of the Member State to a sort of *actio popularis*. In requiring applicants to show a specific effect on their legal situation, a condition comparable to that of standing, the Court reaffirmed the principle that liability will only be available where a specific individual right has been affected.

In this context, it is useful to mention the judgment *Staat der Nederlanden v. Ten Kate Holding Musselkanaal BV and Others.*[17] In this case, the Court was faced with the rather unusual question of whether Community law precludes a national law which contains an obligation to bring an action for annulment or failure to act against the European Commission for the benefit of one of its citizens, or which provides that liability may be imposed on a Member State for not having acted in that regard. The Court, in a very prudent line of reasoning, argued that Community law might actually require the exact opposite, in that the Member State should always retain a degree of discretion as to the appropriateness of bringing an action for failure to act and thereby triggering an action for liability. Otherwise, an automatic right of action and damages for failure to do so would give rise 'to a

14. M. Tison, 'Do Not Attack the Watchdog! Banking Supervisors Liability after Peter Paul', *CMLRev.* 42 (2005): 639.
15. Ibid., at 668.
16. C-366/97 *Criminal proceedings against Massimo Romanelli and Paolo Romanelli* [1999] ECR I-855.
17. Case C-511/03 *Staat der Nederlandse (Ministerie van Landbouw, Natuurbeheer en Visserij) v. Ten Kate Holding Musselkanaal BV and Others* [2005] I-8979.

risk that the Community Courts might be inundated with actions, some of which would be patently unfounded, thus jeopardising the proper functioning of the Court of Justice'.[18]

In this context, the above discussion can and must be linked to the question of whether the breach of a procedural guarantee provided by EU law could give rise to a right for individuals. Where the procedural guarantee is actually an essential part of the right to exercise one of the fundamental freedoms, there is no question that the first condition has to be considered satisfied. More complicated, however, is the question of whether direct effect has been granted to provisions aimed at ensuring the transparency and effectiveness of harmonization mechanisms.[19] Environmental regulatory provisions offer a good example. The *WWF v. Bozen*[20] case concerned the question whether individuals could rely on the previsions of Directive 85/337 EC on the assessment of the environmental effects of certain projects. In its judgment, the ECJ held that where Community authorities have, by directive, imposed on Member States the obligation to pursue a particular course of conduct, not only would the effectiveness of such an act be diminished if individuals were prevented from relying on it in legal proceedings, but also,

> if national courts were prevented from taking it into consideration as a matter of Community law in determining whether the national legislature, in exercising its choice as to the form and methods for implementing the directive, had kept within the limits of its discretion set out in the directive.

This assertion refers to decisions such as *Verholen*[21] and *Kraajeveld*,[22] where the ECJ held that where all the conditions are satisfied for a provision of a directive to be directly applicable, a national court may apply the provision in question – even where the beneficiary has not expressly relied upon it. As to the possible relationship between such case law and the principle of State liability, the *Wells*[23] judgment should be mentioned. The dispute involved a decision of the English Secretary of State for local government to grant a new license to a private mining company to carry out mining operations without first carrying out an Environmental Impact Assessment (EIA). Mrs Wells, a private individual, challenged the decision, complaining that there was a violation of Directive 85/337 ECC on EIAs. The UK tried to demonstrate that allowing an individual to rely directly on the provisions of the directive would amount to imposing obligations under

18. Ibid., para. 31.
19. Prechal raised the question whether an obligation to notify, for instance as provided for by Directive 83/189/EEC, could give rise to liability. S. Prechal, *Directives in EC Law*, 2nd edn (Oxford: OUP, 2006), 9 at 285.
20. C-435/97 *World Wildlife Fund and others v. Autonome Provinz Bozen and others* [1999] ECR I-5613.
21. Cases C-87-89/90 *Verholen and Others v. Speciale Verskeringsbank* [1991] ECR I-3757.
22. Case C-72/95 *Aannemersbedrijf P.K.Kraaijeveld BV v. Gedeputeerde Staten van Zuid-Holland* [1996] ECR I-5403.
23. Case C-201/02 *Wells v. Secretary of State for Transport, Local Government and the Regions* [2004] ECR I-723.

Community law on another individual and was thus contrary to the Court's case law on horizontal effects of directives. The Court, however, reciting its now consolidated case law on 'direct effect as a shield',[24] confirmed that mere adverse repercussions on the rights of third parties, even if the repercussions are certain, do not justify preventing an individual from relying on a directive against a defaulting Member State. Further, although the Court's ruling is somewhat obscure, the availability of an action for damages based on the Directive was confirmed, as the Court stressed that a failure to carry out an assessment of the environmental effects of a specific project would oblige the Member State to make good any harm caused by it.[25]

Most of the comments on this line of case law have centred on the fact that those cases expand the notion of effectiveness and are not grounded in the language of rights. They also make clear, however, that decentralized authorities are under a specific duty to comply with procedural provisions of a directive. Thus, an action under *Francovich* for failure to comply with certain procedural obligations is not beyond imagination. Of course, in this case, damages under *Francovich* amount to an 'indirect remedy, involving a suit against the State rather than the polluter'.[26] Nevertheless, the possibility for individuals to bring an action for damages does exist.

Similarly, a breach of the standstill obligation provided by Article 88(3) EC on the notification procedure in state aid cases might be likely to be considered as a rule intended to confer individual rights. As the Court established in some of its early case law, the prohibition on the implementation of an aid measure has direct effect and 'gives rise to rights in favour of individuals which national courts are bound to safeguard'.[27] Such a development might provide an even firmer incentive for Member States to comply with their obligation to notify.

A final question, provided that both primary law (including case law from the Court of Justice) and secondary law can be considered as possible sources for individual rights, is whether other EU sources can also be considered as conferring rights on individuals. Could, for example, the general principles of EU law perhaps give rise to individual rights? Again, a comparison with the direct effect case law might be instructive. In *Mangold*,[28] a case involving a challenge made against the German law on part-time work and fixed-term contracts, the Court was asked to interpret Directive 2000/78 EC[29] which prohibits both direct and indirect discrimination on the grounds of age. Although at the relevant time of the case the transitional period for the implementation of Directive 2000/78 EC had not expired, the Court found that the national court had an obligation to ensure that the full

24. T. Tridimas, 'Black, White and Shades of Grey: Horizontality of Directives Revisited', *YEL* (2001-2002): 21.
25. Case C-201/02 *Wells v. Secretary of State for Transport, Local Government and the Regions* [2004] ECR I-723, para. 66.
26. M Lee, *EU Environmental Law* (Hart, Oxford, 2005), at 64.
27. Case 120/73 *Lorenz v. Germany* [1973] ECR 1471.
28. C-144/04 *Mangold* [2005] ECR I-9981.
29. Directive 2000/78, OJ 2002, L 303/16.

effectiveness of the principle of non-discrimination was complied with. The Court highlighted the fact that Member States are bound by the terms of the Directive from the date of its publication and during the transitional period for implementation. A Member State may not adopt measures that may seriously compromise the aims and obligations imposed by that Directive. The Court makes reference to both the fundamental rights underpinning modern social policy law and the fact that the principle of non-discrimination on the grounds of age must be regarded as a general principle of Community law. Some criticism has been levelled at this judgment[30] owing to the fact that the Court appears to go further than is necessary in the specific context. The judgment makes clear, however, that the general principles of EU law, such as non-discrimination, are the benchmark against which the legality of national law should be tested.[31] Thus, it could be inferred that the failure to observe those principles could well give rise to individual rights.

In conclusion, the interpretation of the meaning of 'rule intended to confer individual rights' falls within the Court of Justice's jurisdiction.[32] The case law seems to adopt a very practical and non-dogmatic approach. In particular, the Court, on the one hand, confirmed the close link between the direct effect provisions and liability, and, on the other, seems quite ready to lend its authority to protect, through compensation, certain forms of rights, such as consumer or environmental protection, which is in line with the most recent forms of individual redress identified in tort law. Even so, the applicant would still have to show that the rule breached had affected his or her rights or interests. If such a construction seems still too wide and in contradiction to what was previously claimed – that liability should not be transformed into a form of *actio popularis* – it should always be remembered that the 'individual right' condition is the first, but not the only, hurdle that an individual has to overcome to successfully bring an action for compensation. The other two requirements, which will now be analyzed, can be, and are, used as possible filters.

2. SUFFICIENTLY SERIOUS BREACH

The Court stated in *Brasserie du Pêcheur/Factortame* that, as a second condition for State liability, a Member State would not be liable in damages unless it had committed a sufficiently serious breach of Community law. In French, the Court has always used the term '*violation suffisamment caractérisée*'. This is now normally translated into English as 'sufficiently serious breach'. The underlying

30. A. Arnull, 'Out with the Old', *ELRev.* 31(1) (2006): 1-2.
31. See further Joined Cases C-20/00 and C-64/00 *Booker Aquaculture and Hydro Seafood v. The Scottish Ministers* [2003] ECR I-7411, paras 88-93.
32. Another interesting issue would be whether liability might also arise from the violation of provisions of an international agreement. At least as far as the first criteria is concerned, this should be possible on the basis of the traditional ECJ case law on the extension of interpretation of 'internal' Community law provisions to similarly or identically worded provisions in an international agreement. See for instance Case 104/81 *Hauptzollamt Mainz v. Kupferberg* [1983] ECR 3641.

meaning of *caractérisée* however, which gives rise to its inherent implication of seriousness, includes the notion that the breach (or other conduct) has been clearly established in accordance with its legal definition. In other words, the breach must be definite and clear-cut. The introduction of the requirement of a sufficiently serious breach provided a conclusion to the debate that had been going on as to whether a test of strict liability applied in the context of State liability, as per *Francovich*, or whether, as per the Community liability regime under Article 288(2) EC and other certain non-contractual liability regimes in Member States, there has to be something more than just a breach. The new, more refined test would appear to be more suitable for the complex areas of policy and law in which public bodies act, and in particular where they possess discretionary powers as to how and whether to act. The Court's attempt to provide for such a more refined approach in *Brasserie du Pêcheur/Factortame* seems, however, to be somewhat clumsy. It is appropriate to remember that once the Court characterized the breach as sufficiently serious, it went immediately to link seriousness with the exercise of discretionary powers. The Court held that the decisive test for finding that a breach of Community law is sufficiently serious is whether the Member State or the Community institution concerned 'manifestly and gravely disregarded the limits on its discretion'.[33] The Court continued, however, by adding other elements that had to be taken into account in establishing the seriousness of the breach. In *Brasserie du Pêcheur/Factortame*, the Court listed the relevant factors as including

> [t]he clarity and precision of the rule breached, the measure of discretion left by that rule to the national or Community authorities, whether the infringement and the damage caused was intentional or involuntary, whether any error of law was excusable or inexcusable, the fact that the position taken by a Community institution may have contributed towards the omission, and the adoption or retention of national measures or practices contrary to Community law.[34]

It is clear from the above list of factors that the discretion enjoyed by national authorities is just one of the elements to be taken into consideration and is not, as one could have assumed from the previous paragraphs, decisive on its own. This zigzag reasoning has led to many discussions on whether discretion had to be considered as the guiding principle, and, if so, what kind of discretion the Court was referring to; what the meaning of that expression was; and how to apply this test in practice. Conversely, it could also be argued that the satisfaction of all the other factors listed by the Court had to be considered equally fundamental. In our view, the post *Brasserie du Pêcheur/Factortame* case law went a long way in clarifying many of these issues. The section that follows first seeks to group the relevant lines of case law in relation to seriousness of breach, and second, it discusses whether there is a general principle emerging from the case law, before

33. Case 46/93 *Brasserie du Pêcheur v. Bundesrepublik Deutschland and The Queen v. Secretary of State for Transport, ex parte Factortame and others* [1996] ECR I-1029, at para. 55.
34. Ibid., at paras 56-57.

finally analyzing the kind of scrutiny the Court usually employs to determine the seriousness of the breach.

2.1. Cases Where Liability is 'Automatically Established'

2.1.1. Taking ECJ Judgments Seriously

The Court comments in *Brasserie du Pêcheur/Factortame* that a breach of Community law will clearly be sufficiently serious if the Member State has persisted in its conduct despite a previous judgment finding that such behaviour amounts to an infringement of Community law, or if there is a preliminary ruling or settled case law on the matter from which it is clear that such conduct is contrary to EU law. In this sense, State liability can be, and is, a further instrument to enforce more effectively compliance with ECJ judgments, together with the procedure provided by Article 228(2) EC of the Treaty. It will be recalled that the penalty procedure set out by Article 228(2) EC requires that, when a Member State fails to take the necessary measures to comply with a judgment of the Court of Justice, the Court may, following a proposal from the Commission, impose a lump sum or a penalty payment on the violating Member State. The European Commission began to make use of Article 228(2) EC, which had been dormant for some years, and the ECJ has already held several Member States liable under this article.[35] The Court made it clear in *Commission v. France*[36] that it was ready to take the duty to comply with previous judgments very seriously. It went as far as imposing on the defaulting Member States both sanctions – a penalty and a lump sum. The Court clarified that the penalties are not identical, as they perform different functions. The imposition of a penalty payment serves to induce a Member State to put an end to the breach as soon as possible, while the imposition of a lump sum is based more on an assessment of the effects on public and private interests of the Member State's failure to comply with its obligations. This latter point is particularly evident where the breach has persisted for a long period from the time that the initial judgment was given. The Court then continued:

> The order imposing a penalty payment and/or a lump sum is not intended to compensate for damage caused by the Member State concerned, but to place it under economic pressure which induces it to put an end to the breach established. The financial penalties imposed must therefore be decided upon according to the degree of persuasion needed in order for the Member State in question to alter its conduct.[37]

35. Case C-387/97 *Commission v. Greece* [2000] ECR I-5047 and Case C-278/01 *Commission v. Spain* [2003] ECR I-14141.
36. C-304/02 *Commission v. France* [2005] ECR I-6263. See also C-177/04 *Commission v. France* [2006] ECR I-2461.
37. Case C-177/04 *Commission of the European Communities v. French Republic* [2002] ECR I-3827, para. 91.

Some actually argue that such a strict application of the penalty mechanism greatly reduced the scope and usefulness of the liability of the State under *Francovich*.[38] In reality, as both procedures are in very good health and both are fully deployed, it seems that once again the principle of State liability cannot merely be equated to a stick used against Member States, but that it is also as a form of protection for individual rights. Furthermore, it is also not entirely true that Member States will always incur liability with no possible escape. In situations where a previous judgment concerned the same rules at stake in the liability action, such as in the instance of *Brasserie du Pêcheur/Factortame*, both based on previous ECJ rulings, the State would be liable for compensation automatically without any need to discuss the seriousness of the breach. However, in those cases where the action on liability is based on less firm precedents and not perfectly consistent case law, the Member States have some room for manoeuvre. For instance, in areas of fast legal developments, where the legal principles are not entirely settled, a State can try to argue that the breach should not be considered serious because of the fluid character of the case law of the ECJ. The Court itself has recognized this is a legitimate argument. In two cases regarding the compatibility of national tax law with freedom of establishment, despite the fact that the cases revolved around Article 43,one of the cornerstones of the internal market, the Court acknowledged that 'the national court must take into account the fact that, in a field such as direct taxation, the consequences arising from the freedoms of movement guaranteed by the Treaty have been only gradually made clear'.[39] In short, only and in so far the case law of the Court is either directly linked to the case at stake, or it is a settled one, a mere infringement would be enough to establish the seriousness of the breach.

2.1.2. Non-transposition of Directives

A second area where a breach on the part of a Member State will be sufficiently serious per se is when the Member State has failed to adopt the implementing measures to transpose a directive.[40] The *Dillenkofer* judgment is crystal clear in this respect. After having established that the rule infringed conferred rights upon the individual and thereby satisfied the first condition of liability, the Court examined whether the breach was 'sufficiently serious'. Germany had failed to

38. C. Harlow, *State Liability: Tort Law and Beyond* (OUP, Oxford, 2004), 65.
39. Case C-524/04 *Test Claimants in the Thin Cap Group Litigation v. Commissioners of Inland Revenue* [2007] ECR I-2107. See also Case C-424/97 *Haim v. Kassenzahnärztliche Vereinigung Nordrhein (Haim II)* [2000] ECR 1-5123 and Case C-118/00 *Larsy v. Inasti* [2001] ECR I-5063.
40. It should be remembered that for new Member States, the Acts of Accession usually state that new Member States are to put into effect the measures necessary to comply with directives from the date of accession, unless a time limit has been specifically provided. Thus, the Member State cannot be held liable for damage caused to individuals by failure to transpose the directive correctly where the events which give rise to the operation of the guarantee provided for in the directive occurred prior to the date of accession. On this point see Case C-321/97 *Andersson and Wåkerås-Andersson* [1999] I-3551.

implement the Package Travel Directive on time. The intervening governments in the case tried to argue that the mere delay in implementation was not enough to impose damages automatically, but that it had to be shown that the breach was serious. The Court very concisely, but clearly, replied:

> Failure to take any measure to transpose a directive in order to achieve the result it prescribes within the period laid down for that purpose constitutes per se a serious breach of Community law and consequently gives rise to a right of reparation for individuals suffering injury if the result prescribed by the directive entails the grant to individuals of rights whose content is identifiable and a causal link exists between the breach of the State's obligation and the loss and damage suffered.[41]

The Court further elaborated that such a finding did not necessitate a prior finding by the Court of an infringement of Community law, and was not affected by the fact that the Member States are given considerable latitude as regards the choice of means for achieving the intended result:

> The fact that States may choose between a wide variety of means for achieving the result prescribed by a directive is of no importance if the purpose of the directive is to grant to individuals rights whose content is determinable with sufficient precision.[42]

Finally, the Court also seems to have transplanted its case law on the late implementation of directives by Member States. As is well established, a Member State cannot escape its obligation to comply in time by pleading 'provisions, practices or circumstances existing in its internal legal system or any other kind of difficulties of technical or political nature'.[43] In *Dillenkofer*, the Court clearly established that various circumstances which cause the delay in implementation are irrelevant for the purposes of establishing the liability of the State. It should be noted, however, that the main focus for the Court is not just the time elapsed, but the fact that in cases such as *Dillenkofer* (and *Francovich*), the Member States did not take any action at all to give effect to the directives in questions. The seriousness of the breach is thus identified by a total failure to comply. There may be cases, therefore, where, despite the time for implementation having expired, such a breach might not be considered serious. Tridimas suggests that this should be the case where a Member State does not transpose the directive, relying instead on existing national provisions already complying with the directive in question.[44] If it later transpires that these provisions do not actually fully match the directive's provisions, in Tridimas' view, liability should not be automatic. Support for this contention

41. Joined Cases C-178-179/94, C-188-190/94 *Dillenkofer and Others v. Bundesrepublik Deutschland* [1996] ECR I-4845, para. 29.
42. Ibid., para. 45.
43. Case 280/83 *Commission v. Italy* [1984] ECR 2361, See also Case 301/81 *Commission v. Belgium* [1983] ECR 467.
44. T. Tridimas, *The General Principles of EU Law*, 2nd edn (Oxford: OUP, 2006), 506.

can be found in the *Evans* judgment.[45] In this case, the UK implemented the Second Motor Insurance Directive[46] through a series of agreements with a private-law body, of which all insurance companies offering motor vehicle insurance in the United Kingdom were members. The Court held that liability would arise only if an examination of the existing compensation system disclosed a defect in transposition of the Second Directive, and if that defect had adversely affected an individual.

Support can also be found in *Lindöpark*.[47] Lindöpark, a Swedish company which ran a golf course, contended that the 1990 Swedish Value Added Tax (VAT) law, which remained in force after the date of Sweden's accession to the European Union in 1995, was in breach of Article 13 of the Sixth VAT Directive.[48] According to Lindöpark, its activities should have been subject to VAT and the company should have been entitled to deduct input VAT. Under Swedish law, however, up until 1997, all supplies of premises or other facilities for the purposes of sport or physical education, together with the making available of accessories or equipment in that connection, were exempt from VAT. In the main proceedings, Lindöpark did not seek merely to challenge the applicability of the disputed provision, but rather to obtain reparation for the loss it claimed to have suffered as a result thereof. The ECJ held that it was evident from the provisions of the Swedish VAT Law that the general exemption enacted by the Swedish legislature had no basis in the Sixth Directive, and therefore became clearly incompatible with the Directive as from the date of Sweden's accession to the European Union. Given the clear wording of the Sixth Directive, the Member State, by introducing provisions that were clearly contrary to the Directive, automatically committed a serious breach. In those circumstances, the mere infringement of Community law was thought to be sufficient to establish the existence of a sufficiently serious breach.

2.1.3. Absence of Discretion

The third instance where the mere breach of a provision of Community law may be sufficiently serious per se to impose liability in damages on the Member State arises when the Member State has only considerably reduced discretion, or even no discretion under the Community provision. Most of these cases concern breaches of administrative formalities of more mundane situations in applying Community law, and most of those breaches could be attributed to the administrative machinery of the State. The best known example is *Hedley Lomas*.[49] The case concerned an individual decision on the part of a national administration that was

45. Case C-63/01 *Samuel Sidney Evans v. Secretary of State for the Environment, Transport and the Regions* [2003] ECR I-14447.
46. Council Directive 84/5, OJ 1984, L8/17.
47. Case C-150/99 *Sweden v. Lindöpark* [2001] ECR I-493.
48. Council Directive 77/388 EEC, now amended by Council Directive 2004/71 EC OJ 2004, C 27/44.
49. Case C-5/94 *The Queen v. Ministry of Agriculture, Fisheries and Food, ex parte Hedley Lomas* [1996] ECR I-2553.

in breach of a directly effective Treaty provision. Between April 1990 and 1 January 1993, the UK Ministry of Agriculture, Fisheries and Foods (MAFF) refused to issue licenses for the export to Spain of live animals for slaughter, on the grounds that their treatment in Spanish slaughterhouses was contrary to the provisions of EC Directive 74/557 ECC[50] concerning the treatment and welfare of animals in slaughterhouses. The Directive was transposed into Spanish law on 18 December 1987 after Spain joined the Community. MAFF became convinced, however, on the basis of information obtained from the Spanish Society for the Protection of Animals that a number of Spanish slaughterhouses were not complying with the rules contained in the Directive. In 1990, following complaints from animal welfare groups in the United Kingdom and Spain, the Commission contacted the Spanish authorities and held several meetings with them regarding, in particular, the absence of punitive measures for non-compliance with the Spanish law implementing the Directive. The Commission was given assurances by the Spanish national and regional authorities, and declined to bring an action against Spain under Article 226 EC. The Commission also informed the UK Government that it considered the United Kingdom's ban on exports of live animals to Spain to be contrary to the free movement of goods provisions, in particular to the prohibition of restrictions on exports contained in Article 29 EC. In response to this, the UK Government lifted the general ban with effect from 1 January 1993.

On 7 October 1992, Hedley Lomas applied for an export license for a quantity of live sheep intended for slaughter in a specified Spanish slaughterhouse. MAFF did not issue a license even though information provided by Hedley Lomas pointed to the fact that the slaughterhouse had been approved since 1986 and was complying with the Directive. Hedley Lomas therefore brought proceedings in the UK courts against MAFF, seeking a declaration that the refusal to grant an export license was contrary to Article 29 EC, and also claimed damages for loss of revenue. In a reference for a preliminary ruling, the High Court asked, among other questions, whether a Member State is liable as a matter of Community law to compensate a trader in damages for any loss caused to the trader by the failure to grant an export license in breach of Article 29 EC, or, in the words of Advocate General Léger, 'is there, in Community law, a general principle that a State can be liable for the actions of its administrative authorities which are contrary to Community law?'[51] The Court answered with a resounding 'yes':

> The answer to the third question must therefore be that a Member State has an obligation to make reparation for the damage caused to an individual by a refusal to issue an export licence in breach of Article 34 [now Article 29 EC] of the Treaty where the rule of Community law infringed is intended to confer rights on individuals, the breach is sufficiently serious and there is a direct causal link between the breach and the damage sustained by the individuals.[52]

---

50. Council Directive 74/577/EC of 18 Nov. 1974, OJ 1974, L 316/10.
51. AG Léger's Opinion Case C-5/94 *The Queen v. Ministry of Agriculture, Fisheries and Food, ex parte Hedley Lomas* [1996] ECR I-2553, para. 50.
52. Ibid., para. 32.

Therefore, in a case where the administrative body at fault was not called upon to make any legislative choices and had only considerably reduced discretion, or even no discretion, a mere infringement of Community law may be sufficient to establish the existence of a sufficiently serious breach. In reality, in what we can call 'no discretion' cases, the focus is not on the specific powers and choices available to the public authority in question. What the Court concentrates on is the 'European norm' in question, and whether such a norm left any space for interpretation or was so clear that a mere 'rubberstamp' would suffice. A clear example of this distinction arose in the long controversy involving the Larsy family. Mr Larsy, a self-employed gardener in Belgium and France, challenged the decision of the Belgium social security authority to reduce his pension on the grounds that he was receiving a pension from France as well. He brought an action for damages complaining that Belgium had committed a serious breach on two grounds: first, the authority had totally misinterpreted Regulation 1408/71 on the application of social security schemes for self-employed persons,[53] and second, the authority failed to apply a clear-cut precedent of the Court of Justice. In *Larsy I*, the ECJ clearly established that the Belgian law prohibiting the overlapping of benefits where a person had worked in two Member States during the same time and had paid contributions twice, was not compatible with EC law.[54] In the second chapter, *Larsy II*, the Court emphasized that, when Mr Larsy challenged its decision, the Belgian authority was presented with all the possible information necessary to properly take the correct decision. Since it failed to take the correct decision, the breach had to be considered as serious per se.

'No discretion' liability will also be available when the Community measure itself leaves no room for ambiguity or discretion on the part of a Member State. Take, for instance, the following provision in a Directive on machinery safety:[55] 'Member States shall not prohibit, restrict or impede the placing on the market and putting into service in their territory of machinery and safety components which comply with this Directive.' This is a straightforward prohibition with no complex choices to be made or discretion to exercise. Thus, as the Court held in *A.G.M.-COS.MET Srl v. Suomen valtio, Tarmo Lehtinen*,[56] the obligations contained in the Directive did not give the Member State any discretion. Any differing behaviour attributable to the Member State was therefore a sufficiently serious breach. In conclusion, in the context of liability, the Member State will be said to have committed a serious breach whenever the 'meaning of Community law provisions was reasonably beyond dispute and thus it does not give rise to various interpretations'.[57]

---

53. Council Regulation (EC) No. 1408/71 of 14 Jun. 1971 (OJ 1971, L 149, p. 2) (Consolidated version – OJ 1997, L 28, p. 1).
54. Case C-118/00 *Larsy v. Inasti* [2001] ECR I-5063.
55. Art. 4(1) Directive 98/37/EC of the European Parliament and of the Council of 22 Jun. 1998 on the approximation of the laws of the Member States relating to machinery, OJ 1998. L 207, p. 1.
56. Case C-470/03 *A.G.M.-COS.MET Srl v. Suomen valtio, Tarmo Lehtinen* [2007] I-2749.
57. S. Prechal, *Directives in EC Law*, 2nd edn (Oxford: OUP, 2006), 288.

3. ESTABLISHING A 'SUFFICIENTLY SERIOUS' BREACH

The situation becomes somewhat more complicated when the European norm is not so unambiguous, and thus the Member State is presented with different possible options. In those situations the factors listed by the Court in *Brasserie du Pêcheur/ Factortame* are particularly relevant and useful. Once again, in order to establish a serious breach the clarity and precision of the rule breached, the measure of discretion left by that rule to the national or Community authorities, whether the infringement and the damage caused was intentional or involuntary, whether any error of law was excusable or inexcusable, the fact that the position taken by a Community institution may have contributed towards the omission, and the adoption or retention of national measures or practices contrary to Community law have to be taken into account.[58] It should be noted that the Court's language clearly illustrates that this list is not exhaustive. Thus, the test to be used is necessarily a flexible one and substantially practical, depending on the specific features of each case. Despite the tendency of the Court to treat the issue of sufficiently serious breach on a case-by-case basis, it remains possible to classify some of the most typical situations arising out of the Court's case law.

3.1. Incorrect Transposition of Directives

As Advocate General Léger, in the case of *Hedley Lomas*, had predicted, the Court would, at some point, have to deal with the specific problems related to the transposition of directives:

> A more qualified approach to the question of liability would be required where there has been a clumsy or slightly incorrect transposition of complex Community legislation or a bona fide misinterpretation of its requirements. Allowance must also be made for excusable failings: a Member State cannot be held responsible for clumsy or obscure drafting of Community texts, for which the Council or Commission bear sole responsibility and which the Member State simply implements.[59]

The ECJ has been ready to support the Member State in situations where it has implemented the Directive in time, but it has since transpired that such an implementation was erroneous. The leading case developed from the Court's *BT* judgment.[60] The case concerned the implementation of Article 8(1) of Council Directive 90/531/EEC[61] on the procurement procedures of entities operating in

58. Case 46/93 *Brasserie du Pêcheur v. Bundesrepublik Deutschland and The Queen v. Secretary of State for Transport, ex parte Factortame and others* [1996] ECR I-1029, paras 56-57.
59. AG Léger's Opinion in Case C-5/94 *The Queen v. Ministry of Agriculture, Fisheries and Food, ex parte Hedley Lomas* [1996] ECR I-2553, para. 160. On this point, see para. 18 of the judgment in Joined Cases 106-120/87 *Asteris and Others v. Greece* [1988] ECR 5515.
60. C-392/93 *R v. HM Treasury, ex parte British Telecommunications* [1996] ECR I-1631.
61. 90/531/E.E.C OJ 1990, L 297/1.

the telecommunications sector. The article provided that the Directive was not to apply to contracts which contracting entities awarded 'for purchases intended exclusively to enable them to provide one or more telecommunications services where other entities are free to offer the same services in the same geographical area and under substantially the same conditions'. The applicant and other providers of telecommunications services in the United Kingdom were named in an annex to the Directive as contracting entities coming within the Directive. The Directive was transposed into English law by the Utilities Supply and Works Contracts Regulations 1992. Regulation 7(1) and Schedule 2 of the Regulations, which were intended to implement Article 8(1) of the Directive, provided, however, that the Regulations were not to apply to the seeking of offers by the applicant and another telecommunications operators in relation to contracts enabling them to provide all telecommunications services other than certain specified services. The applicant felt that this was in breach of Community law, as instead of leaving the decision to the companies themselves as to which services were excluded from the Regulations, the UK Government had itself specified the services to be excluded. The applicant claimed damages for loss allegedly suffered by it as a consequence of the alleged mis-transposition. The Court, in its judgment, felt that it was not open to a Member State, when transposing the Directive into national law, to determine which telecommunications services were to be excluded from its scope, since Article 8(1) vested that power in the contracting entities themselves. However, given that the article in question was imprecisely worded, and reasonably capable therefore of bearing the interpretation given to it by the UK, in good faith and on the basis of arguments which were not entirely devoid of substance, the Court found that the UK had not manifestly and gravely disregarded the limits of the exercise of its power. Weight was perhaps attributed to the UK's arguments, as other Member States had also adopted the same interpretation as the UK of the article in question. The Court concluded, therefore, that there had not been a sufficiently serious breach. There was, however, some contention in the case as to whether or not the *Brasserie du Pêcheur/Factortame* test should have been applied in the first place. In the words of Advocate General Tesauro, 'widely divergent replies have been given in the course of these proceedings'. The Advocate General himself opined that:

> It must be acknowledged that a decisive factor, for the purpose of setting a limit to the possibility of translating unlawfulness into liability, is not only the discretion which the States may enjoy in the sector concerned but also the greater or lesser degree of precision of the obligation imposed and ultimately the possibility of identifying with a sufficient degree of precision the content of the right asserted by an individual in a particular situation.[62]

62. AG Tesauro's Opinion in Case 46/93 *Brasserie du Pêcheur v. Bundesrepublik Deutschland and The Queen v. Secretary of State for Transport, ex parte Factortame and others* [1996] ECR I-1029, para. 33.

The *Francovich* situation is distinguished, in fact, the Advocate General comments that it is 'undoubtedly different', because in that situation the Member State concerned had no discretion at all in transposing the directive into national law within the prescribed period, and it was precisely that aspect which rendered the infringement per se a serious and manifest breach. The factors highlighted by the Court that needed to be taken into account when assessing the precision and clarity of a measure, therefore, were whether the meaning of the provision in question was reasonably beyond dispute, and whether or not a number of interpretations could be given to the same provision. The assessment should not be conflated with that relating to 'direct effect'. In the case of direct effect, the possible need for clarification by interpretation is no bar to direct application by national courts. In regard to the assessment for State liability, however, the focus is on the breach itself, and whether the act or omission involved was of a kind whose inconsistency with the Community law provision in question cannot be doubted. In the case of *Brinkmann*,[63] for example, a provision of a VAT Directive was found to be sufficiently unconditional and precise so as to have direct effect, but the breach in implementation was not considered 'sufficiently serious', as the wrongful interpretation of the provision made by Denmark was defensible. The case involved a tobacco company, Brinkmann, which produced 'Westpoint', tobacco rolls wrapped in porous cellulose for which cigarette paper was needed. In Germany, the product was taxed as smoking tobacco. On importation in to Denmark, however, the Danish authorities taxed it at the higher rate applicable to cigarettes. Under Danish law, although smoking tobacco was taxed at a much lower rate than cigarettes, the statute in force at that time gave no definition of the various tobacco products, and authority was given to the national tax authorities to make individual decisions on product classification. Brinkmann brought an action against the Danish authorities seeking compensation for the loss suffered by reason of the Danish VAT board's decision, which they felt was contrary to Community law. Various questions were referred to the ECJ, including a request for an interpretation of the applicable Directive 79/32 on VAT,[64] and also concerning the claim for damages. The first issue referred dealt with whether a Member State whose authorities erroneously classified a product, and did not suspend the operation of that decision, were required under Community law to compensate the manufacturer for the damage sustained as a result of the erroneous decision. The Court upheld the first contention, that the Westpoint product had been erroneously classified. The definition for cigarettes laid out the distinctive characteristics of cigarettes as being (1) rolls of tobacco; (2) capable of being smoked as they are; and (3) not cigars or cigarillos. The Westpoint product only fulfilled the first and third characteristics, since they were not capable of being smoked as they were. Therefore, the Court concluded that the Westpoint product should have been classified as smoking tobacco. As for the damage caused to the applicant, the Court identified first, that the articles of the Directive, which contained definitions of the relevant

63. Case C-319/96 *Brinkmann Tabakfabriken v. Skatteministeriet* [1998] ECR I-5255.
64. Directive 79/32, OJ 1979. L 10/8.

products, had not been properly transposed into national law, since the competent minister authorized to introduce the relevant provisions had not adopted any implementing measures. Second, the Danish Tax authorities erroneously interpreted the Directive in making their decision. The Court then proceeded to assess the action of the Danish tax authorities and whether they had committed a sufficiently serious breach of Community law, in particular with regard to the clarity and precision of the provisions. The Court concluded that there was not a sufficiently serious breach, as the product in question did not exactly correspond to either of the definitions given in the Directive, and therefore the classification given was not manifestly contrary to the wording. The same interpretation had in fact been supported by other Member States, and was even in line with the aim of the directive.

In conclusion, a Member State will not incur liability if it can show to the Court that it acted in good faith, and the incorrect implementation was caused by the complexity of the Community measure. A parallel with the case law on the penalty procedure provided by Article 228(2) EC for failure to comply with an ECJ judgment is again useful.[65]

3.2. Serious Breach and the Role of National Courts

In comparison to the criteria of 'rules intended to confer individual rights', the interpretation of which is within the exclusive competence of the Court of Justice, the actual process of ascertaining whether the serious breach formula used by the judges in Luxembourg has been satisfied is left to national courts to determine. As has been seen above, however, in reality, the Court is prepared to intervene in significant cases where it appears that the Court has all the necessary information to assess whether the facts amount to a sufficiently serious breach of Community law. Not only in the first wave of liability cases such as *Brasserie du Pêcheur/ Factortame*, *BT* and *Hedley Lomas*, where arguably the Court felt the pressure of expanding on the rather terse *Francovich* judgment, but also in recent decisions, the Court itself indicated a number of circumstances that the national court should take into account when making a decision on the issue of whether the breach was sufficiently serious.[66] It is true, however, that in other cases the Court is happy to simply reiterate the general formula and leave the national court with greater

65. The Court seems to accept that there might be some attenuating circumstances in cases where non-compliance with a previous judgment of the Court might also been complicated by the specific Community measure involved. So, in *Commission v. Spain*, the Court held that Spain could be excused, as the Bathing Water directive aims for which non-compliance Spain was originally condemned, were hard to achieve and involved complex operations: Case 278/01 *Commission v. Spain* [2003] ECR I-14141. See also Case C-119/04 *Commission v. Italy* [2006] ECR I-6885 and M. Theodossiou, 'An Analysis of the Recent Response of the Community to Non Compliance with Court of Justice Judgments: Art. 288(2) EC', *ELRev*. 27 (2002): 25.
66. See for instance Case C-278/05 *Robins and Others v. Secretary of State for Work and Pensions* [2007] ECR I-1053, paras 61-63.

freedom to decide the issue on the facts before it. In cases such as *Rechberger*[67] and *Konle*[68] the Court made no effort to assess whether the breach was sufficiently serious. In *Konle*, the Court was satisfied to simply comment that

> [i]t is clear from the case-law of the Court that it is, in principle, for the national courts to apply the criteria to establish the liability of Member States for damage caused to individuals by breaches of Community law, in accordance with the guidelines laid down by the Court for the application of those criteria.[69]

Such an on-off approach should not surprise or scandalize, as it is simply yet another example of the continuous dialogue between the national courts and the ECJ. Advocate General La Pergola summed up the position well when he opined in *Konle* that

> [t]his does not mean, however, that the Court itself is not required to define the scope of the principles and rules of Community law that the national courts must then apply in specific cases. This task of centralised supervision, so to speak, is reserved for the Court and is connected with the need to ensure correct and uniform interpretation of Community law, a need that is fulfilled through the permanent dialogue between Community and national courts within the framework of the well-known instrument of judicial co-operation represented by the procedure for preliminary rulings under Article 234 EC. Only the Court therefore may, in general interpretative terms, clarify the concept at issue in this case, that is to say only the Court may define the scope of a 'sufficiently serious' breach, by establishing the conditions in which an individual may claim protection of his right to reparation from a Member State, and only the Court may explain how those conditions are to be understood. It is then for the national court to determine whether or not the facts in the case before it meet the conditions defined by the Court. If in doubt, the national court is, of course, still free to apply to the Court for further interpretative clarification under the preliminary ruling procedure, to help it to solve the problem.[70]

It is arguable that in certain cases the Court has to intervene to aid the general direction of the remedy rather than subsuming the national court's role of application. This appears to strike a reasonable balance between the role of Community and national jurisdictions, and remains fluid enough for the ECJ to provide guidance where it is needed.

---

67. Case C-140/97 *Rechberger and Geindl v. Austria* [1999] ECR I-3499.
68. C-302/97 *Konle v. Austria* [1999] ECR I-3099.
69. Ibid., para. 59.
70. AG La Pergola's Opinion in C-302/97 *Konle v. Austria* [1999] ECR I-3099, para. 24.

4. A FINAL COMMENT ON THE NOTION OF SERIOUS BREACH

It might be questioned whether it is possible to discern from all the ECJ case law a principle of general application in order to determine what a serious breach is. Several attempts have been made to rationalize the Court's case law. The first, presented by van Gerven, focuses on paragraph 55 of *Brasserie du Pêcheur/ Factortame* in relation to the distinction between a serious breach and the manifest and grave disregard by a Member State of its discretion.[71] He argued extra-judicially that, as the case law has developed since *Brasserie du Pêcheur/Factortame*, it has become increasingly clear that there exists what one could term 'a sliding scale' relating to the amount of discretion a State body has in the implementation of Community law. Where a Member State body has a wide degree of discretion in the application of Community law, it will be more difficult to establish a serious breach. Where a State body has little or no discretion, however, the mere infringement of a Community rule may be sufficient to establish the existence of a serious breach.[72] Thus, on a 0-10 scale, we have cases where the Member State has zero discretion, such as the situation in *Francovich* or *Dillenkofer*, where there was a total failure on the part of the Member State to implement a directive; cases where the level of discretion conferred on the Member States would rank as a level 5, such as *BT*, where the Member State incorrectly transposed a directive; and cases where the Member State's discretion could be ranked at level 10, such as *Brasserie du Pêcheur/Factortame*. Although such an approach is a useful, indicative tool, it is easily misunderstood, and could perhaps be willingly interpreted so as to reduce the impact of the EU principle. There is, indeed, a possible temptation to use the kind of power exercised by the Member States as a test. For instance, from a theoretical perspective, a case such as *Brasserie du Pêcheur/Factortame* would probably confer level 10 discretion on the Member State because it deals with two acts of Parliament where the policy choices taken by the State are at their widest. However, in reality, as discussed above, the case is instead one with zero discretion, as in both cases the breach was committed after very clear judgments of the Court, and the EU rules in question imposed very clear prohibitions on the Member States. The 'sliding scale' reconstruction is also somewhat static, as it reproduces a form of Montesquieu division of powers whereby the legislator has full discretion whilst the administration has none. A different argument, developed, for instance, by Prechal, focuses instead on the notion of 'clarity and precision'. Thus the main question is to examine the clarity and precision of the EU legal provisions that

---

71. W. Van Gerven, 'Bridging the Unbridgeable: Community and National Tort Laws after Francovich and Brasserie', *I.C.L.Q.* 45 (1996): 507.
72. See Case C-5/94 *The Queen v. Ministry of Agriculture, Fisheries and Food, ex parte Hedley Lomas* [1996] ECR I-2553. Advocate General Léger in that case comments also 'If the Member State commits a breach of Community law in an area in which it has no discretion, it must incur liability more readily than where it acts in an area in which it has a broad discretion' para. 169.

a Member State has to apply.[73] In our view, the starting point when reconstructing the Court's case law should always be that the determination of what a serious breach is has to be made with reference to Community law and not to national law. 'Serious breach' is a Community concept, and its content has to be defined in a Community context. The Court itself felt it necessary to spell this out:

> The discretion . . . is that enjoyed by the Member state concerned. Its existence and its scope are determined by reference to Community law and by reference to national law. The discretion which may be conferred by national law on the official or the institution responsible for the breach of Community law is therefore irrelevant in this respect.[74]

The subject matter of the case, the powers of the Member State in that area, and the clarity of the measure in question are all Community related. All the factors, discretion included, are elements of assessment in order to determine how negligent the Member State has been. As in many other areas of EU law, the approach of the Court is essentially very functional and practical. A mixture of different elements determines the seriousness of the breach. It seems that the Court itself has candidly acknowledged this state of affairs. In a recent judgment curiously concerning Directive 80/987/EEC on the protection of employees in the event of the insolvency of their employer, which was the object of the *Francovich* judgment, the Court seems to have come full circle. The applicants complained that the legislation in force in the UK did not fully implement the Directive's provisions, as it did not guarantee full protection for employees in case of company insolvency, and in particular, they sustained financial loss because of that. The Court first restated the conditions to establish the liability of the State. In discussing the 'serious breach' condition, the ECJ explained that

> [t]he discretion enjoyed by the Member State thus constitutes an important criterion in determining whether there has been a sufficiently serious breach of Community law. That discretion is broadly dependent on the degree of clarity and precision of the rule infringed.[75]

The Court reiterated that the wording of the Directive was not beyond doubt, and left different choices for Member States. The liability of a Member State by reason of incorrect transposition of that provision is therefore conditional on a finding of manifest and serious disregard by that State for the limits set on its discretion, with such disregard being assessed by taking into account all the factors listed by the ECJ in *Brasserie du Pêcheur/Factortame*. The Court went on to direct the national courts to which factors were particularly relevant. For instance, the fact that neither the applicant nor the Member State nor the Commission was able to suggest with

73. S. Prechal, *Directives in EC Law*, 2nd edn (Oxford: OUP, 2006), 288.
74. Case C-424/97 *Haim v. Kassenzahnärztliche Vereinigung Nordrhein (Haim II)* [2000] ECR 1-5123, para. 40.
75. Case C-278/05 *Robins and Others v. Secretary of State for Work and Pensions* [2007] ECR I-1053, paras 72 and 73.

precision the minimum degree of protection that, in their view, is required by the Directive, should have been taken as suggesting that the Directive was far from being clear. Furthermore, other elements, such as the fact that the Commission had officially considered the UK implementation as appropriate, militated against finding the Member State liable. In conclusion, to use the words of Advocate General Jacobs in *Lindöpark*, 'all various factors are to be taken into consideration globally and are not cumulative requirements the absence of any one of which means that there is no serious breach'.[76] Finally, it was in its judgment in *Brasserie du Pêcheur/Factortame* that the Court first commented on the relevance of fault in the context of State liability. It remarked that certain objective and subjective factors connected with the concept of fault under a national legal system may well be relevant for the purpose of determining whether or not a given breach of Community law is serious. However, 'the obligation to make reparation for loss or damage caused to individuals cannot depend upon a condition based on any concept of fault going beyond that of a sufficiently serious breach of Community law'.[77] This has been understood to mean that although the test is not one of strict liability, i.e., that there must not only be a breach but a sufficiently serious breach, the concept does not extend so far as to include something akin to fault on the part of the State body.

5. CAUSATION

The third condition necessary to establish the liability of the State is the existence of a causal link between the breach committed by the State and the damage incurred by the individuals affected. A chain of causation will have to be established in the light of the context of each case, on the basis of specific facts and conditions. In *Brasserie du Pêcheur/Factortame*, the ECJ was happy to leave the assessment of causation in the hands of the national courts. This is clearly preferable to the question of causation being determined by the ECJ, which would require the Court to evaluate questions of fact, acquire evidence and so on.[78] As such, the Court maintains its control over the first two conditions for holding the Member State liable in damages, while fully decentralizing the third element of the liability test by leaving the national court to determine the question of causation. In leaving this part of the liability test to be determined by national courts, more markedly so than for the 'centralized conditions', there is an inherent risk of diverging interpretations in respect of the causation condition.

Victory before the ECJ can therefore, in certain cases, appear hollow for the individual concerned. A case in point is *Francovich* who was, subsequent to the

76. AG Jacobs Opinion in Case C-150/99 *Sweden v. Lindöpark* [2001] ECR I-493, para. 58.
77. Case 46/93 *Brasserie du Pêcheur v. Bundesrepublik Deutschland and The Queen v. Secretary of State for Transport, ex parte Factortame and others* [1996] ECR I-1029, paras 78-79.
78. See further F. Smith, 'Causation in Francovich: The Neglected Problem', *I.C.L.Q.* 46 (1997): 925.

ECJ judgment, denied damages by the national court on the grounds that the condition of causality had not been fulfilled. The ECJ later confirmed the national court's findings in this respect in a second preliminary reference.[79] In that case, it was found that the directive concerned, while bestowing rights on some individuals, did not confer rights on Mr Francovich individually.

Another good example of possible divergent outcomes derives from the *Brasserie du Pêcheur/Factortame* litigation. It will be recalled that the case dealt with two separate breaches of Community law – one involved the prohibition on the marketing of French beer under the designation 'Bier', and the other was a prohibition on imports because French beer did not comply with German purity requirements. The ECJ had already held that the prohibition on the designation 'bier' was a sufficiently serious breach of Community law[80] so as to fulfil the second requirement of liability. The Court had not, however, made a decision on the issue of causality. The Bundesgerichtshof, in its decision, found that, because the German authorities had taken no proceedings against the company in respect of this rule, the plaintiffs had suffered no direct loss as a result of the rule. The only proceedings that had been taken by the German authorities against the company had related to the prohibition on imports, which the ECJ in its decision had found as not constituting a sufficiently serious breach of Community loss because, up until the decision of the Court in 1987 in *Commission v. Germany (Beer Purity Act)*, the violation was far from manifest.[81] It is particularly pertinent, however, that the German court specifically states that in determining the existence of a causal link it was applying the German rules of causation which require that there be 'necessary and sufficient causation'. In particular, the German Court commented that

> [i]t is a matter for the national legal systems of the individual Member States to implement the conditions for liability as regards "direct causation" into national law while safeguarding the full effectiveness of Community law . . . It is not necessary for present purposes to decide whether, in so doing, the characteristic of directness of causation makes it possible to adopt a narrower approach, possibly oriented towards considerations of protective purpose.[82]

As for the action brought by the French brewery company, the German court found the action in damages to be unfounded. Both the national court and the ECJ found that the damage suffered by the company was causally linked to the national provisions on the prohibition of additives, which could not be considered a serious breach. As for the national rule on designation of the product as beer, which was instead considered by the Court of Justice to be a manifest and clear breach of the

79. Case C-479/93 *Francovich v. Italy (Francovich II)* [1996] ECR I-3843.
80. The Court of Justice had ruled that the prohibition on the designation 'Bier' amounted to a sufficiently serious breach of Art. 30 EC, since the incompatibility of this rule had already been made manifest by the judgments of the Court.
81. Case 178/84 *Commission v. Germany* [1987] ECR 1227.
82. Bundesgerichtshof, *Brasserie du Pêcheur du Pecheur SA v. Germany*, C.M.L.R. 1 (1997): 971.

free movement provision, the national court did not accept the existence of a causal link between this legislation and the damage suffered by the company.

The English courts took a very different approach to that adopted by the German Courts. In a series of judgments, all the different instances of the English judiciary found in favour of Factortame. In a line of reasoning that was clearly influenced by the ECJ case law, the Divisional Court found that in the UK, all the conditions laid down by the ECJ were satisfied, and thus Factortame and the other companies should have been compensated.[83] The national courts' judgments stressed the importance of the EU rules that had been breached by the Merchant Shipping Act, with particular emphasis on principles such as non-discrimination, proportionality and legitimate expectation. The national courts also highlighted that the Government was fully aware that the application of such an act would cause loss to the applicants. The UK government appealed unsuccessfully all the way up to the House of Lords[84] and the claim was finally settled in March 2000, when Factortame and the other claimants accepted an offer from the Secretary of State. Under the terms of the settlement, the claimants, who had originally claimed 285 million pounds sterling (GBP), received GBP 55 million, including interest of GBP 26 million.[85]

The difficulties for applicants, in conclusion, are real and costly, and may prove a great deterrent to the use of the State liability principle by individuals for the protection of rights.[86] The difference between the rhetoric and the reality is therefore somewhat stark.

A possible divergence in the outcome of cases seems nonetheless unavoidable, as this is the nature of both the causation element, so interwoven with questions of fact, and more generally on the dual nature of the judicial systems in EU law, whereby all national courts are a fundamental part of the system. In particular, in any preliminary reference procedure, the only obligation to which the national judge is subject is to provide the ECJ with sufficient elements of law and facts as to provide the necessary information that will enable the Court to give a reply which is of assistance to the national court.[87] As for causation, it might therefore be difficult for the Court of Justice to properly assess the minutiae of the substantive action. The preliminary reference is, however, a procedure of unlimited flexibility, and in a few cases the Court has indeed felt that it was in a position to assess the causation element. The most notable judgment in this respect is *Brinkmann*,[88] which has been labelled 'the first case in which the Court itself relied on causation

---

83. *R v. Secretary of State for Transport ex p Factortame Ltd (No 5)*, Court of Appeal, [1998] 3 C.M.L.R. 192.
84. *R v. Secretary of State for Transport ex p Factortame Ltd (No 5)*, Court of Appeal, [1998] 3 C.M.L.R. 192 and *R v. Secretary of State for Transport ex p Factortame Ltd (No 6)*, House of Lords, [1993] 3 C.M.L.R. 597.
85. House of Lords, Hansard Debates, 8 Feb. 2001.
86. See further comments in conclusion of E. Deards, '*Brasserie du Pêcheur*: Snatching Defeat from the Jaws of Victory', *ELRev.* 22(6) (1997): 620.
87. Information Notice on references from national courts for a preliminary ruling, 2005 C143/01.
88. Case C-319/96 *Brinkmann Tabakfabriken v. Skatteministeriet* [1998] ECR I-5255.

to restrict liability'.[89] In its judgment, the Court pointed out that while it is generally for national courts to decide whether or not the conditions of State liability for breach of Community law are met, in this case, the Court had before it all the information necessary to judge whether the facts presented were to be characterized as a sufficiently serious breach of Community law and, if appropriate, whether there was a causal link between the breach of the State's obligation and the damage sustained. The Court recalled that it is settled law that a failure to take any measure to transpose a directive in order to achieve the result it prescribes, within the period laid down for that purpose, constitutes per se a serious breach of Community law. The Court went on to say that there must also be a direct causal link between the breach and the damage allegedly suffered. In the present case the action of the Danish tax authorities – although they wrongly classified the Westpoint tobacco rolls as cigarettes and thus taxed them at a higher rate – by giving immediate effect to the relevant provisions of the Directive, broke the causal link between damage and conduct of the State. Therefore, the failure to implement the Directive by ministerial decree did not in itself give rise to liability on the part of the State.

The case of *Brinkmann* introduced a degree of uncertainty and disparity, it would seem, into the remedies available to litigants. The actions and interpretation of administrative bodies may vary from State to State, and it is only where their actions are manifestly contrary to the provisions of Community law that the individuals have redress, despite the fact that the State as a whole has committed a sufficiently serious breach of Community law by failing to implement the Directive in the first place. Furthermore, different administrative bodies in the same Member State could also interpret provisions differently, leading to liability being incurred in some situations and not in others. A criticism levelled by some is that the case appears to muddle the issue of causation: Why was the alleged loss of the applicants more attributable to the erroneous interpretation of the Directive by the national tax authorities than to the failure to adopt implementing measures? The Court has always been clear that a change in practice by the national authorities would not be sufficient to comply with the Community obligation of implementing a directive.[90] The decision, therefore, appears to dilute the strength of the finding that failure to implement a directive is a sufficiently serious breach, per se. This result could, in some ways, be compared to the principle in the field of Community liability that, where wrongful conduct by a Member State has been made possible by an illegal failure of a Community authority to exercise supervisory powers conferred upon it, then it is this second failure which will be seen as the direct cause of the damage.[91] In this latter situation, it is clear that the Community institution had a duty to act. This flexible attitude of the Court was not repeated in the case of *Rechberger, Geindl and Others v. Austria.*[92] The case dealt

89. T. Tridimas, *The General Principles of EU Law*, 2nd edn (Oxford: OUP, 2006), 530.
90. Case C-167/73 *Commission v. France (Re French Maritime Code)* [1974] ECR 359.
91. Joined Cases 9 and 12/60 *Vloeberghs v. High Authority* [1961] ECR 197 at 240. See Ch. 3 for a full discussion.
92. Case C-140/97 *Rechberger and Geindl v. Austria* [1999] ECR I-3499.

with the Austrian implementation of the Package Travel Directive.[93] The Court first found that the Directive was intended to confer rights on individuals, and that the Austrian government's failure to properly implement the Directive had to be considered as a serious breach. What is interesting, in terms of the condition of causality, is the Court's comments in reply to the national court's sixth question. The Austrian government argued that there was no direct causal link between the late or incomplete implementation of Article 7 on the protection of travellers, and the loss or damage suffered by the applicants because of the intervention of a chain of wholly exceptional and unforeseeable events. In connection with this question, the UK and Swedish governments highlighted the fact that it is for the national court to decide on the issue of causality. The Court referred to the passage in *Brasserie du Pêcheur/Factortame* that set out this principle. It also remarked that in the present case, the national court had already found that there was such a direct causal link between the conduct of the Member State and the damage sustained by the individuals. The Court went further by pointing out that 'Article 7 of the Directive imposes an obligation of result, namely to guarantee package travellers the refund of money paid over and their repatriation in the event of the travel organisers bankruptcy',[94] and in those circumstances the Member State's liability for breach of Article 7 of the Directive cannot be precluded by imprudent conduct on the part of the travel organizer or by the occurrence of exceptional and unforeseeable events. If Article 7 had been properly implemented, the imprudent conduct and the occurrence of exceptional and unforeseeable events would not have prevented the refund of monies. As Advocate General Saggio comments,

> If the Directive is concerned with imposing upon Member States an obligation to provide a system for the protection of consumers that will provide them with security in the event of the insolvency of the organisers or retailers of package services, it is clear that that concern has the specific aim of protecting consumers as the weak parties to the contract.[95]

In conclusion, the principles one can draw from these cases are that it has been made clear that it is for the national court to determine whether or not the condition of causality is fulfilled. What is implicit in these judgments, however, is that it is for the national court to determine whether there is a direct causal link on the facts according to Community law principles, and not according to national law. To conclude otherwise would contradict the nature of the remedy as a whole, and would create great uncertainty. The condition remains as of yet undeveloped in a sense, as in the examples given above – *Brinkmann* and *Rechberger* – where the analysis of the causal link operated by the ECJ is far from accurate. In the *AGM* case, the ECJ hinted that the statements made by a Finnish official in the media, suggesting that elevators produced by an Italian company were unsafe, could give rise to compensation. According to the ECJ, evidence of a fall in company turnover

93. Council Directive 90/314/EEC of 13 June 1990, 4.
94. Case C-140/97 *Rechberger and Geindl v. Austria* [1999] ECR I-3499, para. 74.
95. Ibid., AG Saggio's Opinion, at para. 54.

and a decrease in profit after the statements were made might have been enough to establish a casual link between the conduct of the State and the loss suffered by the individual.[96]

It seems that, in reality, the Court treats causation as a further element to characterize the seriousness of the breach without detracting from the main finding (that is, that a failure to implement a directive properly is a serious breach per se). Thus, causation can be used so as to 'provide an exit route in cases of non-transposition'.[97] A State that has not transposed a directive can rely on the actions of national administrative bodies to bridge the gap and protect it from damages claims. The State would only then be liable if the actions of the administrative bodies were contrary to Community law, and inexcusable according to the test set out in the *BT* case.[98]

6. STATE LIABILITY AND NATIONAL PROCEDURAL LAW

6.1. Introduction

As has been seen from the foregoing sections, the development of the principle of State liability is centred on a mechanism of duality of reparation. The ECJ has laid down the core principles of the State liability doctrine, while, at the same time, emphasizing the procedural autonomy of national states in deciding whether damages should be paid in any specific case. The Court of Justice in the cases discussed above provides a detailed analysis of whether the conditions for liability are met according to the circumstances of the case before it, and has remained slightly reticent with regard to the condition of causality. This approach can be praised for ensuring uniformity of approach in a complicated area of law but does, as is demonstrated in many other areas of law, stretch the borders of its accepted role in the context of preliminary rulings. The Court is certainly seen to stray into answering questions about the application of law to facts rather than merely answering abstract questions on the interpretation of Community law. A discussion of State liability would therefore be incomplete without exploring the range of questions that have generally been left to national courts to decide, and the circumstances in which the ECJ will decide the concrete outcome itself.[99]

96. Case C-470/03 *A.G.M.-COS.MET Srl v. Suomen valtio, Tarmo Lehtinen* [2007] I-2749, para. 84.
97. T. Tridimas, 'Liability for Breach of Community Law: Growing up and Mellowing Down?,' *CMLRev.* 38 (2001): 306.
98. C-392/93 *R v. HM Treasury, ex parte British Telecommunications* [1996] ECR I-1631.
99. A detailed analysis of the national courts case law in applying the principle of state liability goes beyond the scope of this work. For some interesting data see M. Claes, *The National Courts' Mandate in the European Constitution* (Oxford: Hart, 2006), 11.7, 346 ss. and M.P.F. Granger, 'National Applications of Francovich and the Construction of a European Administrative jus commune', *ELRev.* 32 (2007): 157.

The three conditions discussed above are those necessary to make the State liable in damages. Still, as in any system of tort law, to make such an action 'workable', other requirements and conditions will have to be satisfied. The section that follows will try to highlight the other essential elements for an action in damages. Once more, such an analysis will have to take into account the case law of the Court and its 'cohabitation' with national elements.

6.2. The State as Defendant

So far, we have been examining the notion of liability. The first extra element that has to be analyzed is the second element in the *Francovich* principle: the notion of 'State'.

In certain respects, the Court in *Francovich* was presented with the easiest case – total failure on the part of the State to implement a directive. There was no real need, therefore, for the Court to touch upon questions of the definition of 'State'. The question remained, however, whether breaches on the part of the legislator, regulatory authorities, administrative bodies, courts and private bodies could be subject to the same liability requirement. Before embarking on the specific remedial questions, it is first necessary to examine what is meant by the expression 'State'. Such an analysis will not only confirm the theoretical justification, but will also shed light on a very import question: Who is to be held responsible for breaches of EU law?

6.2.1. The Notion of the State in EU Law

As in most areas of European law, the definition of 'State' in the context of State liability has to be a Community concept. As the Court has often repeated, such a definition is not and cannot be totally independent from traditional national law concepts of the State, but it is relevant and instrumental to the aim of harmonization of European integration. It is therefore perhaps useful to briefly examine how the ECJ has dealt with this question in related areas.

The ECJ's case law on the determination of the scope of application of the doctrine of direct effect of directives provides useful guidance in this context. It is now well established that non-implemented directives can only be enforced against the State. In this context, the Court has taken a broad view of what constitutes a State body,[100] which includes all administrative organs, decentralized authorities, such as municipalities,[101] constitutionally independent authorities which are responsible for the maintenance of public order,[102] public authorities which

100. See further Case 152/84 *Marshall v. Southampton and South-West Hampshire Area Authority (Teaching)* [1986] ECR 723; reaffirmed in Case C-91/92 *Paola Faccini Dori v. Recreb* [1994] ECR I-3325.
101. See Case 103/88 *Fratelli Costanzo SpA v. Comune di Milano* [1989] ECR 1839.
102. Case 222/84 *Johnston v. Chief Constable of the Royal Ulster Constabulary* [1986] ECR 1651.

provide health services[103] and nationalized industries.[104] The test, set out in *Foster* to determine whether or not a body is a 'State body', includes organizations or bodies which are subject to the authority or control of the State or have special powers beyond those which result from normal relations between individuals.[105] Whether or not these two factors are alternative or cumulative has been left unclear, although it is now generally accepted that the test should be read widely. From the perspective of Community law, therefore, the internal allocation of power on the legislative, executive or even judicial branch of the State does not matter.

Furthermore, it is also useful to refer to the case law of the Court under Article 226 EC, which regulates direct actions brought by the Commission against defaulting States guilty of breaching EU law. In several early cases, the state concerned complained that such an action could not have been brought against the central government, when in reality, the breach committed could have been attributed to independent authorities on whom the State did not have any, or had only partial, control. The Court consistently refused to accept such an argument.[106] The *Commission v. Italian Republic* of 2003 judgment deserves a special mention.[107] The case laid down the clear principle that an enforcement action can be brought against a State even if the non-compliance with EC law can be attributed to national courts. A provision of an Italian law of 1990 implemented the obligation that customs duties and other taxes that were levied contrary to Community law were to be reimbursed to the taxpayer. The legislation also provided, however, that those duties and taxes were to be reimbursed only if the corresponding burden had not been passed on to third parties. The national courts interpreted the provision to the effect that in most practical scenarios there was a presumption that the charge had been passed on to third parties. The applicant was a commercial enterprise, the company had not gone bankrupt and the tax had been uncontestedly levied for a number of years throughout the country. The ECJ found this presumption to be inadmissible, as it rendered reimbursement practically impossible or excessively difficult. Thus, through the actions of the national court, the ECJ found that the Italian Republic had failed to fulfil its obligations under the Treaty.

To go back to liability, most of the principles developed by the ECJ have been transposed in this area of EC law as well. The crucial statement is to be found in *Brasserie du Pêcheur/Factortame*. In establishing the universality of the right of reparation, the Court not only repeated the dictum of *Francovich* – that the principle of State liability is inherent in the system of the Treaty – but also drew the relevant conclusion that the principle 'holds good for any case in which a Member State breaches Community law, whatever be the organ of the

103. Case 152/84 *Marshall v. Southampton and South-West Hampshire Area Authority (Teaching)* [1986] ECR 723.
104. Case C-188/89 *Foster v. British Gas Plc* [1990] I ECR 3313.
105. Ibid.
106. Case 77/69 *Commission v. Belgium* [1970] ECR 237; and Case 169/82 *Commission v. Italy* [1984] ECR 1603.
107. Case C-129/00 *Commission v. Italy* [2003] ECR I-14637.

State whose act or omission was responsible for the breach'.[108] Thus, liability does not vary according to the specific authority that is actually responsible for the breach.

6.2.2. Who Can be Sued?

In EU law, there are no specific rules on the issue of who can be sued. In theory, who and how the State will defend itself in an action in liability before domestic courts should be an issue to be left to national courts. Still, one could argue that even in respect of this procedural condition, the two principles of effectiveness and equivalence would still apply. The ECJ itself has actually laid down some broad guidance on the issue, most notably in the cases of *Konle*[109] and *Haim II*.[110]

The first case concerned Mr Klaus Konle, a German national, who was the successful bidder in an enforcement sale by auction of a parcel of land in Osttirol, Austria on 11 August 1994. Mr Konle submitted his own application for authorization for acquisition of the land, declaring that he intended to use the land he had acquired to establish his principal residence and the head office of his own undertaking, EUVAT GmbH. This declaration was essentially similar to the declaration Austrian nationals were allowed to submit under regional law instead of having to make an application for authorization. The Lienz District Administration, as land transfer authority of first instance, nevertheless rejected the application on the ground that the conditions applying to foreigners under the relevant legislation were not met. It also considered that Mr Konle's application had not provided the necessary proof, without which authorization could not be granted, that the acquisition in question was not to be used to establish a secondary residence, which was contrary to the objectives of the law on the transfer of land. After a further change in the law, Mr Konle was eventually given authorization, after long delays and appeal procedures. He considered that he had been discriminated against, and his freedom of establishment and free movement of capital affected, by having to prove that he would not establish a secondary residence rather than making a simple declaration, and further, in that he had to submit to an authorization procedure before acquisition of the land. This authorization procedure had delayed the completion of Mr Konle's acquisition, preventing him from entering into possession of the property. A question that arose in the proceedings was who Mr Konle could claim against – the offending law applicable to him was regional law rather than federal law. The question was,

> Is the principle of the liability of Member States for the damage caused to an individual by breaches of Community law complied with, on a proper interpretation of Article 5 of the E.C. Treaty (now Article 10), if the national law on

---

108. Case 46/93 *Brasserie du Pêcheur v. Bundesrepublik Deutschland and The Queen v. Secretary of State for Transport, ex parte Factortame and others* [1996] ECR I-1029, para. 32.
109. C-302/97 *Konle v. Austria* [1999] ECR I-3099.
110. Case C-424/97 *Haim v. Kassenzahnärztliche Vereinigung Nordrhein (Haim II)* [2000] ECR 1-5123.

> liability of a Member State with a federal structure lays down that in the case of infringements imputable to a part of the State, the injured party may claim only against the part State, not the State as a whole?[111]

The Court first of all underlined the responsibility that each Member State has in ensuring that individuals obtain reparation for damage caused to them by non-compliance with Community law, no matter which public authority was responsible for the breach, and no matter which public authority was, in principle, under the law of the Member State concerned, responsible for making reparation. The Court continued that a Member State 'cannot, therefore, plead the distribution of powers and responsibilities between the bodies which exist in its national legal order to free itself from liability on that basis'.[112] Subject to that reservation, and the obligation as to result – effective protection of individual rights – Community law does not require Member States to make any changes in their system of governance or in the way they distribute powers and responsibilities between the public bodies of their territory. The answer in the immediate case was that reparation did not necessarily need to be provided by the federal structure for a Member State's obligations under Community law in the context of State liability to be fulfilled.

The case of *Haim II* offered the Court the chance of further elaborating on the findings in *Konle*. The case concerned not a federal structure, but rather geographically or otherwise decentralized bodies – taking the *Konle* jurisprudence a step further. Mr Haim was an Italian national who, on completion of his dental studies in Turkey, obtained a diploma in dentistry in Turkey and practised as a dentist there until 1980. In 1981, he obtained permission to practise as a dental practitioner in Germany. It was in Belgium, however, that his Turkish diploma was recognized by the competent authorities in 1982 as equivalent to the Belgian diploma in dentistry. He practised as a dentist under a social security scheme in Belgium until 1991. At the end of that year, he returned to Germany to work as an assistant in his son's practice, returning to his previous work in Belgium in 1993. In the meantime, Mr Haim applied to the Nordrhein Association of Dental Practitioners of Social Security Schemes in Germany ('the KVN') for enrolment on the register of dental practitioners so that he could treat patients affiliated to social security schemes. That application was refused on the ground that the relevant German rules required applicants to have completed a preparatory training period of at least two years, which Mr Haim had not done. That requirement could only be waived in the case of dental practitioners who had obtained a qualification recognized in another Member State under Community law, and who were authorized to practise that profession. That was not true of Mr Haim, whose Turkish qualification had only been recognized as equivalent in Belgium. The case led to two references to the ECJ, the first on the possible breach of Mr Haim's right of free movement, and a second one, some ten years into Mr Haim's litigation process, with which we are now

111. C-302/97 *Konle v. Austria* [1999] ECR I-3099, para. 20 N.4.
112. Ibid., para. 62.

concerned. Mr Haim sought compensation for the pecuniary damage arising from a loss of earnings, which he claimed to have suffered because, in breach of Community law, he was prevented from working in Germany as a dental practitioner under a social security scheme from 1988 until the end of 1994. One of the questions raised in the second preliminary ruling was whether both the legally independent public body and the Member State could be held liable if an official of the independent public body breached Community law. Relying on the Court's judgment in *Konle v. Austria*, all the Member States that submitted observations in the case, together with the Commission, agreed that it was for each Member State to ensure that individuals obtained reparation for loss and damage caused to them by non-compliance with Community law, no matter which public authority was responsible for the breach, and no matter which public authority was in principle, under the law of the Member State concerned, responsible for making reparation. While acknowledging that this argument was obviously correct, the Court in *Haim* continued that there is nothing in the *Konle* case to suggest that reparation for loss and damage caused to individuals by national measures taken in breach of Community law must necessarily be provided by the Member State itself in order for its obligations under Community law to be fulfilled:

> That is also true for those Member States, whether or not they have a federal structure, in which certain legislative or administrative tasks are devolved to territorial bodies with a certain degree of autonomy or to any other public-law body legally distinct from the State. In those Member States, reparation for loss and damage caused to individuals by national measures taken in breach of Community law by a public-law body may therefore be made by that body. Nor does Community law preclude a public-law body, in addition to the Member State itself, from being liable to make reparation for loss and damage caused to individuals as a result of measures which it took in breach of Community law.[113]

As Advocate General Mischo commented in his Opinion in the *Haim* case: '[A]s regards individuals, however, there is nothing to prevent the State from standing back and letting its authorities face the consequences of a breach of Community law which those authorities have committed in the exercise of their own powers'.[114]

In general, one could argue that since liability should be the corollary of allocation of power in a democratic system, it would be irrational for the State to have to take responsibility for the actions of local authorities, whose autonomy it is bound to respect under the constitution. However, it might be instead claimed that it would hardly be rational, in view of the strict hierarchy of norms which applies in theory under domestic law, to hold an independent body in any way

113. Case C-424/97 *Haim v. Kassenzahnärztliche Vereinigung Nordrhein (Haim II)* [2000] ECR 1-5123, paras 31 and 32.
114. AG Mischo's Opinion in Case C-424/97 *Haim v. Kassenzahnärztliche Vereinigung Nordrhein (Haim II)* [2000] ECR 1-5123, para. 31.

liable for an act where, although that act is legally attributable to it, the content of the act is predetermined by legislation with which it is bound strictly to comply. The only indications provided by the Court are that the conditions for reparation of loss and damage laid down by national legislation must not be less favourable than those relating to similar domestic claims, and must not be so framed as to make it in practice impossible or excessively difficult to obtain reparation.

Although it appears, therefore, that there is no objection in principle under Community law to making the decentralized public body liable in the event of a breach of Community law, such as that in Mr Haim's case, the condition is that the plaintiff is not led down a 'cul-de-sac'. This sort of situation may arise if national law provided only for the possibility of a claim against the decentralized public body, but then added extra conditions for finding such liability. This issue closely relates to that of causation. The case of *Brinkmann* illustrates the point well, as in that case the breach was caused by the legislature in not transposing a directive. This was found not to have caused the damage, but rather, it was held that the intervention of the tax authorities in applying the relevant law broke the chain of causation. Since their breach was not 'sufficiently serious', State liability was not triggered. Both the issue of which body should be sued under national law, and which body caused the damage, are complex. As such, there is a real possibility that an applicant may get it wrong, and in pursuing one body, which is deemed not to be responsible, may be left time-barred as regards the proper defendant. What should be borne in mind in this instance is that Community law also imposes a requirement of legal certainty. The national rules pertaining to the issue of which body should be sued should therefore be sufficiently clear and precise for citizens to understand them, and for them to be able to effectively assert their rights. It needs to be remembered that the case law on supremacy of EC law as to administrative authorities should also be taken into account. It is now well established that such a principle binds administrative authorities and is not dependent on any internal allocation of powers. In the case of *Ciola*, for instance, the Court clearly established that the obligation to set aside 'any conflicting provision of national law is incumbent on all administrative bodies, including decentralized authorities'.[115]

7. THE UNIVERSALITY OF LIABILITY AGAINST THE STATE

In *Brasserie du Pêcheur/Factortame*, the Court firmly declared the irrelevance of the question of which authority committed the breach. But is this always the case? Two delicate questions need to be examined. The first concerns when the breach is attributable to the national court, and the second is when individuals are responsible for the breach.

115. Case C-224/97 *Erich Ciola v. Land Vorarlberg* [1999] ECR I-2517.

7.1. National Courts as Tortfeasor

The thought that courts could also be considered as organs of the State for the purposes of State liability was initially regarded by academics as questionable: 'In view of the need to protect the independence of the judiciary, and to foster a spirit of cooperation in national judges in matters concerning Community law the possibility of State liability under *Francovich* in respect of judicial failure is surely unthinkable.'[116] Advocate General Léger also comments in *Hedley Lomas* that 'State liability incurred by reason of judgments of national courts contrary to Community law is certain to pose many difficult constitutional questions.'[117] In the case of *Brasserie du Pêcheur/Factortame*, however, the Court made it clear that State liability can in principle apply even where the breach of Community law is committed by the judiciary. The logic of this is clear. National courts, as well as other State bodies, are subject to the obligation of cooperation under Article 10 EC, as confirmed explicitly in the case of *Von Colson*, where the Court ruled that

> the Member States obligation arising from a directive to achieve the result envisaged by the directive and their duty under Article 5 of the Treaty [now Article 10 EC] to take all appropriate measures, whether general or particular, to ensure the fulfilment of that obligation, is binding on all the authorities of Member-States including, for matters within their jurisdiction, the courts.[118]

The *Gerhard Köbler v. Republic of Austria*[119] decision confirmed the principle that Member States are obliged to make good damage caused to individuals by decisions of national courts which infringe Community law. The case concerned an action by a German professor who had applied for a special length-of-service increment in Austria. The increment was normally paid to professors who had fifteen years of experience exclusively at Austrian universities. Mr Köbler, who had only ten years' experience in an Austrian university, but completed the requisite length-of-service teaching in Germany, argued that the duration of service in other Member States should be taken into consideration. After applying for, and then withdrawing, a reference for a preliminary ruling, the *Verwaltungsgerichtshof* (administrative court of last instance) decided that the refusal to take into account service in other Member States was justified. The national court reasoned that the special length-of-service increment was a loyalty bonus, and therefore, the derogation from the freedom of movement for workers was objectively justified. Mr Köbler then brought an action for damages before the *Landesgericht für Zivilrechtssachen*, Vienna (Civil Law division of the regional court in Vienna), against

116. T. Tridimas, *The General Principles of EU Law*, 2nd edn (OUP, Oxford, 2006), 506.
117. AG Léger's Opinion in Case C-5/94 *The Queen v. Ministry of Agriculture, Fisheries and Food, ex parte Hedley Lomas* [1996] ECR I-2553, at n. 124, quoting E. Szyszczak, 'European Community Law: New Remedies, New Directions', *MLR* 55 (1992): 690, at 696.
118. Case C-14/83 *Von Colson and Kamann v. Land Nordrhein-Westfalen* [1984] ECR 1891, para. 26.
119. Case C-224/01 *Köbler v. Austria* [2001] ECR I-10239.

the Republic of Austria on the grounds that the judgment was contrary to Community law. He based his action on the EC's previous ruling in *Schöning-Kougebetopoulou*,[120] which established that duration of service in other Member States should be taken into consideration. The referring court submitted several questions to the ECJ in connection with this second action. In its preliminary ruling, the ECJ confirmed the principle laid out in *Brasserie du Pêcheur/Factortame* that every organ of the State could be held liable. In particular, the Court referred very rapidly to the liability of courts in the context of international law, and in the context of the European Convention of Human Rights. More importantly, because of the essential role played by the judiciary in the protection of the rights derived by individuals from Community rules, and the fact that a court adjudicating at last instance is by definition the last judicial body before which individuals may assert the rights conferred on them by Community law, the Court of Justice inferred that the protection of those rights would be weakened – and the full effectiveness of the Community rules conferring such rights would be brought into question – if individuals were precluded from being able, under certain conditions, to obtain reparation when their rights were affected by an infringement of Community law attributable to a decision of a court of a Member State adjudicating at last instance.[121]

The Court also rejected any claims that the recognition of liability could affect the independence of the judiciary. On the contrary, according to the Court, it would instead 'enhance the quality of a legal system and thus in the long run the authority of the judiciary'.[122] After such a strong reaffirmation of the universality of the action of liability, however, the Court softened its stance considerably. With regard to the second condition, concerning the seriousness of the breach, the Court made it clear that for a breach to be sufficiently serious in the case of an infringement by a national court, 'it must be manifest, taking into account the specific nature of the judicial function'.[123] Whether or not the breach is manifest is to be determined by the court designated as competent by the national legal system. In the case at hand, however, instead of leaving this determination to the national court, the ECJ felt it had sufficient facts to make the decision itself. Accordingly, although the ECJ found that the Austrian legislation was incompatible with Community law and not justified, ultimately, the breach by the national court was not manifest. The Court based its reasoning first, on the fact that there was no Community law which expressly covered the point of law at issue, and second, on the infringement not being intentional, but rather a result of an incorrect reading of a judgment of the Court. Thus, *Köbler* could be listed as another example of a Member State escaping liability as the Community norms – in this instance a judgment of the Court itself – did not provide an unequivocal answer. Even so, the Court of Justice very clearly

120. Case C-15/96 *Kalliope Schöning-Kougebetopoulou v. Freie und Hansestadt Hamburg* [1998] ECR I-47.
121. Case C-224/01 *Köbler v. Austria* [2001] ECR I-10239, paras 33-35.
122. Ibid., para. 43.
123. Ibid., para. 53.

acknowledged the specificity of the judicial function, and declared that liability would arise in exceptional circumstances. The judgment has attracted many comments. Tridimas is right in calling it a very significant constitutional case, emphasizing a federal character whereby it is reaffirmed that 'in a polity governed by the rule of law, why should the judicial branch be the only one which is exempt from the possibility of challenge'?[124] In our view, the *Köbler* judgment certainly has a very high symbolic value. On a practical level, however, its impact may not be so great. It is, of course, to be accepted that when there is a general principle of State liability, it would be difficult to make an exception for national courts. Nonetheless, the judgment might prove to be applicable in many situations. First, it is not clear what kind of breach could be imputable to the courts. From the factual context of *Köbler*, it could be argued that liability will arise where the national courts fail to refer a question under Article 234 EC, and/or when they fail to apply a clear and unconditional Community norm. Second, it could be questioned whether these are two cumulative conditions, or whether they are independent of one another. If one considers that they might be kept as separate issues, then it is necessary to infer that liability will incur only for supreme courts or courts against whose decisions there is no further remedy – which is a violation of Article 234(3) EC, the only provision which seems to impose an obligation to refer questions to the ECJ. Such an interpretation would certainly introduce an element of rigidity in the otherwise rather flexible interpretation of the supreme court's duty to refer. It would also have to be established whether a violation of Article 234(3) EC would be automatically classified as a rule intended to confer an individual right, or whether it would be necessary to show that the rule of Community law, which the national court was supposed to apply, was intended to confer individual rights. Furthermore, imposing liability for failure to refer questions, even if limited to supreme courts, would insert an element of strain in the relationship between supreme courts and the ECJ, which the Luxembourg court has so far tended to avoid. Such an approach is best exemplified by the very flexible and ambiguous *CILFIT* principles, where the Court of Justice considered that in certain cases no reference should be made, in particular where the question of interpretation is irrelevant; where the ECJ has already ruled on the point; or in a case where the interpretation of Community law is self-evident.[125] It would still be necessary, however, to demonstrate the seriousness of the breach and the alleged damage. The mere failure to refer would thus be just another factor that would have to be taken into account when establishing the seriousness of the breach, and would not be enough on its own to establish the liability.

The complications continue at the level of procedural application of the ruling. In *Köbler*, the Court was at pains to stress that an action in damages would not affect well established principles such as that of res judicata. This latter principle is based on the idea that there must be finality in litigation, despite the possibility that

124. T. Tridimas, *The General Principles of EU Law*, 2nd edn (OUP, Oxford, 2006), 525.
125. Case 283/81 *CILFIT and Lanificio di Gavardo SpA v. Ministry of Health* [1982] ECR 3415.

mistakes in the judgment might emerge in the future. In reality, bringing an action for damages in this context involves impugning the final decision of a domestic court.

As of yet, the full consequences of *Köbler* have not been assessed, but, if the judgment were to be read strictly and closely, it would require drastic changes to be made to domestic legal systems. It would probably be necessary first, to introduce a specific procedure for this kind of action, or else there could be a real possibility that the same issues would be litigated twice before the same Supreme Court, raising problems of impartiality in respect of the judicial body in question. On occasion, this may require the court to give a ruling on whether it itself was responsible for breaching EC law. The judgment, as has already been pointed out, may also lead to certain paradoxical results. As Zuckerman notes:

> Suppose that in an action for damages, the House of Lords reaches the same conclusion as that reached by the House of Lords in the original claim. Should the claimant still have a right to complain before yet another court that his Community rights have been denied?[126]

In addition, there are many other practical problems that may arise. It could be questioned whether a right of reparation could arise for a breach committed by a lower court, whether the original judgment would continue to bind the parties, or whether damages could be recovered exclusively by the parties that participated in the original trial.[127]

In conclusion, *Köbler* is certainly a case which reaffirms the universality of the principle of State liability. It also reaffirms that liability for a breach committed by a national court cannot be excluded a priori.[128] However, the actual award of damages would arise only in exceptional circumstances. Such a reconstruction seems to be confirmed by the only other case that has so far dealt with the

126. A. Zuckerman, *Appeal to the High Court against House of lords decisions on the interpretation of Community law – Damages for judicial error* [2003] CLJ 177.

127. A similar case is Case C-453/00 *Kühne & Heitz* [2004] ECR I-837. The Court held that the principle of loyal cooperation imposes on an administrative body an obligation to review a final administrative decision, whenever an application for such a review is made, in order to take account of the interpretation of the relevant provision given in the meantime by the ECJ even – inter alia – where 'the administrative decision in question has become final as a result of a judgment of a national court ruling at final instance'. See also on the application of the principle of res judicata in EC law C-392/04 and C-422/04 *i-21 v. Germany* [2006] ECR I-8559; Case C-234/04 *Kapferer v. Schlank & Schick* [2006] ECR I-2585; and Case C-119/05 *Ministero dell'Industria, del Commercio e dell'Artigianato v Lucchini Siderurgica SpA* [ECR] 2007 I-6199. For an overview of these cases see X. Groussot & T. Minssen, 'Res Judicata in the Court of Justice Case-Law: Balancing Legal Certainty with Legality?', *ECLRev.* 3 (2007): 385.

128. If the objective is to try to ensure that national courts do not stray too far from the correct application of EC law, it is suggested that the appropriate procedure against 'devious' national case law in this context is that of Art. 226 EC under which the Court performs not an interpretative function, as under Article EC, but acts as an adjudicator. See Case C-129/00 *Commission v. Italy* [2003] ECR I-14637.

issue. In *Traghetti del Mediterraneo SpA* [TDM], an Italian maritime transport company sued the Italian State for compensation for damage suffered as a result of an incorrect interpretation by the Corte Suprema di Cassazione (Italian Supreme Court of Cassation) of the Community rules on competition and State aid, as interpreted by the ECJ.[129] The questions referred by the Italian court before which the action for damage was brought concerned liability for breaches committed by national courts, and a further question on a specific piece of Italian legislation on judicial liability. Italian law excluded all State liability for damage caused to individuals where that infringement was the result of an interpretation of provisions of law, or of an assessment of the facts and evidence carried out by that court, and individuals were only allowed to bring an action in damages in cases of intentional fault and serious misconduct on the part of the court. TDM argued that these conditions were so restrictive that they made it excessively difficult, indeed virtually impossible, to obtain compensation from the State for damage caused by judicial decisions. The Court replied, once again, in a manner that was very respectful of the role played by the judiciary. The ECJ recognized that the 'interpretation of provisions of law and the evaluation of facts and the evidence forms part of the very essence of judicial activity'.[130] However, the Italian legislation was formulated in such an absolute way as to exclude all State liability, and was therefore

> [t]antamount to rendering meaningless the principle laid down by the Court in the *Köbler* judgment. That remark is even more apposite in the case of courts adjudicating at last instance, which are responsible, at national level, for ensuring that rules of law are given a uniform interpretation.[131] . . . If State liability were to be wholly excluded by reason of the assessments of facts carried out by a court, those individuals would have no judicial protection if a national court adjudicating at last instance committed a manifest error in its review of the above operations of legal classification of facts.[132]

This judgment clearly represents a proper application of the *Köbler* judgment. The Italian statute, imposing a total bar on liability for judgments of courts of last resort, had to go. Nevertheless, in the decisive passage on whether the referring court should have awarded damages, the ECJ reiterated the *Köbler* dictum whereby State liability for damage caused to individuals by reason of an infringement of Community law, attributable to a national court adjudicating at last instance, could be incurred in exceptional cases where that court had manifestly infringed the applicable law.

129. Case C-173/03 *Traghetti del Mediterraneo* [2006] ECR I-5177.
130. Ibid., para. 34.
131. Ibid., para. 36.
132. Ibid., para. 41.

7.2. Private Parties

A further dimension that has to be examined is whether the principle of State liability can be extended to those cases where the culprit is actually an individual. Although this seems to be something of a contradiction in terms, it is not unforeseeable that such an obligation may arise in certain contexts. As is already the case in respect of Treaty provisions that the ECJ has declared to be horizontally applicable,[133] the question is whether, despite the fact that the cases of *Francovich* and *Brasserie du Pêcheur/Factortame* only relate to the liability of Member States, such a principle may, under certain circumstances, be transferred to cases in which individuals breach Community rules. The clearest example of this arises in the field of competition law. The possibility for individuals to claim compensation for a breach of EC antitrust rules has been long discussed and a right to damages, in some jurisdictions, has actually already been recognized.[134] As for ECJ case law, such a possibility was fully discussed in a seminal Opinion by Advocate General Van Gerven in *Banks.*[135] The case concerned litigation between Banks, a mining company, and the British Coal Corporation, which controlled coal reserves in the UK, and had the power to authorize other companies in the extraction of coal, and to sell it to third parties, subject to a fixed amount payable to British Coal. Banks claimed that such a licensing agreement was in breach of the competition provisions of the European Coal and Steel Community (ECSC) Treaty, and that it was entitled to compensation from British Coal for excessive license fees and for the unreasonably low prices paid by British Coal under the license/purchase agreement. Whilst the ECJ did not address the issue, as it held that Articles 65 and 66 of the (now expired) ECSC were not directly applicable, the Advocate General strongly argued in favour of conferring on the claimant the right to bring an action for compensation before the national court. In his view, as State liability has to be considered as a fundamental principle of EU law, its rationale should apply where an individual infringes a provision of Community law to which he is subject, thereby causing loss and damage to another individual. Paraphrasing *Francovich*, he argued that:

> the full effect of Community law would be impaired if the former individual or undertaking did not have the possibility of obtaining reparation from the party who can be held responsible for the breach of Community law – all the more so, evidently, if a directly effective provision of Community law (such as competition law) is infringed.[136]

---

133. See for instance Case 43/75 *Defrenne v. SABENA (Defrenne II)* [1976] ECR 455, para. 39; Case C-281/98 *Angonese v. Cassa di Risparmio di Bolzano* [2000] ECR I-4139, para. 13.
134. *See further, Garden Cottage Foods Ltd v Milk Marketing Board*, [1983] 3 C.M.L.R. 43.
135. Case C-128/92, *Banks Ltd v. British Coal Corp* [1994] ECR I-1209.
136. Ibid., AG Van Gerven's Opinion, para. 44.

The ECJ eventually tackled the question in *Courage v. Crehan*,[137] where the Court held that a right in damages against another private party for breach of the competition rules enshrined in Article 81 EC must in principle be available where the first party bears no significant responsibility for the distortion of competition. The Court ruled that

> the full effectiveness of Article 85 of the Treaty (now Article 81) and, in particular, the practical effect of the prohibition laid down in Article 85(1) would be put at risk if it were not open to any individual to claim damages for loss caused to him by a contract or by conduct liable to restrict or distort competition.[138]

A preliminary ruling was sought in this case by the English Court of Appeal in the context of proceedings initiated by Courage Ltd, a beer supplier, against Mr Crehan, a tenant of one of the plaintiff's pubs. The claimant sought to obtain payment of GBP 15,000 for the sale of beer to the defendant. The defendant had refused to pay for the beer, as he felt he was being charged more as a tenant contractually tied with Courage than independent tenants who were free to choose between different brewers. In his defence, the respondent pleaded that the 'beer tie' agreement was void, as it infringed Article 81 EC, and he also filed a counterclaim for damages suffered as a result of the agreement. The Court of Appeal, despite accepting that the agreement in question had breached Article 81(1) EC, found that the plaintiff was barred from claiming compensation in damages, as he had been a party to the anti-competitive agreement, and his action was barred under the principle of public policy *ex dolo malo non oritur* action, the effect of which being that one may not profit from one's own wrongdoing. The ECJ in its judgment was mindful of the possible inherent conflict raised by the case: on the one hand, the need to ensure the effectiveness of Article 81 – 'the practical effect of the prohibition laid down in Article 85 (now Article 81) would be put at risk if it were not open to any individual to claim damages for loss caused to him by a contract or by conduct liable to restrict or distort competition'[139] – and on the other, the rule of public policy preventing a wrongdoer from benefiting from his own wrongdoing. The ECJ highlighted the centrality of Article 81 EC in the system of the Treaty, and in particular its nature as a directly effective prohibition. The availability of an action for damages was considered to be a 'significant contribution to the maintenance of effective competition in the Community'.[140] Therefore, there should not be an absolute bar to such an action being brought by a party to a contract that is held to violate the competition rules. The action is subject, however, to a set of conditions aimed at assessing whether the applicant bore any significant responsibility for the restriction of competition arising from the anti-competitive agreement. Community law does not prevent national courts from taking steps to ensure

137. Case C-453/99 *Crehan v. Courage Ltd* [2001] ECR I-6297.
138. Ibid., para. 26.
139. Ibid., para. 25.
140. Ibid., para. 27.

that the protection of the rights guaranteed by Community law does not entail the unjust enrichment of those who enjoy them. In particular, it is for the national court to ascertain whether the party who claims to have suffered loss through concluding a contract that is liable to restrict or distort competition found himself in a markedly weaker position than the other party, such as to compromise seriously or even eliminate his freedom to negotiate the terms of the contract, and his capacity to avoid the loss or reduce its extent, in particular by availing himself in good time of all the legal remedies available to him.

Article 81 EC can operate in different ways, and different circumstances of breach may require different remedies. Since the Court of Appeal incorrectly held that illegality barred any potential claim for restitution or compensatory damages, and the Court of Justice ruling can be limited to the finding that such an absolute bar was not possible, there was no determination as to whether restitution or compensatory damages could have been awarded on the facts of the *Courage* case. The matter has been left to the national court.[141]

The *Crehan* decision sparked a lively academic debate[142] and the drafting of an ad hoc Commission Green Paper on Damages Actions for breach of the EC antitrust rules.[143] Apart from the specific issues dealing with the enforcement of competition law, the *Crehan* decision raises some general issues on the extent of the principle of liability in EU law. Questions arise in particular in respect of the extent of the right of an individual to claim compensation against another, and in respect of the possibility of extending *Crehan* outside the realm of antitrust enforcement. As for the first question, as noted by Advocate General Van Gerven, writing extra-judicially, *Banks* and *Crehan* are atypical cases, in that they have not been triggered by the 'natural' injured party (competitor, indirect purchaser or consumer) against the restrictive practice. However, 'both cases concern a claim made by a contracting party who relies on Community law to get rid of a contract which he no longer wishes to perform under its initial terms'.[144] Nevertheless, the language used by the Court in *Crehan* is very broad, and suggests that

141. See further O. Odudu & J. Edelman, 'Compensatory Damages for Breach of Article 81', *ELRev.* 27(3) (2002): 327-339.

142. See in general ed. C.D. Ehlermann & I. Atanasiu, *European Competition Law Annual 2001: Effective Private Enforcement of EC Antitrust Law* (Oxford: EUI, Hart, 2003); A.P. Komninos, 'New Prospects for Private Enforcement of EC Competition Law: Courage v. Crehan and the Community Right to Damages', *CMLRev.* 39 (2002): 447; and with an extensive bibliography, N. Reich, 'Horizontal Liability in EC Law: Hybridization of Remedies for Compensation in Case of Breaches of EC Rights', *CMLRev.* 44 (2007): 707.

143. European Commission, *Green Paper – Damages Actions for Breach of the EC Antitrust Rules*, COM(2005)672 final; see also European Commission, *Annex to the GREEN PAPER: Damages Actions for Breach of the EC Antitrust Rules* (Commission Staff Working Paper), SEC(2005)1732. See for a comment T. Eilmansberger, 'The Green Paper on Damages Actions for Breach of the EC Antitrust Rules and Beyond: Reflections on the Utility and Feasibility of Stimulating Private Enforcement through Legislative Action', *CMLRev.* 44 (2007): 431.

144. W. Van Gerven, 'Substantive Remedies for the Private Enforcement of EC Antitrust Rules Before National Courts', in *Modernisation of European Competition Law*, eds J. Stuyck & H. Gilliams, vol. 2 (Intersentia: Leuven CCLE series, 2002), 93-136.

the individuals concerned are not just those which were parties in the restrictive agreement. Confirmation can be drawn from the case of *Manfredi and others,*[145] a case brought by some individual policy holders against a unilateral collective insurance company's increase in the cost of premiums for compulsory civil liability insurance. The insurance policies related to car accidents were declared unlawful by the Italian competition authority. The Court reiterated that, as Article 81 EC is a norm of '*ordre publique*', the violation of which causes an agreement to be totally void, and which can be relied upon by individuals, the full effectiveness of Article 81 EC would be put at risk if it were not open to an individual to claim damages for losses caused to him by a contract or by conduct liable to restrict or distort competition. The Court insisted that the only requirement was for the individual to show that there was a causal link between the harm and the agreement or practice prohibited under Article 81 EC, thereby suggesting that damages should be available even to final consumers.[146]

The most challenging question, thus is how far horizontal liability can be extended. A consensus seems to have emerged that it is possible to link the question of damages with that of horizontal direct effect.[147] In a series of decisions, the Court held that, on the one hand, Treaty provisions are applicable horizontally even to private bodies when those bodies have the power to collectively regulate a specific sector of the market,[148] and, on the other hand, the Court also read into the Treaty the possibility of imposing obligations on individuals, even where the provision in question was primarily addressed to Member States.[149] Very recently, the Court confirmed in *Viking* and *Laval* that the free movement provisions in the Treaty may be relied on by a private undertaking against a trade union or an association of trade unions. In particular, the Court referred to the idea that the fact that certain provisions of the Treaty are formally addressed to the Member States does not prevent rights from being conferred at the same time on any individual who has an interest in compliance with the obligations thus laid down.[150] It could be further added that damages against individuals might not be limited to cases of Treaty violations. In *Antonio Munoz*[151] the Court held that the full effectiveness of certain regulations concerning quality standards

145. Case C-295/04 *Vincenzo Manfredi et al. v. Lloyd Adriatico Assicurazioni SpA et al.* [2006] ECR I-6619.
146. N. Reich, 'Horizontal Liability in EC Law: Hybridization of Remedies for Compensation in Case of Breaches of EC Rights', *CMLRev.* 44 (2007): 707, at 719.
147. See in general M. Dougan, *National Remedies before the Court of Justice* (Oxford: Hart, 2004).
148. Case 36/74 *Walrave and Koch* [1974] ECR 1405, para. 17; Case C-415/93 *ASBL v. Bosman* [1995] ECR I-4921, paras 83-84; Joined Cases C-51/96 and C-191/97 *Chr. Deliège v. Ligue francophone de judo et disciplines associées ASBL* [2000] ECR I-2549; Case C-176/96 *Jyri Lehtonen and Castors Canada Dry Namur-Braine, ASBL v. FRBSB* [2000] ECR I-2681.
149. Case 43/75 *Defrenne v. SABENA (Defrenne II)* [1976] ECR 455, para. 39; and Case C-281/98 *Angonese v. Cassa di Risparmio di Bolzano* [2000] ECR I-4139, para. 13.
150. Case C-438/05 *International Transport Workers' Federation and Finnish Seaman's. Union* [2007] ECR I-10779.
151. Case C-253/00 *Muñoz v. Frumar Ltd* [2002] ECR I-7289.

applicable to table grapes, compliance with which was entrusted to Member States' public authorities, would have been enhanced by conferring the right of traders to bring civil proceedings against competitors. The Court concluded that:

> The possibility of bringing such proceedings strengthens the practical working of the Community rules on quality standards. As a supplement to the action of the authorities designated by the Member States to make the checks required by those rules it helps to discourage practices, often difficult to detect, which distort competition. In that context actions brought before the national courts by competing operators are particularly suited to contributing substantially to ensuring fair trading and transparency of markets in the Community.[152]

Interestingly, the Court cited *Courage v. Crehan* as authority for the above statement. It is arguable, therefore, that for those provisions that have been acknowledged as imposing an obligation upon individuals 'in a clearly defined manner', an action in damages might be available.[153] As discussed above, it is again tempting to transform an action in liability into a form of *actio popularis*. It should be reaffirmed, however, that a damages action would still be dependent on the satisfaction of all the other requirements, including that of serious breach and causation, which will automatically limit the number, and the 'quality', of actions for compensation.

8. PROCEDURAL RULES *STRICTU SENSU*

As has been made clear above, it is for national courts to ultimately decide whether or not the conditions governing State liability for a breach of Community law are fulfilled. They are also charged with ensuring that this 'newly' qualified individual right against the State is effectively protected in the context of national rules both procedural and substantive. In the reconstruction proposed by Van Gerven, the notion of rights refers to a legal position which a person may have and which can be enforced before a court of law by means of one or more remedies, in accordance with procedures governing the exercise of classes of actions. The latter comprises procedural conditions, evidential rules and substantive conditions, such as rules concerning the content or form of the reparation to be given to the individual affected. As has already been mentioned, the Court of Justice has qualified such autonomy by insisting that national law ensure that Community rights are protected effectively. With specific reference to liability claims, the Court reiterated that

> [i]t must also be observed that the material and formal conditions laid down by the various national laws on compensation for damage cannot be less favourable in such a context than those relating to similar domestic claims and cannot

152. Ibid., para. 31.
153. W. Van Gerven, 'Non-contractual Liability of Member States, Community Institutions and Individuals for Breaches of Community Law with a View to a Common Law for Europe', *M.J.* 1 (1994): 6.

> be so framed as to make it in practice impossible or excessively difficult to obtain compensation.[154]

The difficulty is that there is no hard and fast dividing line between what is governed by Community law and what is left to the national legal system. In any case, there exists what could be described as a partial 'Communitarization' of national conditions of liability, in that they must comply with Community principles such as equivalence and effectiveness. Once again, such questions affect the debate on whether Community-specific remedies are being created rather than the protection of rights being left to Member State determination, as has been traditionally thought. As vividly put by Reich, the coexistence, on the one hand, of national procedural autonomy and the necessity of properly enforcing EC law results in a 'hybridization' of remedies based on national law, but reshaped under the influence of EU law.[155] The following section attempts to deal with some of the issues deriving from the cohabitation of EC and national procedural rules.

8.1. The Extent of Reparation

Procedural rules governing the quantification of compensation provide a perfect example of the relationship between EU and national law in this context. The Court laid down some general conditions but did not shy away, in particular circumstances, from imposing very clear requirements upon national procedural law. In *Brasserie du Pêcheur/Factortame* the Court held that the damage 'should be commensurate with the loss of damage sustained so as to ensure the effective protection of their rights'.[156] This implies that an injured person must be able to seek compensation not only for actual loss (*damnum emergens*) but also for loss of profit (*lucrum cessans*) plus interest. In particular, the Court always insisted on the importance of including economic loss:

> Total exclusion of loss of profit as a head of damage for which compensation may be awarded cannot be accepted in the case of a breach of Community law since, especially in the context of economic or commercial litigation, such a total exclusion of loss of profit would be such as to make reparation of damage practically impossible.[157]

154. See, to that effect, Joined Cases C-6 and C-9/90 *Francovich and others v. Italy* [1991] ECR I-5357, para. 43, and C-127/95 *Norbrook Laboratories Ltd v. Ministry of Agriculture, Fisheries and Food* [1998] ECR I-1531, para. 111.
155. N. Reich, 'Horizontal Liability in EC Law: Hybridization of Remedies for Compensation in Case of Breaches of EC Rights', *CMLRev.* 44 (2007): 707, at 709.
156. Case 46/93 *Brasserie du Pêcheur v. Bundesrepublik Deutschland and The Queen v. Secretary of State for Transport, ex parte Factortame and others* [1996] ECR I-1029, at para. 82.
157. Ibid., para. 87, and Joined Cases C-397/98 and C-410/98 *Metallgesellschaft and Others* [2001] ECR I-1727, para. 91.

As in many other areas of the law of remedies, the Court has been rather selective in its interventions, sometimes striking down certain domestic national rules, while at other times being content to leave it to the national courts. For instance, in *Brassiere du Pêcheur*, the Court pointed out explicitly that some restrictions present in the German non-contractual liability regime would be incompatible with Community law. In particular, the ECJ commented that the German requirement of *Drittbezogenheit*, a condition which makes reparation dependent on the legislature's act or omission being referable to an individual situation (the 'third party'), would be such as to make it impossible or excessively difficult in practice for individuals to exercise their rights and thereby obtain an effective remedy. As for the British system, which came under the spotlight in *Factortame*, the condition in English law requiring proof of misfeasance in public office was deemed to make it, in practice, impossible or excessively difficult for individuals to obtain reparation from the State. Another example can be derived from *Traghetti del Mediterraneo*, where the Court found that an Italian law that excluded liability of national courts when such liability would have arisen from an interpretation of provisions of law, or where the infringement arose from the national court's assessment of the facts and evidence, would have been tantamount to rendering meaningless the principle of State liability. Similarly, in the *AGM* case, which concerned liability of the Finnish State for televised declarations made by one of its officials in relation to the suspected risk associated with elevators produced by an Italian company, the Court strongly hinted that Finnish law could have made the exercise of such a right excessively difficult. National law provided that State liability could arise only as a result of a criminal offence, or from the exercise of public authority, or where there were particularly serious reasons for awarding compensation. The conduct of the official in question did not fall within any of those cases, making it impossible for the company involved to obtain compensation.[158] In observance of the principle that liability has to represent an efficient remedy, the Court has been very alert to dismantling national procedural conditions that place excessive burdens on individuals. For instance, the Court always required that, in order to determine the loss or damage for which reparation may be granted, the national court must enquire whether the injured person showed reasonable diligence in order to avoid the loss or damage or limit its extent, and whether, in particular, the applicant availed itself in time of all the legal remedies available to it.[159] As far as the relationship between liability and other remedies is concerned, although the case law is somewhat complicated, it is clear that in dealing with the effective application of EC law, a hierarchy between remedies is not appropriate. Liability in damages is one of the options available to individuals to enforce their Community rights, and should therefore be considered as an independent remedy in the sense that its use should not be conditioned on a prior or concomitant use of some other

158. Case C-470/03 *A.G.M.-COS.MET Srl v. Suomen valtio, Tarmo Lehtinen* [2007] I-2749
159. Case 46/93 *Brasserie du Pêcheur v. Bundesrepublik Deutschland and The Queen v. Secretary of State for Transport, ex parte Factortame and others* [1996] ECR I-1029, para. 84.

remedy.[160] Furthermore, the Court made it very clear that the principle of mitigation should not be construed so as to deny any real possibility of compensation. Thus, in the area of taxation, the Court held – in a case involving a possible breach of the right of establishment with respect to tax legislation which did not afford the same benefits to non-resident parent companies as it did to resident companies – that the exercise of such a fundamental right would be rendered impossible or excessively difficult by national provisions rejecting a company claim for restitution or compensation

> solely because the persons concerned had not applied for a tax advantage which national law denied them, with a view to challenging the refusal of the tax authorities by means of the legal remedies provided for that purpose, invoking the primacy and direct effect of Community law.[161]

Similarly, an action for compensation against discriminatory taxation benefits on non-resident companies would be made excessively difficult if claims for restitution or compensation based on infringement of those provisions were rejected or reduced solely because the companies concerned had not applied to the tax authorities to be allowed to pay interest on loans granted by a non-resident parent company without that interest being treated as a distribution when national law provided for such treatment to apply.[162]

The Court has, however, stopped short of imposing on national courts new forms of compensation or other positive duties. For instance, a recurrent question has been whether Community law requires the imposition of certain forms of damages such as punitive or exemplary damages. The Court in these instances adhered strictly to the equivalence/effectiveness analysis. As such, in respect of the possibility of an award of punitive damages in the absence of Community rules governing the matter, the Court merely reiterated that it is for the domestic legal system of each Member State to set criteria for determining the extent of the damages subject to compliance with the principles of equivalence and effectiveness. Of course, if domestic law provides that such damages may be awarded in

---

160. See Case C-66/95 *Eunice Sutton* [1997] ECR I-2163; Joined Cases C-192-218/95 *Comateb and Others v. Directeur général des douanes et droits indirects* [1997] ECR I-165; and Joined Cases C-231-233/06 *National Pension Office v. Jonkmann and Others* [2007] ECR I-5149. See for a discussion A. Biondi & L. Johnson, 'No Small Matter: The Right to Recovery of Charges Levied in Breach of Community Law', *EPL* 4 (1998): 313; and P. Eeckhout, 'Liability of Member States in Damages and the Community System of Remedies', in *New Directions in European Public Law*, eds A. Beatson & T. Tridimas (Oxford: Hart, 1998), 63. For a slightly different approach see G. Anagnostaras, 'State Liability and Alternative Courses of Action: How Independent Can an Autonomous Remedy Be?', *YEL* (2002): 355.
161. Joined Cases C-397/98 and C-410/98 *Metallgesellschaft and Others* [2001] ECR I-1727, para. 106.
162. Case C-524/04 *Test Claimants in the Thin Cap Group Litigation v. Commissioners of Inland Revenue* [2007] ECR I-2107.

accordance with the principle of equivalence, it must be possible to award particular damages even in actions founded on Community rules.[163]

8.1.1. Interest

Individuals are entitled to recover interest on any damages awarded, since this is considered to be an essential component of compensation. After some initial hesitation, this principle has now become well established.[164] The national courts seem not to have particular difficulties with such a question. For instance, in the case of *Sempra Metals Ltd*, in the latest instalment of a long-running battle between Sempra Metals Ltd (formerly Metallgesellschaft Ltd) and the Inland Revenue, the English House of Lords has required that a full Community remedy be provided in so far as the rules concerning interest payments are concerned.[165] The case originally concerned a discriminatory tax system in the UK by which companies which had both parents and subsidiaries resident, for tax, purposes, in the UK, benefited from a later payment of Advance Corporation Tax (ACT) than those subsidiaries based in the UK whose parent company was based in another Member State. This timing disadvantage in payment of ACT led, so the ECJ held, to a right to compensation, as the scheme was contrary to Article 43 EC. The ECJ also held that the amount of compensation in the case was to be decided by the national court.[166] Upon the case being returned to the national court, there was disagreement over whether compensation should be calculated on the basis of compound interest or on the basis of simple interest. The House of Lords, in July 2007, held that domestic rules regarding interest were unlikely to be of any assistance in the instant case, and that the task of the English court was to provide a Community remedy in the circumstances. By this, the House of Lords meant that the remedy to be given should be 'full' in the sense that it should restore the equality of treatment guaranteed by Article 43 EC. Therefore, in commercial cases, an award based on compound, rather than simple interest was more likely to reflect the economic reality and to provide full, rather than partial, recompense for the loss of the use of the money.

---

163. See, to that effect Case 46/93 *Brasserie du Pêcheur v. Bundesrepublik Deutschland and The Queen v. Secretary of State for Transport, ex parte Factortame and others* [1996] ECR I-1029, para. 90; and Case C-295/04 *Vincenzo Manfredi et al. v. Lloyd Adriatico Assicurazioni SpA et al.* [2006] ECR I-6619, para. 93.
164. Joined Cases C-397/98 and C-410/98 *Metallgesellschaft and Others* [2001] ECR I-1727, paras 93-95, in which the Court makes an effort to distinguish the case from Case C-66/95 *Eunice Sutton* [1997] ECR I-2163, where the claimant was denied an award of interest. See also Case C-295/04 *Vincenzo Manfredi et al. v. Lloyd Adriatico Assicurazioni SpA et al.* [2006] ECR I-6619, para. 97 and the Opinion of AG Jacobs in Case C-150/99 *Sweden v. Lindöpark* [2001] ECR I-493, para. 81.
165. *Sempra Metals Limited. Her Majesty's Commissioners of Inland Revenue* [2007] UKHL 34.
166. Joined Cases C-397/98 and C-410/98 *Metallgesellschaft and Others* [2001] ECR I-1727, para. 91.

8.2. Limitation Periods

Time limits are another classic procedural rule *strictu sensu* that all Member States apply in cases of non-contractual liability. The ECJ has always made it clear that the question should be governed by national law. The possibility of challenging a national time limit was raised, however, in the *Rosalba Palmisani* judgment.[167] The facts of the case were similar to those in *Francovich*: An Italian firm was declared insolvent on 17 April 1985 while owing salary money to Ms Palmisani. By that date, Italy should have implemented Directive 80/987 EC relating to the protection of employees in the event of the insolvency of their employer, but had failed to do so. Italy was subsequently found[168] to have failed to fulfil its obligations under the directive, and the Court of Justice in *Francovich* held that the Member State was required to make good the loss caused to individuals by its failure to transpose the Directive on time. On 27 January 1992, Italy adopted a legislative decree which belatedly transposed the directive, and which also laid down conditions governing reparation for loss caused by the delay in transposition. Although actions under Italian domestic law for non-contractual liability were normally subject to a five-year limitation period, this legislation provided that actions for reparation were to be brought within a year of the entry into force of the decree. After the one-year limitation period had expired, Palmisani brought an action against the national social service authority (INPS), which managed the guarantee fund now set up by Italy pursuant to the directive, for reparation under the decree. INPS pleaded the time-bar in its defence. The Italian court referred a question to the Court of Justice asking whether a national court was bound to disapply the one-year limitation period and, if so, whether it should apply the five-year period available for domestic non-contractual actions, or the one-year period for claims of social security payment or for payments under the guarantee system which had been set up to implement the directive. The Court of Justice first made it clear that Member States were to grant compensation according to national procedures, but that the time limits laid down by national law were not to be less favourable than those relating to similar domestic claims (principle of equivalence), and were not to be so framed as to make it virtually impossible or excessively difficult to obtain reparation (principle of effectiveness). As to the principle of equivalence, as Advocate General Cosmas commented in the case, the national court must assess what would happen in a similar procedure in which satisfaction of a similar claim based on national law would be sought. For that comparison to take place, 'there must be a comparison of like with like'.[169] Therefore, to enable a comparison to be made between procedural rules in accordance with the foregoing, first, the claims in respect of which judicial satisfaction is sought must be similar; second, the procedural rules on which the comparison is based must not be considered in isolation, but in their procedural context; and third, those procedures

167. Case C-261/95 *Palmisani v. INPS* [1997] ECR I-4025.
168. Case C-22/87 *Commission v. Italy* [1989] ECR 143.
169. Ibid., Advocate General Cosmas' Opinion, para. 26.

must not be chosen at random, but must be of a similar kind. In its judgment, the ECJ ruled that the time limit of a year, per se, could not be seen to be rendering difficult or virtually impossible a claim by an individual, as it complies with the principle of legal certainty. As regards equivalence, the Court remarked that, although in principle it is for the national courts to ascertain whether the procedural rules intended to ensure that the rights derived by individuals from Community law and which are safeguarded under national law comply with the principle of equivalence, certain aspects of the case provided a basis for some remarks by the Court itself. First, the Court commented that the measures implementing the Directive contained in the Legislative Decree pursued an objective that differed from that of the compensation scheme established by that Decree. While the former aimed to provide employees with protection under Community law in the event of the insolvency of their employer by means of specific guarantees of payment of unpaid remuneration, the latter sought to make good the loss or damage sustained by the beneficiaries of the Directive as a result of its belated transposition. Therefore, the two schemes could not be objectively compared. The Court commented that, for the same reasons, this must also be true of actions under national law for obtaining social security benefits other than pensions. Furthermore, as far as the ordinary five-year limitation period for non-contractual liability provided by Italian law is concerned, the Court highlighted that the system was, in terms of its objective, more similar to that introduced by the original Legislative Decree, in as much as it intended to guarantee reparation for the loss or damage sustained as a result of the conduct of the perpetrator. However, to make a full and complete comparison, the Court would need more information on national law than was available to it, and so it therefore fell to the national court to undertake that examination. If the conclusion was that the two systems were not comparable, then the result must be that Community law does not preclude a Member State from requiring any action for reparation of the loss or damage sustained as a result of the belated transposition of the Directive to be brought within a limitation period of one-year from the date of its transposition into national law.[170]

The issue of national time limits was raised again in the *Manfredi* case. The national court enquired whether the limitation period for an action for compensation for harm caused by an agreement or practice prohibited under Article 81 EC could be considered as making the exercise of a Community right excessively difficult. In particular, the national court was concerned with the moment in time from which the time limit has to be calculated – whether it had to run from the day on which that prohibited agreement or practice was adopted, or from the day on which the agreement or concerted practice came to an end. The ECJ, in a rather 'intrusive' judgment, replied that making the time limit run from the day of the adoption of the agreement would make it practically impossible to exercise the right to damages. In particular,

170. Ibid., para. 39.

> [i]n such a situation, where there are continuous or repeated infringements, it is possible that the limitation period expires even before the infringement is brought to an end, in which case it would be impossible for any individual who has suffered harm after the expiry of the limitation period to bring an action.[171]

The case law on time limits applicable to liability actions follows the general tendency of the case law on national procedural law, with the Court sometimes engaging in close scrutiny and sometimes not. As argued above, the principle of effectiveness has an enhanced role to play in the area of limitation periods, and should be carefully balanced with the need to preserve legal certainty.

8.3. Form of Redress

Although in most cases individuals seek to obtain full compensation for the damage caused to them by the State's breach of Community law, the question has been raised as to whether there are instances in which other forms of action are more appropriate. For instance, in the aftermath of *Francovich*, the Italian legislator decided to implement Directive 80/987/EEC by limiting liability retrospectively to compensation payable to employees who had suffered a loss because of the late implementation of the Directive. Italian law also imposed an upper limit to the compensation awarded. In substance, the workers were belatedly paid their wages directly from the INPS, the national social service authority, subject to certain restrictions. In an ensuing controversy over the compatibility of the solution with Community law, the ECJ emphasized that this was a possible option.[172] Retroactive and proper application in full of the measures implementing the Directive will be considered to be compliant with Community law unless the beneficiaries establish the existence of complementary loss sustained on account of the fact that they were unable to benefit, at the appropriate time, from the financial advantages guaranteed by the Directive, with the result that such loss must also be made good. In conclusion, it should be reaffirmed that the Court is not concerned here with entering into a debate on what forms of compensation are the most adequate or to suggest possible alternatives. Its focus is only on the action for damages and on its effective application.

171. Case C-295/04 *Vincenzo Manfredi et al. v. Lloyd Adriatico Assicurazioni SpA et al.* [2006] ECR I-6619, para. 79.
172. Cases C 94-95/95 *Bonifaci and Others and Berto and Others* [1997] ECR I-3969; and Case C-373/95 *Maso and Others v. INPS and Repubblica Italiana* [1997] ECR I-405.

Chapter 3
Non-contractual Liability in Damages: Article 288(2) EC

INTRODUCTION

In the celebrated *Les Vertes* case, the Court of Justice cast the EU constitutional framework as defined by its founding Treaties, as a 'Community based on the rule of law, inasmuch as neither its Member States nor its institutions can avoid a review of the question whether the measures adopted by them are in conformity with the basic constitutional charter, the Treaty'.[1] A constitutive element of an efficient and responsive system of judicial review provides individuals with an opportunity to bring an action in damages if their rights have been violated by one of the EU institutions.

Unlike State liability which was developed by the European Court of Justice (ECJ), the European Community (EC) Treaty has always provided that an individual shall be entitled to compensation in the event that a Community institution has caused loss in the performance of its duties. Article 288 EC addresses Community liability in relation to contractual situations, non-contractual situations, and liability in respect of Community servants. The following pages focus principally on Article 288(2) EC,[2] which regulates the non-contractual liability of the Community. Article 288(2) EC provides that:

> In the case of non-contractual liability, the Community shall, in accordance with the general principles common to the laws of the Member States, make

---

1. Case 294/83 *Partie Ecologiste 'Les Verts' v. European Parliament* [1986] ECR 1339, para. 23.
2. Art. 288(3) EC was amended by the Treaty of the European Union (the Maastricht Treaty) and extends the term '*institution*' under Art. 288(2) EC to cover damage caused by the European Central Bank (ECB) and its servants, and is considered at section 2.2 below.

good any damage caused by its institutions or by its servants in the performance of their duties.

The first question to be asked is, what is meant by non-contractual liability? The easiest way to approach this question is by comparing the respective ambits of Articles 288(1) and (2) EC. Article 288(1) EC regulates the situation where a Community institution has entered into a formal contract with an individual and subsequently breached the terms of that contract. Article 288(2) EC however, seeks to address the situation where a Community institution has caused an individual to suffer loss through the exercise of its general legislative, administrative or executive functions. Article 288 EC is thus the key provision in ensuring an effective right to damages. The need to ensure the satisfaction and the protection of individual rights needs to be considered in relation to the equally important need of ensuring that the legislative and executive action of the EU are not excessively impaired and to avoid an excessive proliferation of damages claims. As will become clear throughout the course of this chapter, the pervasive thread running through much of both the ECJ and the CFI, upon which jurisdiction on action for damages was conferred since 1989, reasoning is an attempt to strike a balance between ensuring effective judicial recourse for individuals, by providing them with a means by which to seek financial compensation for any losses suffered, and ensuring that the Community institutions have sufficient protection from liability so as to be able to perform their legislative functions.

1. EXPLORING NON-CONTRACTUAL LIABILITY

While at first glance this chapter may seem to be somewhat cumbersome in length, it has been divided into specific areas designed to deal with each stage of a claim for damages: admissibility, substance, causation, and compensation. To this end, the chapter begins with a discussion of the way in which the Court has approached the admissibility criteria for bringing a claim under Article 288(2) EC. Failure to observe these criteria often has the effect of requiring the Court to strike out the claim on the grounds of admissibility, and has meant the end of many otherwise meritorious claims. This is followed by an analysis of the substantive elements that need to be satisfied to succeed once a claim has been judged admissible. As with other areas dominated by case law, these substantive criteria have developed gradually over time, in a piecemeal fashion, and have lead to periods of contradiction and uncertainty in the law. The Court sought to sweep away these contradictions however, and bring the law of Community liability in line with that of Member State liability. in its ruling in Bergaderm.[3] While the Court's ruling in *Bergaderm* reflects the current state of the law in relation to Community liability, in order to appreciate its significance, it must be appraised in light of the legal context in which it was decided. As such, the section dealing with the substantive rules of

3. Case C-352/98 P *Laboratoires Phramaceutiques Bergaderm and Groupil v. Commission* [2000] ECR I-5291.

Community liability first examines the legal situation as it existed *pre-Bergaderm* before exploring the *Bergaderm* ruling itself and how the case law in this area has developed since.

While a claim in damages is inherently linked with the idea of the measure in question breaching a Community rule, the Court has never ruled out the possibility of liability existing in respect of legal acts of the Community that have caused individuals to suffer damage. This situation, which is covered in section 6 below, is something of a recent development and increasingly, applicants are seeking damages under this heading, often as an alternative, once the Court has ruled that the Community institution has not breached its obligations under the Treaty.

Article 288(2) EC makes it clear that the Community will only be liable in damages where it has caused the loss suffered by the applicant. Where causation cannot be proved, an applicant will not be entitled to compensation, regardless of the losses suffered. After years of having been a secondary test to that of breach, the issue of causation has come to prominence in recent cases, with the CFI preferring to deal with cases on the basis of causation rather than on the existence of breach. The test of factual causation applied by the Community Courts is considered below.

The final part of this chapter explores what an applicant can expect to receive once it has successfully brought a claim for damages. This section deals predominantly with how an applicant needs to structure a claim and the burden of proof that needs to be discharged in order to demonstrate firstly the existence of loss and secondly how that loss is to be quantified.

2. ADMISSIBILITY UNDER ARTICLE 288(2) EC

Before the merits of an action for damages under Article 288(2) EC can be presented before the Court, the claim brought by the applicants must be deemed admissible. The admissibility criteria under Article 288(2) EC have been the undoing of many potentially meritorious claims, and must therefore by complied with if an applicant is going to stand any chance of recovering damages. The following paragraphs seek to answer the following questions: Who may bring a claim (the applicant)? Against whom may a claim be brought (the defendant)? Has the claim been brought within the limitation period? Whether or not it is first necessary to bring an alternative claim prior to bringing an action under Article 288(2) EC – for example, an action for annulment under Article 230 EC? Whether the claim amounts to an abuse of process? Before which court should the claim be brought (CFI or national court)? Only where the answers to each of these questions satisfy the requirements of the Court will the substantive elements of the case be heard.

2.1. WHO MAY BRING A CLAIM UNDER ARTICLE 288(2)?

Unlike Article 230 EC which sets down judicial review procedures that allow an individual to challenge the legality of a measure enacted by the Community, or

Article 232 EC, which allows an individual to challenge the Community's failure to act when it was under a duty to do so, the text of Article 288(2) EC does not set out strict limits as to who may bring a claim in damages. To this end, the ECJ has held that any natural or legal person, who claims to have been injured by an act of the Community or by one of its servants, must have the possibility of bringing an action against the Community.[4] This applies regardless of whether or not the applicant is a European citizen.[5] The language of Article 288(2) EC is not, however, specifically limited to claims arising from individuals. The general terms in which Article 288(2) EC is phrased are also wide enough to encompass a potential claim by a Member State against the Community for damages. Such an action has never been brought, and as such, neither the ECJ nor the CFI has had to rule on the admissibility of a claim brought by a Member State, and what is more, in view of the overall judicial scheme provided by the Treaty, it is unlikely that such a claim will ever be brought. Given their privileged applicant status, Member States are more likely to challenge a Community measure that they consider to be invalid by means of an action for annulment under Article 230 EC, before they suffer any damage.

In the case of legal persons, applicants must show that the damage affects their own assets, and that they are bringing their claim in their capacity as a legal person.[6] While this criterion will not ordinarily pose any difficulty for private enterprises, it does have a significant bearing on the possibility for trade unions and associations to bring claims. In the *Civil Servants' Union* case, a trade union representing the interests of EC officials sought the annulment of Regulation 2/74 European Economic Community (EEC) on the adjustment of its members' salaries. The union claimed that the readjustment of its members' salaries resulted in errors adversely affecting their interests. The applicant brought a claim for damages under Articles 235 and 288(2) EC for the monies that it felt were owed to its members. The Court held that, in order to bring an action for damages, a trade union must either bring an action on the basis of a loss suffered by it in its capacity as a trade union or association,[7] or show that the right has been assigned to it by its members.[8] In the *Civil Servants' Union* case, the Court considered that the union was seeking to enforce the personal proprietary interests of the officials and servants rather than a right held by the trade union itself.[9] It was therefore for the

4. Case 118/83 *CMC Cooperativa muratori e cementisti and others v. Commission* [1985] ECR 2325, para. 31.
5. Case 119/77 *Nipon Seiko v. Council and Commission* [1979] ECR 1303; Case 239/82 *Allied Corporation a.o. v. Commission* [1984] ECR 1005.
6. Case 114/83 *Société d'Initiatives et de Coopération Agricole v. Commission* [1984] ECR 2589, paras 3-5; Case 289/83 *Groupement des Associations Agricoles pour l'Organisation de la Production et de la Commercialisation des Pommes de Terre et Légumes de la Région Malouine (GAARM) a.o. v. Commission* [1984] ECR 4295 paras 4-5; Joined Cases T-481/93 and T-484/93 *Vereniging van Exporteurs in Levende Varkens a.o. v. Commission* [1995] ECR II-2941, para. 76.
7. Case 114/83 *Société d'Initiatives et de Coopération Agricole v. Commission* [1984] ECR 2589, paras 3-5.
8. Case 238/78 *Ireks-Arkady GmbH v. Council and Commission* [1979] ECR 2955, para. 5.
9. Case 72/74 *Union syndicale-Service public européen and others v. Council of the European Communities* [1975] ECR 401, paras 20-22.

members of the union, and not the trade union itself, to bring the case before the Court, and the claim was therefore inadmissible. The Court did, however, leave the option of assignment open to the trade union. Upon valid assignment, the assignor, in this case the trade union members, would cease to be entitled to compensation for the damage, and the trade union would be able to bring the claim on their behalf.[10] An assignment of the right to bring an action for damages will only be valid, however, where there is no cause to believe that the assignment may have led to an abuse.[11] The Court has not however elaborated on what it might consider to constitute an abuse.

2.2. Against Whom May an Action be Brought?

While Article 288(2) EC makes it clear that only acts or omissions of the institutions or their servants can be challenged, it also states that it is the Community that must make good any damage. Against whom then, must the action be brought – the Community as a whole, or the institution responsible for the alleged act? In *European Parliament v. Council*, the ECJ held that it is the Community that must be regarded as the defendant in actions brought under Article 288(2) EC and not the institutions, for they have no legal personality, and cannot therefore be sued.[12] The Community will, however, be represented by the institution or institutions against which the matter giving rise to liability is alleged.[13] Despite the clear division drawn by the Court between the institutions, which could amount to a potential pitfall for applicants who institute proceedings against the wrong institution, the Court has tended to be flexible in its approach to the institution that is called upon to represent the Community. The Court has been prepared to accept both cases that bring an action against a specific institution, as well as claims brought against the Community as a whole, provided that it does not affect the rights of the defence.[14]

The Court has also been flexible in respect of those institutions whose actions could cause the Community to be liable in damages. It is clear from its wording, that the scope of Article 288(2) EC is wide enough to encompass measures adopted by the five principal Community institutions listed in Article 7(1) EC – the Council, the Commission, the European Parliament, the Court of Auditors, and the Court of Justice. The Treaty of European Union ('Maastricht Treaty') further increased the scope of Article 288(2) EC by amending Article 288(3) EC so as to include the European Central Bank as an 'institution' for the purposes of Article 288(2) EC.

---

10. Case 267/80 *Birra Wührer SpA and others v. Council and Commission* [1984] ECR 3693.
11. Case 238/78 *Ireks-Arkady GmbH v. Council and Commission* [1979] ECR 2955, para. 5.
12. Case 302/87 *European Parliament v. Council* [1988] ECR 5615, para. 9.
13. Joined Cases 63-69/72 *Wilhelm Werhahn Hansamühle a.o. v. Council of the European Communities* [1973] ECR 1229.
14. Compare the claims brought in Case 106/81 *Julius Kind KG v. European Economic Community* [1982] ECR 2885 and Case T-246/93 *Günther Bühring v. Council of the European Union and Commission of the European Communities* [1998] ECR II-171.

The Court has been prepared to go even further and hear cases brought against acts of the European Investment Bank,[15] and the European Ombudsman.[16]

The generally broad interpretation of the term 'institution' used by the Court of Justice is designed to prevent the Community from escaping possible liability where it acts through bodies and agencies that are not institutions within the meaning of Article 7(1) EC, since national courts have no jurisdiction to find the Community non-contractually liable.[17] This approach is justified on the basis that if the Community truly does constitute a system based on the rule of law, as Article 6 EU requires that it should, then no Community institutions should be able to avoid being held accountable, through the provision of damages or otherwise, for any liability that it has incurred either through its own actions, or through the actions of a body to which it has delegated responsibility.

The European Courts do appear, however, to have drawn the line when it comes to the European Council. Following a strict reading of the wording of Article 288(2) EC, the CFI held in its ruling in *Krikorian* that acts of the European Council could not render the Community liable under Article 288(2) EC.[18] Such a strict interpretation could be justified on the basis that the European Council has traditionally been viewed as a European Union political institution and that the legal basis for its existence is found in Article 4 EU as opposed to the EC Treaty. Given the three-pillar structure of the European Union, and the fact that Article 288(2) EC is applicable only in respect of the first pillar, the CFI's reasoning is not without merit. Following similar reasoning, the CFI has also held in some of its more recent case law that a Community institution will only be an 'institution' for the purposes of Article 288(2) EC when it is acting in respect of its powers under the EC Treaty as opposed to the EU Treaty. In the case of *Segi*,[19] the applicants sought compensation for damage suffered as a result of their being included in a list annexed to a Council Common Position on the application of specific measures to combat terrorism. The Common Position was adopted under the Common Foreign and Security Policy (CFSP) and Justice and Home Affairs (JHA) pillars, and was therefore a European Union measure opposed to a Community measure. The CFI found that Article 34 EU was the only relevant legal basis upon which such measures could be based. The Court therefore concluded that it had no jurisdiction to hear a claim in damages since the only remedies provided for under Title VI of the EU Treaty are references for a preliminary ruling, actions for annulment and rulings in disputes between Member States.

15. Case C-370/89 *SGEEM and Etroy v. EIB* [1992] ECR I-6211, para. 16.
16. Case T-209/00 *Lamberts v. European Ombudsman* [2002] ECR II-2203.
17. K. Lenaerts, D. Arts & I. Maselis, *Procedural Law of the European Union*, 2nd edn (London: Sweet & Maxwell, 2006), 11-011.
18. Case T-346/03 *Krikorian a.o. v. European Parliament a.o.* [2003] ECR II-6037, para. 17.
19. Case T-338/02 *Segi and Others v. Council* [2004] ECR II-1647 upheld on appeal in Case C-355/04 P *Segi and Others v. Council* [2007] ECR I-1657.

The *Segi* decision appears to be at odds with the CFI's ruling in *Kadi*, however,[20] which also concerned the Council's Common Position to combat terrorism. The applicant sought to annul a Community regulation enforcing the provisions of the Common Position on the grounds that the Community lacked competence to pass legislation to further the objectives of the second and third pillars of the EU. The CFI held, however, that despite the lack of an express attribution of powers to the Community, provisions of the EC Treaty could form the legal basis of measures passed to attain the objectives pursued by the CFSP. If provisions of the EC Treaty can be used to form the legal basis of measures enacted to further the aims of the CFSP and JHA pillars, it seems contradictory to rule that remedies available under the EC Treaty should not also be available where those measures contravene a principle of Community law. Certainly, a strict delineation between the European pillars is increasingly untenable as both the draft Constitution and the Treaty of Lisbon have sought to do away with it.

The Court has also taken a liberal approach when ruling whether or not a claim for damages can be brought against a particular institution. The wording of Article 288(2) EC makes it clear that, in order to bring a claim for non-contractual damages against the Community, one must be able to point to an act adopted either in the name of a Community institution (*fautes de service*: for example, the adoption of a regulation by the Commission) or an act of one of its servants undertaken in the performance of his or her duties (*fautes personnelles*). A claim cannot be brought, however, for damage caused arising out of an act of primary law, for example, for damage caused as a direct result of a Treaty amendment. The Court has held that any Treaty which seeks to amend the original EC Treaty is an act of the Member States and cannot be ascribed to the Community.[21] It follows, therefore, that although the Community must take all necessary steps to ensure the proper performance of Community law, where the implementation of Community law has been delegated to the Member States, the Community cannot be held liable where a Member State fails to comply with its Community obligations.[22] Under Article 288(2) EC, it is necessary that the injury derive from an act or omission on the part of a Community institution. Although this line of reasoning can be justified on the basis of Article 10 EC, which requires Member States to act in conformity with the Community rules, the distinction between acts of the Community and acts of Member States implementing Community law has caused many applicants to have their claims struck out on the basis of admissibility. Where the Court considers that the damage has been caused by the implementation of a Community act

20. Case T-315/01 *Yassin Abdullah Kadi v. Council of the European Union and Commission* [2005] ECR II-3649. At the time of this writing, the CFI's judgment in *Kadi* was awaiting an appeal to the ECJ.
21. Case 169/73 *Compagnie Continentale France v. Council of the European Communities* [1975] ECR 117, para. 16; Joined Cases 31 and 35/86 *Levantina Agricola Industrial SA (LAISA) and CPC España SA v. Council of the European Communities* [1988] ECR 2285, paras 19-22.
22. Case 99/74 *Société des Grands Moulins des Antilles v. Commission* [1975] ECR 1531.

by a Member State rather than as a direct result of the Community act itself, it will refuse jurisdiction and require the applicant to bring proceedings before its national courts. This issue of concurrent liability, where the loss suffered can be attributable to an act of the Community that has been actively executed by national authorities, is discussed in greater detail below.[23]

2.3. Acts of Community Servants

In respect of acts of servants of Community institutions (*fautes personnelles*), an applicant is not required to bring an action directly against the servant involved. Indeed, the servant involved need not even be identified. It is sufficient for the applicant to lodge the action for damages against the Community per se, as represented by the institution employing the servant.[24] This is consistent with Article 12(a) of the *Protocol on the Privileges and Immunities of the European Communities* which grants immunity to servants of Community institutions, as against third parties, for 'acts performed by them in their official capacity, including their words spoken or written'. While under certain circumstances, the institution may be in a position to waive its staff members' immunity, this does not prevent the applicant from bringing a claim for damages against the Community under Article 288(2) EC.[25] The justification for continuing to hold the Community liable once immunity has been removed from the servant is to prevent the Community from evading damages claims by waiving immunity, which would ultimately leave the applicant open to the risk that his or her sole claim would be against an insolvent debtor in the form of the staff member responsible.[26] A claim may lie between the responsible staff member and the Community, but this is an internal matter, and as such, it is governed by internal staff regulations.[27]

In its seminal case on the issue of damage caused by civil servants, the Court of Justice ruled that the Community would only be liable for damage where the injury had been caused by an official act. The *Sayag* case concerned an official of the European Coal and Steel Community (ECSC), who caused a traffic accident in his private car while in possession of a travel order for the performance of Community business. An action was brought to recover damages under Article 188 ECSC, which was the equivalent of Article 288(2) EC. The Court held that:

> By referring at one and the same time to damage caused by the institutions and to that caused by the servants of the Community, Article 188 indicates that the Community is only liable for those acts of its servants which, by virtue of an

23. See Ch. 4.
24. AG Lagrange's Opinion in Case 23/59 *Acciaieria Ferriera di Roma (FERAM) SpA v. High Authority* [1959] ECR 253.
25. See further, Case 5/68 *Claude Sayag and S.A. Zurich v. Jean-Pierre Leduc a.o.* [1969] ECR 329.
26. K. Lenaerts, D. Arts & I. Maselis, *Procedural Law of the European Union*, 2nd edn (London: Sweet & Maxwell, 2006), 11-014.
27. See Art. 288(4) EC.

internal and direct relationship, are the necessary extension of the tasks entrusted to the institutions.[28]

The Court concluded that the driving of a private car by a servant could not in principle constitute the performance of duties within the meaning of the second paragraph of Article 188(2) ECSC, because there was no internal or direct relationship between the act of driving and the task entrusted to the servant. The Community will only be liable for the acts of its servants, therefore, where the act was undertaken in the performance of the servant's duties. Where this is not the case, the servant will be personally liable before the national courts. He or she will not be able to avail him or herself of the immunity clause found in Article 12(a) of the *Protocol*, as this only covers acts of servants performed in their official capacity.

2.4. Limitation Period

Article 46 of the Statute of the Court of Justice provides that matters arising from non-contractual liability shall be barred after a period of five years from the occurrence of the event, giving rise thereto. This stands in sharp contrast to the two-month limitation period provided for by Article 230(5) EC to begin proceedings for the annulment of Community measures. Furthermore, in *Birra Wührer*,[29] the Court ruled that the period of limitation could not begin before all the requirements governing an obligation to provide compensation for damage had been satisfied. This means, in particular, that the time limit does not begin to run until the damage complained of has materialized. The case dealt with a complaint by maize producers, brought after the Council abolished (by regulations), certain grants to which they were previously entitled. The Court concluded that because the limitation period could not start before the injurious effects of that measure had been produced, the time only began to run once the applicants had completed the transactions entitling them to refunds. It was at this point that it became sufficiently clear that the applicants were bound to incur damage.

Given that it is conceivable that damage could potentially arise more than five years after the publication of the Community measure in the Official Journal, in the interests of individual justice, the Court was undoubtedly correct to hold that the limitation period should not begin to run until such damage has in fact materialized. One of the consequences of the Court's ruling, however, has been to create uncertainty on at least two levels. The first is the uncertainty caused due to the possibility of individuals challenging a Community act more than five years after its publication in the Official Journal, depending upon when the damage materialized. One could validly argue that the Community should not be held responsible

28. Case 5/68 *Claude Sayag and S.A. Zurich v. Jean-Pierre Leduc a.o.* [1969] ECR 329, para. 7.
29. Joined Cases 256, 257, 265 and 267/80 and 5/81 *Birra Wührer a.o. v. Council and Commission* [1982] ECR I-85.

for damage arising more than five years after the implementation of the measure given the institutions' understandable inability to predict the consequences of their actions over a period greater than five years. Requiring the institutions to have regard for possible damages claims arising more than five years after the implementation of a measure would have serious negative effects on the Community's ability to legislate effectively. In addition, it may be extremely difficult, if not impossible, to determine the exact date that the damage was suffered, and therefore fixing a date for the end of the limitation period becomes equally difficult. This is particularly so where the damage complained of is either ongoing or has continued over a period of time.

The issue of limitation periods in respect of damage that develops over time arose in the case of *Biret*. The applicant company sought compensation for losses suffered, which eventually led to its liquidation, as a result of the prohibition on imports into the Community of beef and veal, as provided for by Council Directives 81/602 and 88/146 EEC. The CFI held that the applicant was only time-barred in so far as it sought compensation for damage allegedly suffered prior to the five-year period before the action was brought.[30] The applicant brought the action in 2000 and was therefore time-barred only in respect of damage occurring prior to 1995. Therefore, where the full extent of the damage does not materialize immediately, but rather develops over a period of time, the damages claim will continue to be admissible, but only in so far as the applicant seeks compensation for damage arising during a period not longer than five years from the time at which he brought the action.

The possibility of claims for damages arising more than five years after the publication of the act was raised in the case of *Adams.*[31] The case concerned an employee of a Swiss company that the Commission suspected of being engaged in anti-competitive practices. Adams sent a letter to the Commission stating that he was about to leave the company and was prepared to give evidence against it in court. Based on Adams' evidence, the Commission subsequently issued a decision that the Swiss company was carrying on anti-competitive practices. Believing Adams to be the informant, the company had him arrested for economic espionage when he returned to Switzerland in 1974. In 1975, the Commission confirmed that Adams was indeed the informant, and he was eventually given a one year suspended sentence, after having been held in solitary confinement, without being able to contact his family. He claimed damages on the grounds that the Commission had wrongly disclosed his identity to the company when it was under a duty of confidentiality. With regard to the limitation period, the ECJ concluded that:

> The expiry of the limitation period cannot constitute a valid defence to a claim by a person who as suffered damage where that person only belatedly became aware of the event giving rise to it and thus could not have had a reasonable

30. Case T-174/00 *Biret International SA v. Council* [2002] ECR II-17.
31. Case 145/83 *Stanley George Adams v. Commission of the European Communities* [1985] ECR 3539.

> time in which to submit his application to the Court or to the relevant institution before the expiry of the limitation period.[32]

The expiry of the limitation period is governed by Article 80 of the *Rules of Procedure of the Court of Justice*. Accordingly, where a limitation period is expressed in years, it shall end with the expiry of whichever day in the last year falls on the same date, as the day during which the event or action from which the period is to be calculated occurred or took place. Where a defendant wishes to rely on the expiry of the period of limitation as a bar to admissibility for an action under Article 288(2) EC, then it must raise this issue before the Court. The Court of Justice will not raise the issue of limitation of its own motion. In *Roquette Frères*, the Court justified this approach on the basis that when one compares the legal systems of the Member States, one finds that, as a general rule, and subject to very few exceptions, a court may not of its own motion raise the issue of time limitation.[33] Such reasoning falls in line with the express requirement of Article 288(2) EC, that in developing the law of non-contractual liability of the Community, the ECJ should have regard for the general principles common to the laws of the Member States.

Article 46 of the Statute of the Court of Justice also provides that the period of limitation will be interrupted once proceedings before the ECJ or CFI have been brought. The effect of this is to 'stop the clock'. Where an application has been lodged within five years of the events giving rise to the damage, the relevant institution will not be able to claim that the action is out of time, even if the case is not heard by the CFI until more than five years after the damage has arisen. The period will not, however, be interrupted if proceedings are only commenced before the national courts,[34] a point which can be crucial in deciding before which court to bring a case in the instance of concurrent liability.[35]

2.5. Independent Form of Action

As has been mentioned above, the EC Treaty provides for a series of actions that can be brought by individuals to protect their Community rights. Included in these actions are the judicial review procedures set out in Articles 230 and 232 EC, which allow the individual to seek a declaration from the Court that a Community measure is illegal and therefore null and void. An action for damages under Article 288(2) EC also inherently requires the Court to pass judgment on the validity of the Community measure in question. Damages have only ever been awarded where the

32. Ibid., para. 50.
33. Case 20/88 *SA Roquette Frères v. Commission* [1989] ECR 1553, para. 12.
34. Case C-136/01 *P Autosalone Ispra dei Fratelli Rossi Snc v. EAEC* [2002] ECR I-6565, para. 57; Case T-246/93 *Günther Bühring v. Council of the European Union and Commission of the European Communities* [1998] ECR II-171.
35. See below, p.163.

applicant has been able to show that the Community measure breached a higher norm of Community law. As such, issues arise in respect of the hierarchical relationship between Article 288 EC and Articles 230 and 232 EC. Articles 230 and 232 EC seek predominantly to ensure the effectiveness of Community law and the manner in which the institutions conduct their affairs. Article 288(2) EC, however, is concerned with protecting the individual where he has suffered loss. The question of which article takes precedence, therefore goes to the heart of establishing how the Court seeks to strike a balance between these two, often competing, principles.

The question of which article takes precedence first came before the Court of Justice in the *Plaumann* case.[36] The action was a combined action for annulment under Article 230 EC and an action for damages under Article 288(2) EC. The Court first ruled the action for annulment to be inadmissible on the grounds that the applicant lacked standing, for he was not directly and individually concerned by the Community act. The Court then continued to dismiss the action for damages, stating that:

> In the present case the contested decision has not been annulled. An administrative measure which has not been annulled cannot of itself constitute a wrongful act on the part of the administration inflicting damage upon those whom it affects. The latter cannot therefore claim damages by reason of that measure.[37]

The Court, therefore, took the view that in order to be able to claim damages against the Community under Article 288(2) EC, it was first necessary not only to bring a claim for the annulment of the relevant act (or omission), but to also have standing to bring such a claim, and then successfully prove the unlawfulness of the act. The effect of this was to place an incredibly heavy burden upon applicants and effectively served to close the door to claims under Article 288(2) EC. Nine years later, the Court had the opportunity to reassess the scope and prerequisite conditions for a claim in damages against the Community. In the first of two cases brought around the same time, the applicants in *Lütticke*[38] sought damages from the Commission for losses suffered as a result of its failure to act against Germany when the country levied illegal taxes. Similarly, in the *Schöppenstedt* case,[39] the applicants brought a claim against the Council for its failure to make special provisions for the applicants in a regulation on sugar. In neither case were the applicants eligible to bring direct claims against the institutions under Article 232 EC. While the defendants in both cases sought to rely on the Court's earlier ruling in *Plaumann* to the effect that the claim for damages was inadmissible on the basis

36. Case 25/62 *Plaumann & Co. v. Commission* [1963] ECR 199.
37. Ibid., para. 12.
38. Case 4/69 *Alfons Lütticke GmbH v. Commission* [1971] ECR 325.
39. Case 5/71 *Aktien-Zuckerfabrik Schöppenstedt v. Council* [1971] ECR 975.

that the claimants had not succeeded in an action under Article 232, the Court of Justice held that:

> The action for damages provided for by Article 178 [now Article 235 EC] and the second paragraph of Article 215 [now Article 288 EC] was established as an independent form of action with a particular purpose to fulfil within the system of actions and subject to conditions for its use, conceived with a view to its specific purpose. It would be contrary to the independent nature of this action as well as to the efficacy of the general system of forms of action created by the Treaty to regard as a ground of inadmissibility the fact that, in certain circumstances, an action for damages might lead to a result similar to that of an action for failure to act under Article 175 [now Article 232 EC].[40]

The Court, therefore, established that it was no longer necessary either to first bring an action for a failure to act (or, by analogy, an action for annulment) before bringing a claim for damages, or even to have standing to do so, for such a prerequisite would be contrary to the intended independent nature of Article 288 EC and the principle of efficiency.

While the Court's rulings in *Lütticke* and *Schöppenstedt* were welcome, they did open the door to the possibility of abuses of process. There may arise a situation where the applicant is entitled to challenge a Community act directly under Article 230(4) EC or a failure to act under Article 232 EC, but given the Courts restrictive approach to the issue of standing for private individuals under the *Plaumann*[41] line of case law, together with the strict limitation period of two months contained in Article 230(5) EC, an applicant may prefer to simply bring an action for damages under Article 288(2) EC, and thereby avoid the disadvantages of a direct action under these provisions. Alternatively, given the generous limitation period under Article 288(2) EC of five years, applicants may seek to annul an action 'through the back-door', where they would otherwise be time-barred under Article 230(5) EC. This has necessitated the Court ruling on the admissibility of a claim for damages where the applicant could have brought an action for annulment under Article 230 EC.

2.6. Standing under Articles 230 and 288(2) EC

The question arises as to whether, despite the Court's rulings in *Lütticke* and *Shöppenstedt*, that Article 288(2) EC is an independent form of action, there are situations where an applicant must seek the annulment of an act before being able to bring a claim in damages. In subsequent cases, the Court of Justice has sought to make a distinction between situations where damage was caused by acts of which the applicant was the addressee and those where the damage was caused by a measure of general application.

40. Case 4/69 *Alfons Lütticke GmbH v. Commission* [1971] ECR 325, para. 6.
41. Case 25/62 *Plaumann & Co. v. Commission* [1963] ECR 199.

Where the case deals with damage caused by an act that has been addressed to the applicant, then he or she will clearly have standing to bring an action for annulment under Article 230(4) EC. In this situation, the Court of Justice will declare an action for damages under Article 288(2) EC as inadmissible, if the applicant has failed to first bring an action for annulment, compliant with Article 230 EC. This stance is justified in that it seeks to prevent applicants from by-passing the strict limitation period found in Article 230(5) EC and is in line with the Court's reasoning with regard to an indirect challenge to the legality of a Community act brought by means of a preliminary ruling or through a plea of illegality. This point was illustrated by the Court in the staff case of *Müller-Collignon.*[42] Mrs. Müller-Collignon filed an action for annulment against a decision of the Commission, appointing another person, Mrs. Graf, to a post that she desired. Upon discovering that she had filed her claim for annulment of the appointment decision too late, she brought an action seeking damages against the Commission under Article 288 EC. The Court held that:

> It is clear from this that the damage is founded on the non-appointment of the applicant and more exactly on the appointment of Mrs. Graf. The applicant could have avoided this damage by contesting the measures in question in good time. It is apparent from the foregoing that she has failed to do so. In these circumstances she cannot repair this omission, and so to speak, acquire the opportunity of bringing a new appeal by means of a claim for damages. Accordingly the inadmissibility of the request for annulment must inevitably bring with it inadmissibility of the claim for damages.[43]

Whenever the action for damages can, therefore, be said in reality to be aimed only at obtaining the withdrawal of an individual act which was addressed to the applicant and which is no longer open to challenge under Article 230 EC, and is not designed to obtain separate damages, the Court will consider the claim to be an abuse of process and declare it inadmissible. The abusive purpose of the damages action will be inferred by the Court where the reparation sought by the applicant coincides with the benefit which he or she would have obtained had an action for annulment been brought.[44]

This is not the case, however, where the applicant seeks to challenge a Community act that is of general application, or for which he or she has no standing to challenge it directly. As seen above, in *Lütticke* and *Schöppenstedt*, the applicants brought a claim in damages as they had no standing to bring a direct action for failure to act under Article 232 EC. Both claims were held to be admissible, and did not require the applicants to bring what would have been a futile claim under Article 232 EC.

In the *Merkur* case,[45] the Court went even further. The case concerned Regulation 974/71 EEC, which regulated the export of products processed from

42. Case 4/67 *Anne Muller (née Collignon) v. Commission* [1967] ECR 469.
43. Ibid., paras 11-13.
44. Case 59/65 *Heinrich Schreckenberg v. Commission* [1966] ECR 785.
45. Case 43/72 *Merkur Außenhandel-GmbH & Co. KG v. Commission* [1973] ECR 1055.

barley. The Regulation provided for compensatory amounts to be paid to exporters of barley products. The applicants claimed that they were entitled to 50,000 deutsch marks (DM) from the Commission on account of its failure to award it the compensation to which it considered that it was entitled under Regulation 974/71 EEC. The Court held the applicant's claim to be admissible, even though the applicants could potentially have challenged the decision under Article 232 EC. The Court based its reasoning on the principles of proper administration and procedural efficiency by holding that:

> the Court already has the case before it and within its jurisdiction and is therefore bound to see whether or not these regulations are tainted with the alleged irregularities. It would not be in keeping with the proper administration of justice and the requirements of procedural efficiency to compel the applicant to have recourse to national remedies and thus await for a considerable length of time before a final decision on his claim is made.[46]

As Schermers and Waelbroeck rightly assert,[47] the conclusion to be drawn from the Court's case law is that a claim for damages is admissible in cases where the injuries result from an act or a failure to act which the individual either could or could not challenge, or which was of a general character.[48] However, where the individual is the direct addressee of the act, and in reality only seeks the withdrawal of the act, then an action for damages will be declared inadmissible, unless or until the applicant has first brought an action for annulment under Article 230 EC.

3. SUBSTANTIVE RULES UNDER ARTICLE 288(2) EC

The law governing the substantive rules of liability under Article 288(2) EC have, as with much of EC law, evolved over time. As is often the case in areas dominated by case law, this development has been done gradually and in a piecemeal fashion, and has lead to periods of contradiction and uncertainty in the law. Eventually, however, the time comes when the Court decides to start fresh so as to re-instil order and clarity to its case law by significantly altering the criteria for establishing liability. In respect of Article 288(2) EC, this moment came with the Court's ruling in *Bergaderm*.[49] To reflect this evolution, and to put the current law in context, the subsequent paragraphs are arranged to reflect the three evolutionary stages of Article 288(2) EC: first, the Court's case law prior to its ruling in the *Bergaderm* case; second, the *Bergaderm* case itself, and the way in which the Court sought to

---

46. Ibid., para. 6.
47. H.G. Schermers & D.F. Waelbroeck, *Judicial Protection in the European Union*, 6th edn (The Hague: Kluwer International, 2001), 1085.
48. See, for example, Case 281/82 *Société à responsabilité limitée Unifrex v. Commission and Council* [1984] ECR-1969.
49. Case C-352/98 P *Laboratoires Phramaceutiques Bergaderm and Groupil v. Commission* [2000] ECR I-5291.

change the substantive test for damages liability; and third, the post-*Bergaderm* case law, and whether or not the Court – and particularly the CFI – has followed the changes introduced by the ECJ in *Bergaderm.*

3.1. Pre-*Bergaderm*

Article 288(2) EC provides that the conditions for incurring liability are to be determined by the Court '*in accordance with the general principles common to the laws of the Member States*'. At the time that Article 288(2) EC was written, there were only six Member States. Even then, however, deducing any meaningful 'general principles' that could be relied upon to any great extent was no easy task. Instead, the Court has drawn on those principles only as a source of inspiration to develop an independent Community law on liability.[50] Throughout the evolution of the case law on non-contractual liability, the Court has remained faithful to, at least what English lawyers consider as, the fundamental elements of a civil action – duty, breach, loss, and causation. This is evident from the Court's ruling in *Lütticke*, where it stated that liability on the part of the Community 'presupposes the existence of a set of circumstances comprising actual damage, a causal link between the damage claimed and conduct alleged against the institution, and the illegality of such conduct'.[51]

Traditionally, therefore, the first element of the substantive test that requires proving in order for liability to exist is that the act of the Community institution was unlawful.[52] The Court's case law has not always been clear as to whether, when establishing the unlawfulness of a Community act, the unlawfulness arises simply out of breach of a superior rule of law (objective or strict liability) or whether 'fault' is also required (subjective liability).[53] The original approach adopted by the Court was to tackle the issue of fault by distinguishing between those acts that were fundamentally administrative in nature and those that were legislative in nature. In relation to administrative acts, the Court determined that the requirement of unlawful conduct would be satisfied by any infringement of law (objective liability). In relation to legislative measures, however, an act would only be unlawful where it constituted a serious breach of a superior rule of law for the protection of individuals. Furthermore, where, in the adoption of the legislative measure the institution was afforded a wide discretion of how to act, the measure would only be unlawful

50. See F. Fines, 'Etude de la responsibilité extracontractuelle de la Communauté économique européenne', in Bibliothèque de droit international, vol. 101 (Librairie générale de droit et de jurisprudence, Paris, 1990), 501.
51. Case 4/69 *Alfons Lütticke GmbH v. Commission* [1971] ECR 325, para. 10.
52. More recent case law has raised the possibility of a claim in damages existing even where the act of the Community institution was not illegal. See below s. 6.
53. K. Lenaerts, D. Arts & I. Maselis, *Procedural Law of the European Union*, 2nd edn (London: Sweet & Maxwell, 2006), 11-025; see also Case 153/73 *Holz & Willemsen v. Council and Commission* [1974] ECR 675, para. 7.

where it could be shown that the measure constituted a 'sufficiently serious breach of Community law'.[54]

3.1.1. Distinction between Administrative and Legislative Acts

In assessing whether or not an act is administrative or legislative in nature, the Court is not interested in the title or form of the measure in question, but rather whether or not the measure produces effects of general application.[55] Administrative acts may be defined as those acts by which the administration applies general rules in individual cases or otherwise exercises its executive powers in an individual manner.[56] Legislative measures on the other hand often deal with broad policy areas and require the institutions to make a choice as to the way in which an issue should be resolved.

The Court's focus on the generality of the measure in determining whether an act is administrative or legislative in nature – and therefore whether a simple breach of Community law is sufficient or whether a 'serious breach' is required – was illustrated by the CFI in *Levende Varkens (Live Pigs)*.[57] The case concerned a challenge brought by Dutch pig farmers against Council Directive 90/425 EC on veterinary checks concerning intra-Community trade in live animals. In 1993 there were reports of outbreaks of swine vesicular disease in Italy and the Netherlands and, acting pursuant to the provisions of Council Directive 90/425 EC, the Commission adopted Decision 93/128 EC, preventing both countries from exporting live pigs to other Member States. The applicant sued for damages, claiming that the ban was disproportionate. In bringing the claim the applicant argued that it was not necessary to prove that there had been a sufficiently serious breach of Community law. It claimed that the Decision was not a legislative measure because it only imposed specific obligations on the two countries in question. The measure was therefore of only individual and not general effect. The Court of First instance disagreed, stating that:

> It is true that the decision produces, vis-à-vis those two Member States, the legal effects of an individual measure. In relation to the applicants however, the decision produces the effects of a generally applicable measure, in the same way, for example, as a regulation prohibiting exporters established in the Netherlands and Italy from exporting live pigs to other Member States.[58]

---

54. Joined Cases T-481/93 and T-484/93 *Vereniging van Exporteurs in Levende Varkens a.o. v. Commission* [1995] ECR II-2941, para. 76; Joined Cases 261/78 and 262/78 *Interquell Strärke-Chemie v. EEC* [1979] ECR 3045.
55. M. Brealey & M. Hoskins, *Remedies in EC Law*, 2nd edn (London: Sweet & Maxwell, 1998), 361.
56. See E. Grabitz, 'Liability for Legislative Acts', in *Non-contractual Liability of the European Communities*, eds H. Schermers, T. Heukels & P. Mead (The Hague: Kluwer, 1988), 1-11.
57. Joined Cases T-481/93 and T-484/93 *Vereniging van Exporteurs in Levende Varkens a.o. v. Commission* [1995] ECR II-2941, para. 76.
58. Ibid., para 87.

In establishing whether or not a measure is administrative or legislative, the Court therefore has regard not only for the effects that the measure has on those to whom it is addressed (in *Levende Varkens* the Italian and Dutch States) but also the wider effects that the measure has on the citizens of those States and ultimately the applicants themselves. Consequently, a measure must be looked at in the context of what it sets out to achieve, and the generality of that aim. There are, therefore, no hard and fast rules as to when a measure will be administrative or legislative. That is a decision to be taken on a case-by-case basis having regard to the situation as it comes before the Court.

As in any context where the Court is required to make an assessment based almost exclusively on the facts of an individual case, there is a large scope for inconsistencies to arise, particularly in borderline cases. Although somewhat clichéd, the old English saying that hard cases make bad law is certainly appropriate in respect to the Court of Justice's rulings on Community liability. The situation is further complicated when one considers why the Court chose to draw such a distinction. As will become apparent, the common thread running throughout the case law in this area is the balance that the Court seeks to strike between effective judicial protection for the individual and, as the Court stated in its ruling in the *BT* case, ensuring '*that the legislative function is not hindered by the prospect of actions for damages whenever the general interest requires the institutions . . . to adopt measures which may adversely affect individual interests*'.[59]

The administrative/legislative distinction is the Court's attempt to identify those situations where compensating individual applicants for the loss they have suffered outweighs the general aims of the measure in question. The Court recognizes however, that in certain circumstances, even when dealing with measures of general, legislative application, an individual may have the right to compensation. In order to be entitled to such compensation, however, the applicant will need to prove to the Court the higher fault threshold and that the Community institution has committed a 'sufficiently serious breach' of its duty.

In attempting to strike this balance, the unofficial tendency of the Court is to consider a measure to be legislative, unless the applicant can show that it is administrative. This places a heavy evidential burden on the applicant, and few have succeeded in discharging it. Those applicants that were successful in pleading that the act in question was administrative have, however, made it possible to identify certain situations in which the Court is more likely to define a measure as administrative rather than legislative. The list of situations where this is the case is not exhaustive. If an application does not fall within one of the categories set out below, this does not mean that the Court will determine that the measure is legislative. Similarly, where an act does fall within one of the categories below, there is no guarantee that the Court will not find that the act is legislative. The question turns very much on the facts of the case. Where an applicant can bring its case within one of the categories below, however, then he stands a better chance of

59. Case C-392/93 *The Queen v. H.M. Treasury, ex parte British Telecommunications* [1996] ECR I-1631, para. 40.

the Court defining the act as administrative, and therefore only having to satisfy the lower fault threshold applicable to administrative acts.

3.2. Administrative Acts

The following constitute different situations in which applicants have successfully pleaded that the measure in question was administrative as opposed to legislative in nature.

3.2.1. Abusive or Erroneous Application of Power

The Court has held that a Community institution may be liable in damages either where it has abused its powers,[60] or where there has been an error in the application of the rules.[61] The *Meskens* case provides a good example of when liability in damages can arise as a result of a failure on the part of an institution to apply the appropriate rules correctly.[62] The applicant had been working as a temporary staff member for a political group of the Parliament. While holding this position, she applied for a post within the Parliament. The Secretary-General of the Parliament wrongfully rejected her application. Mrs. Meskens successfully challenged the Secretary-General's decision by means of an action for annulment. By the time the CFI had heard the case, however, the period for application was over, and the applicant was no longer permitted to apply for the post. Mrs. Meskens returned to the Court of First Instance seeking compensation on the basis that she had suffered loss as a result of the Secretary-General's wrongful rejection of her application. The CFI ruled that the decision of the Secretary-General to refuse to take any specific measures vis-à-vis the applicant so as to allow her to participate in the application process amounted to a breach of duty for which Mrs. Meskens could receive compensation.[63]

3.2.2. Inadequate Organization of the Administration

In the *First Feram Case*,[64] the Court was faced with the fraudulent certification, by a national institution, of Community ferrous scrap as scrap coming from outside of

60. Joined Cases 5, 7, 13-24/66 *Kampffmeyer and others v. Commission* [1967] ECR 317.
61. In Joined Cases 363/88 and 364/88 *Finsinder and Falk v. Commission* [1992] ECR I-359, para. 22, the Court cited examples of the numerous terms used to determine liability in relation to the erroneous application of rules: 'inexcusable mistakes' Joined Cases 14/60 and 1/61 *Meroni v. High Authority* [1961] ECR 161, at 171; 'gravely neglected the duties of supervision' Joined Cases 19 and 21/60, 2 and 3/61 *Fives Lille Cail v. High Authority* [1961] ECR 281, at 297; 'lack of care' which was 'increasingly obvious' Joined Cases 29 and 51/63 *Usines de la Providence v. High Authority* [1965] ECR 911, at 937.
62. Case C-412/92 P *Parliament v. Meskens* [1994] ECR I-3757.
63. See also Case T-47/93 *C. Case* [1994] ECR-SC II 743.
64. Case 23/59 *Acciaieria Ferriera di Roma (FERAM) SpA v. High Authority of the European Coal and Steel Community* [1959] ECR 245.

the Community. The purpose behind the fraudulent certification of the scrap was to allow it to benefit from subsidies from the Community. The scrap was sold through a Community body, the Office Commun des Consommateurs de Ferrailles (OCCF), on the basis of the fraudulent certificates. The certificates were issued by the Head of the Iron and Steel Department of the Netherlands Ministry of Economic Affairs. The fraud had continued for three years before the High Authority intervened, and resulted in USD 646,200 being wrongfully paid out. FERAM brought a case against the High Authority for the damage that it had suffered, claiming that the High Authority was liable for having failed to avoid a situation whereby, during a three-year period, considerable quantities of ferrous scrap were sold through the OCCF, supported by fraudulent material. The Court considered whether there was a wrongful act on the part of the High Authority because of its failure to provide a better organized system for issuing the certificates of origin for ferrous scrap, and, in particular, its failure to provide for the investigation of the authenticity of those certificates:

> In leaving to the competent national authority the task of issuing the necessary certificates, the defendant pursued the course which appeared the most appropriate.... It was natural to entrust [the issuing of the certificates] to the national authorities, who ... were the best qualified to carry out the necessary checks.... In these circumstances, the defendant cannot be blamed for having adopted this system and the fact of its having done so cannot in any case be described as a wrongful act or omission.[65]

It is clear from the Court's ruling that while the Community in this instance was not required to compensate the applicant, in general, inadequate organization of an administration may be a 'fault' for which damages are recoverable, provided that it can be blamed on the Community.[66] This point was further elucidated by the Court in *Gratreau*.[67] The case concerned a complaint on the part of a scientific officer in the Commission who, upon having issued a complaint to the Commission regarding a report on his personal file, did not receive a reply for four months, which caused him to be passed over for promotion. In its judgment, the Court held 'that the Commission may not put forward its internal administrative organization as a justification for the non-observance of its obligations towards its officials'.[68] The Court therefore employs a form of estoppel-reasoning in awarding the applicant compensation, by holding that the Commission may not avoid liability through reliance on its own failings. The Court has utilized this type of reasoning in other areas – most notably in the context of granting direct effect to directives where Member States have failed to enact implementing legislation within the prescribed time period. As such, it is a good, early example of an instance

65. Ibid., at 251-252.
66. H.G. Schermers & D.F. Waelbroeck, *Judicial Protection in the European Union*, 6th edn (The Hague: Kluwer International, 2001), 1093.
67. Joined Cases 156/79 and 51/80 *Gratreau v. Commission* [1980] ECR 3953.
68. Ibid., para. 15.

where the Court attempts to judge Community and national institutions equally – a principle to which the Court later expressly committed itself in its ruling in *Bergaderm.*

3.2.3. Erroneous Information

In the *First Richez-Parise* case,[69] the Court held that the simple adoption of an erroneous interpretation of Community law was not, in itself, a wrongful act. Such an act could, however, become wrongful where the institution failed to rectify its mistake within a reasonable period:

> Apart from the exceptional instance, the adoption of an incorrect interpretation does not constitute in itself a wrongful act. However, whilst it may be possible to doubt the existence of a wrongful act concerning the supply of incorrect information, the same cannot be said of the department's delay in rectifying the information.... A failure to make such a correction is... a matter of such a nature as to render the Communities liable.[70]

3.2.4. Abusive Criticism of a Person

The Court has ruled that 'redundant criticism' of staff members would constitute a wrongful administrative act, since it harms the individual position of the staff members concerned, and therefore leads to liability on the part of the Community.[71]

3.2.5. Breach of Internal Rules

The Court of Justice in the *Di Pillo* Case[72] accepted that a breach of internal rules could be a ground for liability, and would ordinarily be an administrative act. The Court awarded damages where the Community, in breach of its own internal rules, failed to make probation reports within five months of the beginning of the trial period of its officials. The Court argued that the promulgation of internal Community institution rules governing institutional administration were essential in the interests of legal certainty. Similarly, the Court has ruled that in the absence of special circumstances, an institution will be liable for a wrongful act where it fails to complete an official's report within the period allowed.[73]

---

69. Joined Cases 19, 20, 25 and 30/69 *Denise Richez-Parise a.o. v. Commission* [1970] ECR 325.
70. Ibid., paras 36-42.
71. See further H.G. Schermers & D.F. Waelbroeck, *Judicial Protection in the European Union*, 6th edn (The Hague: Kluwer International, 2001), 1097.
72. Case 10 and 47/72 *Nunzio di Pillo v. Commission of the European Communities* [1973] ECR 763, para. 58.
73. Case 207/81 *Dietrich v, Commission* [1983] ECR 1274, para. 28.

3.2.6. Failure to Comply with a Previous Judgment of the Court

Failure to comply with a judgment of the Court is not only an infringement of Article 233 EC, but also gives rise to liability in damages on the part of the institution concerned. This was exemplified by the CFI's ruling in *Stahlwerke Peine-Salzgitter*, where the Court concluded that:

> Following the judgment of the Court of Justice . . . annulling the individual decisions . . . the Commission was under an obligation to eliminate from the measures already adopted when the annulling judgment was delivered any provisions with the same effect as the provisions held to be illegal.[74]

3.2.7. Breaches of Confidentiality

In the *Adams* case outlined above,[75] an employee of a Swiss company engaged in anti-competitive practices sent a letter to the Commission stating that he was about to leave the company and was prepared to give evidence against it in court. He was later arrested for economic espionage. He claimed damages on the ground that the Commission had wrongly disclosed his identity to the company when they were under a duty of confidentiality. The Court acknowledged that in handing documents over to the Swiss company, the Commission aided the company in identifying Adams which eventually led to his arrest. The Commission was fully aware of the risk that handing over the documents might reveal Mr. Adams' identity, and it should therefore have consulted and warned him before handing over the documents. The Commission's failure to do this amounted to an administrative act, which breached the principle of confidentiality and therefore entitled Mr. Adams to compensation under Article 288(2) EC for the resulting loss that he suffered.

3.3. Legislative Acts

In contrast to the four basic elements for liability arising out administrative acts – duty, breach, loss, and causation – the Court requires proof of a higher standard of breach when bringing an action for an alleged contravention of a legislative act. In its ruling in *Schöppenstedt*,[76] where the Court first established its formula for grounding a claim in damages based on a legislative measure, the Court required that there be a violation of a superior rule of law; the rule must be intended for the protection of the individual; and such violation must be sufficiently serious. While the issue in *Schöppenstedt* related to an alleged breach of an economic measure, the Court has since applied the same test to measures governing other aspects of

74. Case T-120/89 *Stahlwerke-Salzgitter v. Commission* [1991] ECR II-279.
75. See above p. 94.
76. Case 5/71 *Zuckerfabrik Schöppenstedt v. Council* [1971] ECR 975.

Community law.[77] While the weight attributed to each of these elements has evolved over time, the fundamental requirements remained the same – up until the Court's ruling in *Bergaderm*.

Much of the Court's early case law in this area developed out of the Common Agricultural Policy (CAP), under which the Community institutions had to make difficult discretionary choices. Assessed in this context, the Court's rationale of requiring a higher standard for liability is justified when one considers that in introducing legislation the Community institutions will often be engaged in a complex weighing process designed to balance the conflicting variables identified in Article 33 EC.[78] Requiring a mere breach (as opposed to a 'sufficiently serious breach'), would render decision-makers susceptible to a potentially wide liability, and would run the risk that the Court might 'second guess' decisions made by the Commission and Council.[79]

Furthermore, as Tridimas rightly argues,[80] where an action for damages is successful, it is ultimately the taxpayer who covers the cost. A public authority should only incur liability as a result of legislative action where the interest of compensating the persons who suffered loss is judged more worthy of protection than the interest of the taxpayer. The *Schöppenstedt* formula therefore engenders the Courts aim of striking a balance between the need to provide sufficient protection for legislators so as not to stifle the effectiveness of their legislative initiative, while, at the same time, satisfying the general principle of providing effective judicial protection to individuals whose EC rights have been infringed.

3.3.1. Superior Rule for the Protection of the Individual

As is evident from the formulation used by the Court in *Schöppenstedt*, the first requirement for claiming a breach of a legislative act contains two elements: the rule breached by the Community measure must be a superior rule, and must be for the protection of individuals. In respect of the first strand of the test, the Treaty is conspicuously silent as to the hierarchy of the various sources of EC law. Despite there being no express provision governing the relationship between the sources of European law, Lenaerts and Van Nuffel argue that the authors of the Treaties nevertheless assumed the existence of a hierarchy of norms.[81] Their reasoning is based on Article 230 EC, under which an action may be brought for the

77. See, for example, Case C-62/89 *Assurances du Crédit v. Council and Commission* [1991] ECR I-1799; and Joined Cases T-481/93 and T-484/93 *Vereniging van Exporteurs in Levende Varkens a.o. v. Commission* [1995] ECR II-2941, para. 76.
78. Article 33 EC lists the objectives of the common agricultural policy as being: to increase agricultural productivity by promoting technical progress; to ensure a fair standard of living for the agricultural community; to stabilize markets; to assure the availability of supplies; and to ensure that supplies reach consumers at reasonable prices.
79. P. Craig & G. de Burca, *EU Law*, 4th edn (OUP, Oxford, 2007), 585.
80. T. Tridimas, *The General Principles of EC Law*, 3rd edn (OUP, Oxford, 2006), 480.
81. K. Lenaerts & P. Van Nuffel, *Constitutional Law of the European Union*, 2nd edn (London: Sweet & Maxwell, 2005), 17-052.

annulment of acts of Community institutions, inter alia, on the ground of 'infringement of this Treaty or of any rule of law relating to its application'. The conclusion to be drawn from this is that judicial review extends to examining whether the acts in question are compatible with superior rules of law.

Following on from this, Lenaerts and Van Nuffel helpfully construct the following hierarchy of European law: At the top of the hierarchy are the Treaties and the Acts of Accession which constitute the basic constitutional charter of the European Union.[82] Beyond the Treaties themselves, there is a series of quasi-constitutional decisions, such as the Decision on Own Resources[83] or the Decision on the Direct Election of the European Parliament.[84] Further, and on the same hierarchical footing as the Treaties and quasi-constitutional decisions, are the general principles of law, including fundamental rights, which constitute unwritten constitutional norms. The second level of the hierarchy contains rules of international law which permeate the legal order of the Community, including agreements and customary international law. The third level is where we find acts of the Community institutions based directly on Treaty provisions. Finally, there are acts of Community institutions which seek to implement previous acts of the institutions.[85]

From the Court's case law, it is clear to see that the superior rules that are usually said to have been breached by Community measures are generally found in the top two levels of the normative hierarchy. In relation to provisions of the Treaty prior to the *Bergaderm* ruling, the Court heard cases based on alleged breaches of Article 12,[86] Articles 28 and Article 29,[87] Article 33(1)[88] and Article 34(3)[89] of the EC Treaty. In respect of general principles of law, the Court has ruled that the protection of legitimate expectation,[90] the principle of proportionality,[91] the principle of equal treatment,[92] and the principle of proper administration[93] were all superior rules for the purposes of Article 288(2) EC.

An action under Article 288(2) EC cannot however, be brought to challenge a provision of the Treaty itself. In *Dubois et Fils*,[94] a French company providing custom agency services brought an action for damages, claiming that the completion of the internal market and the abolition of internal frontiers directly led to it being put out of business. The CFI ruled, however, that the Single European Act,

82. Case 294/83 *Partie Ecologiste 'Les Verts' v. European Parliament* [1986] ECR 1339, para. 23.
83. See Art. 269 EC.
84. See Art. 190(3) EC.
85. See further K. Lenaerts & P. Van Nuffel, *Constitutional Law of the European Union*, 2nd edn (London: Sweet & Maxwell, 2005), at 17-052-17-055.
86. See Joined Cases 71 and 72/84 *Surcouf and Vidou v. EEC* [1985] ECR 2925.
87. See Case 265/85 *Van den Bergh and Jurgens v. Commission* [1987] ECR 1155.
88. See Case 27/85 *Vandemootele v. Commission* [1987] ECR 1129.
89. See Case 281/82 *Unifrex v. Council and Commission* [1984] ECR 1969.
90. See Case 74/74 *CNTA v. Commission* [1975] ECR 533.
91. Case 27/85 *Vandemootele v. Commission* [1987] ECR 1129.
92. Case 238/78 *Ireks-Arkady GmbH v. Council and Commission* [1979] ECR 2955, para. 5.
93. See Case T-105/96 *Pharos v. Commission* [1988] ECR II-285.
94. Case T-113/96 *Dubois et Fils v. Council and Commission* [1998] ECR II-125.

which was the direct cause of the applicant's loss, formed a part of the Community's constitution, and was not an act of the institutions for the purposes of Article 288(2) EC. Although never having come before the Court, the position is probably the same in relation to all constitutional sources of European law falling within the top level of the hierarchical chain.

Even where the applicant is able to show that the legislative act in question infringes upon a rule from one of the higher hierarchical levels, this will not, however, in itself, be sufficient for the applicant to be awarded damages. In drawing on the general principles of the Member States, the Court's interpretation of Article 288(2) EC requires that liability in damages for the alleged breach of a legislative act only be available where the measure in question breaches a legal norm that protects the individual. This is based on the German *Schutznormtheorie*, according to which, the State is only liable where it breaches a subjective public right of the injured party. Under German law, in order for an individual to be able to claim damages from the State, the legal norm in question must be intended to protect not only individuals in general, but also the group of individuals to which the injured party belongs.[95] The Court of Justice has not, however, been as strict in its interpretation of when a rule will be for the protection of the individual as is required under German law. As the *Kampffmeyer*[96] case illustrated, for the purposes of Article 288(2) EC, it is sufficient to show that the superior rule of law is for the protection of individuals generally. It is neither necessary to show that the applicant belongs to a certain class as is required under German law, nor is it necessary for the applicant to be directly and individually concerned, as would be the case for the purposes of standing under Article 230(4) EC.

The *Kampffmeyer* case concerned a series of German grain dealers who wanted to import maize from France. At the time, the relevant provisions of Community law specified that the applicants required import permits from the German government. In its judgment, the Court rejected the argument that the applicants could not claim damages because the rule of Community law that had allegedly been infringed was only of general application and was not intended to protect the interests of the applicants. The Court continued:

> The fact that these interests are of a general nature does not prevent their including the interests of individual undertakings such as the applicants.... Although the application of the rules of law in question is not in general capable of being of direct and individual concern to the said undertakings, that does not prevent the possibility that the protection of their interests may be – as in the present case it is in fact – intended by those rules of law. The defendant's argument that the rule of law [in question] is not directed towards the protection of the interests of the applicant cannot therefore be accepted.[97]

95. E. Grabitz, 'Liability for Legislative Acts', in *Non-contractual Liability of the European Communities*, eds H. Schermers, T. Heukels & P. Mead (The Hague: Kluwer, 1988), 1-11.
96. Joined Cases 5, 7, 13-24/66 *Kampffmeyer and others v. Commission* [1967] ECR 317.
97. Ibid., at 263.

In determining whether a rule is designed to protect individuals, the Court therefore adopts a case-by-case approach, based on the objectives to be achieved by the rule in question.[98] As the *Kampffmeyer* ruling and subsequent case law has shown, the threshold employed by the Court when assessing whether or not a rule protects individuals is not particularly difficult to achieve. Recent case law confirms that this element of the test for the recovery of damages will be satisfied where the rule in question is designed to protect individuals generally. In *Camós Grau v. Commission*,[99] which concerned an investigation by the European Anti-Fraud Office into the conduct of Commission employees, the requirement of impartiality, to which all the Community institutions are subject in carrying out their tasks, is intended to ensure that the public interest is respected as well as to protect individuals and confer on them a right to see that the corresponding guarantees are complied with. It is not necessary, therefore, that the applicant be part of a particular group or show that a duty was owed to him specifically. Provided that the underlying objective of the rule is the general protection of individuals the test of individual protection will be satisfied.

The fact that the test adopted by the Court in relation to claims based on Article 288(2) EC is more liberal than that for actions for annulment brought under Article 230 EC, should not, however, be read as implying that the criterion will be satisfied in every case. The rule must still have as its purpose the protection of individuals. This point was well illustrated in *Vreugdenhil II* where the applicant sought to claim damages for losses that the applicant argued had been caused by a Commission regulation. The Regulation had previously been declared invalid on the grounds that the Commission had acted *ultra vires* by adopting the measure. The Court refused to award compensation, reasoning that:

> The aim of the system of the division of powers between the various Community institutions is to ensure that the balance between the institutions provided for in the Treaty is maintained, and not to protect individuals. Consequently, a failure to observe the balance between the institutions cannot be sufficient on its own to engage the Community's liability towards the traders concerned.[100]

98. Case T-271/04 *Citymo v. Commission* [2007] ECR II-1375. The case arose out of negotiations between the Community public authority and a tenderer in a public tendering procedure. The applicant claimed that the Commission had committed a sufficiently serious breach of the principle of good faith and had misused the right conferred on it by Art. 101 of Regulation 1605/2002 EC, on the Financial Regulation applicable to the general budget of the European Communities which granted the awarding authority a wide discretion to decline to award the public contract. The CFI ruled that the principle of good faith could be regarded as a rule protecting individuals who were in a position to negotiate with the Commission and that by failing to advise the applicant immediately of its decision not to award the contract, the Commission had breached this principle and caused the applicant to lose a serious opportunity to contract with a third party for a period of two months.
99. Case T-309/03 *Camós Grau v. Commission* [2006] ECR II-1173.
100. Case C-282/90 *Vreugdenhil v. Commission* (Vreugdenhil II) [1992] ECR I-1937, paras 20-21; See also Case 74/74 *CNTA v. Commission* [1975] ECR 533.

Further, in *Kind v. EEC*,[101] the Court of Justice held that insufficient reasoning – which normally is a ground for illegality – is not a breach of a superior rule for the protection of individuals, and is not therefore sufficient to ground a claim in damages under Article 288(2) EC. In curt fashion, the Court rejected the applicants' arguments by declaring 'any inadequacy in the statement of the reasons upon which a measure contained in a regulation is based is not sufficient to make the Community liable'.[102] Similarly, a mere technical error in the text of a regulation, which might suffice to have the measure annulled under Article 230 EC, will not suffice as a basis for the award of damages under Article 288(2) EC.[103]

3.3.2. Economic Acts?

The Court, when setting out the test in *Schöppenstedt*, left open the issue of what constitutes a legislative act for the purposes of Article 288(2) EC. In its ruling the Court declared:

> Where legislative action involving measures of economic policy is concerned, the Community does not incur non-contractual liability for damage suffered by individuals as a consequence of that action . . . unless a sufficiently flagrant violation of a superior rule of law for the protection of the individual has occurred.[104]

A literal interpretation of the Court's formula would mean that the Court only intended its ruling to apply in instances involving economic policy measures. As Schermers and Waelbroeck argue,[105] there is no compelling reason why the Court should exclude legislative measures based on, for example, social policy or transport. They submit rather, that the correct interpretation of the Court's meaning in *Schöppenstedt* is that the formula should be used to limit the amount of control that can be exercised where the decision-makers have to make policy choices.

Subsequent case law appears to affirm Schermers' and Waelbroeck's argument. For instance, in *Assurances du Crédit*[106] the Court applied the *Schöppenstedt* formula to establish whether the Community was liable for an alleged breach of the principle of non-discrimination by a harmonization directive. The applicants were companies engaged in export credit assurance, and brought a claim for compensation against the Community on the basis that they suffered losses as a result of their being wrongfully excluded from the scope of a Council Directive on the

101. Case 106/81 *Kind v. EEC* [1982] ECR 2885.
102. *Ibid.*, para. 14.
103. Joined Cases 194-206/83 *Asteris v. Commission* [1985] ECR 2815.
104. Case 5/71 *Aktien-Zuckerfabrik Schöppenstedt v. Council* [1971] ECR 975, para. 11.
105. H.G. Schermers & D.F. Waelbroeck, *Judicial Protection in the European Union*, 6th edn (The Hague: Kluwer International, 2001), 1102.
106. Case C-62/89 *Assurances du Crédit v. Council and Commission* [1991] ECR I-1799.

coordination of laws governing insurance. The Court ruled that the harmonizing legislation was a legislative act, on the grounds that:

> The implementation of harmonising provisions of that kind is generally difficult because it requires the competent Community institutions to draw up, on the basis of diverse, complex national provisions, common rules which conform to the objectives laid down by the Treaty and obtain, as appropriate, either the unanimous agreement of the Council or the agreement of a qualified majority of its members. It is because of that difficulty in particular that the competent Community institutions must be recognised as enjoying a discretion in relation to the stages in which harmonisation is to take place, having regard to the particular nature of the field subject to coordination.[107]

While the case arose out of the economic setting of the provision of financial and insurance services, the reasoning given by the Court for classifying that act as legislative is not grounded on this basis. The Court focused instead on the discretion open to the Commission in adopting harmonizing legislation; the general nature of the measure; and the relative complexity of the issue at hand. In doing so, it concluded that the term legislative act covers all decisions adopted in the exercise of wide discretion, in particular where concerned with the organization of a market. The CFI's case law has not, however, been consistent as to whether it considers that the existence of wide discretion is an element which contributes to the legislative character of the act or whether discretion is a cumulative condition separate from the legislative nature of the act. This appears to have been resolved in *Levende Varkens*[108] where the CFI explicitly held that the conditions were separate and cumulative, and therefore, for the *Schöppenstedt* formula to apply, the act needed to be a legislative measure and the Community institution needed to have adopted the decision in the exercise of a wide discretion.

It is evident, therefore, that while many of the cases arising before the Court do concern measures of economic policy, the Court will not limit itself to only classing these as legislative acts. Instead, it will assess whether the measure is of general application; the level of discretion afforded to the Commission; and the general complexity of the matter dealt with by the act in question.

3.3.3. Sufficiently Serious Breach

Once the Court has established that the measure in question is a legislative act, it is up to the applicant to prove that the measure constitutes a serious breach of a superior rule. This second element of the *Schöppenstedt* formula once again reflects the Court's reluctance to find the Community liable for loss caused by acts involving policy choices. The Court sought to clarify what it meant by

107. Ibid., paras 10-11.
108. Joined Cases T-481/93 and T-484/93 *Vereniging van Exporteurs in Levende Varkens a.o. v. Commission* [1995] ECR II-2941, paras 81-82.

'sufficiently serious breach' in the *HNL* case.[109] The case was the fourth in a series of actions brought by a group of chicken farmers. The applicants claimed losses allegedly resulting from a Council Regulation aimed at reducing the mounting stocks of skimmed-milk powder. The Regulation required producers to use skimmed-milk powder in the manufacture of feeding-stuffs. In the first three rulings on the issue the Court held that the Regulation was invalid on the basis that the purchase price of skimmed-milk powder was fixed at a level that was so much higher than alternative products used in the production of feeding-stuffs that it amounted to a breach of Article 40(3) EC by discriminately distributing the cost burden between various agricultural sectors. The fourth case dealt with a subsequent claim for damages brought by end-users of the feeding-stuffs. The applicants claimed that they had suffered loss because the producers of feeding-stuffs had increased their prices to take account of the elevated price of the skimmed-milk powder that they were obliged to use. After ruling that the measure in question was a legislative act, the Court stated that compensation could only be awarded where there was evidence of a sufficiently serious breach:

> Individuals may be required, in the sectors coming within the economic policy of the Community, to accept within reasonable limits certain harmful effects on their economic interests as a result of a legislative measure without being able to obtain compensation from public funds even if that measure has been declared null and void. In the legislative field such as the one in question, in which one of the chief features is the exercise of a wide discretion . . . the Community does not therefore incur liability unless the institution concerned has manifestly and gravely disregarded the limits on the exercise of its power.[110]

In order for there to be a sufficiently serious breach, therefore, the Court required evidence of there having been a manifest and grave disregard by the institution for the limits on the exercise of its power. In *HNL*, the Court decided that this high threshold had not been satisfied. It pointed out that the contested measure affected all buyers of compound feeding-stuffs, so that its effects on the individual were reduced. The fact that the Court refused to grant compensation to a very wide group of traders appears to infer that, as with claims for the annulment of a Community measure brought under Article 230(4) EC, an applicant will only succeed if it can show that it is part of a very small number of individuals who have been so affected. While this argument appears to have been approved in the *Quellmehl and Gritz* cases,[111] Advocate General Van Gerven later rebuffed it in his Opinion in *Mulder II*.[112] Furthermore, the Court found that the effect of the

109. Joined Cases 83 and 94/76, 4, 15 and 40/77 *HNL v. Council and Commission* [1978] ECR 1209.
110. Ibid., para. 6.
111. Case 238/78 *Ireks-Arkady GmbH v. Council and Commission* [1979] ECR 2955, para. 5; Joined Cases 261/78 and 262/78 *Interquell Strärke-Chemie v. EEC* [1979] ECR 3045.
112. See below at 128 ff.

Regulation on the price of feeding-stuffs was small when compared to the increases resulting from variations in the world market prices. It went on to dismiss the claim. Advocate General Capotorti, in his Opinion in *HNL*, however, came to the opposite conclusion. While the process by which Capotorti came to his final decision is interesting in itself, the point of greatest interest for present purposes is the way in which he defined 'sufficiently serious breach'. He opined that the question of whether a breach is sufficiently serious turns on three issues: The importance of the infringed rule (which if the first part of the *Schöppenstedt* formula (i.e. breach of a superior rule) has been complied with, is a non-contentious issue); the degree of blame to be attributed to the author of the measure; and the extent of the loss suffered. While the Court did not refer to the Advocate General's comments in its judgment, it did not reject them out of hand. Nor is the Court's ruling incompatible with the criteria suggested by Advocate General Capotorti. The Court and the Advocate General came to opposite conclusions due to a difference in the weight that each attributed to the factors of the case, rather than through the adoption of different sets of criteria. An analysis of paragraph 6 of the Court's judgment, where the Court tests the facts of the case against the criterion of serious breach, illustrates that the factors relied on by the Court all fall into the third category set out by Advocate General Capotorti (i.e., the extent of the loss suffered). While the Court in *HNL* refrained from referring directly to the definition of 'serious breach', the Advocate General's Opinion has nonetheless had a substantial impact on subsequent case law on Community liability. Perhaps contrary to the Advocate General's intentions, however, the initial impact of his definition was to make the test of serious breach more, rather than less, strict. In the case of *Amylum*,[113] the applicants sought to recover compensation for loss suffered as a result of the introduction by means of a Council Regulation, of a production levy on isoglucose, an artificial sweetener in direct competition on the market with sugar. In a previous preliminary ruling the Court held the Regulation to be invalid on the basis that the levy amounted to a charge which was manifestly unequal to the charges imposed on sugar and thereby contravened Article 40(3) EC.[114] In the subsequent claim for damages, after reiterating the operative parts of the *HNL* ruling, the Court continued:

> In fact, even though the fixing of the isoglucose production levy . . . was vitiated with errors, it must nevertheless be pointed out that, having regard to the fact that an appropriate levy was fully justified, these were not errors of such gravity that it may be said that the conduct of the defendant institutions in this respect was verging on the arbitrary and was thus of such a kind as to involve the Community in non-contractual liability. . . . It follows from these considerations that the Council and the Commission did not disregard the limits which they were required to observe in the exercise of their discretion in

---

113. Joined Cases 116 and 124/77 *Amylum v. Council and Commission* [1979] ECR 3497.
114. Joined Cases 103 and 145/77 *Royal Scholten-Honig v. Intervention Board for Agricultural Produce* [1978] ECR 2037.

> the context of the common agricultural policy in such a serious manner as to incur the non-contractual liability of the Community.[115]

By focusing on the behaviour of the Council and the Commission, the Court focused on and quantified the second criterion outlined by Capotorti in his Opinion (i.e., the degree of blame to be attributed to the author of the measure), as opposed to the third criterion as it had done in *HNL*. Taken together, therefore, the test for serious breach contained two elements: To be successful, the applicant must show that the institutions involved had behaved in a manner which verged on the arbitrary, and that the consequences of that behaviour were serious, to the extent that they exceeded the bounds of the economic risks inherent in carrying on business in the relevant sector of the market.[116] Not only does the simple fact of having to prove both of these elements place a heavy burden on the applicant, but the first element is excessively difficult to prove in practice. It will be rare that a Community institution introduces an act which is wholly unrelated to the general ends that the institution has been granted power to achieve. Mistakes are far more likely to occur in acts which seek to attain general, legitimate policies, but which do so in an erroneous manner.[117] After the Court's ruling in the *Isoglucose* cases, it appeared to be almost impossible for applicants to succeed in a claim against a legislative act under Article 288(2) EC. *Amylum* appears, however, to have been the high-water mark in relation to the Court's strict approach to 'seriousness of breach'. Since then, the Court has adopted a more liberal approach in respect to breach. One example of where the Court employed a more liberal interpretation of serious breach is the *Quellmehl and Gritz* cases.[118] Taking the action in *Dumortier Frères* as an example of one of those cases, the applicants sought compensation for a loss which they claimed they had suffered as a result of a Council Regulation abolishing refunds available to producers of maize 'gritz', which was used to brew beer. In earlier proceedings,[119] the Court had ruled that the abolition of the refunds infringed on the principle of equality. The Court based its ruling on the fact that gritz could be substituted in the beer-making process with maize starch for which production refunds were still in place. By only abolishing refunds in respect of gritz and not maize starch, the Council had caused significant disparities in the market to the detriment of gritz producers. In the subsequent *Dumortier Frères* action for damages, the Court found that there was a grave and manifest disregard on the part

115. Joined Cases 116 and 124/77 *Amylum v. Council and Commission* [1979] ECR 3497, paras 19-21.
116. AG Van Gerven's Opinion in Joined Cases C-104/89 and C-37/90 *Mulder and Others v. Council and Commission (Mulder II)* [1992] ECR I-3061.
117. P. Craig & G. de Burca, *EU Law*, 4th edn (Oxford: OUP, 2007), 595.
118. Case 238/78 *Ireks-Arkady GmbH v. Council and Commission* [1979] ECR 2955, para. 5; Joined Cases 261/78 and 262/78 *Interquell Strärke-Chemie v. EEC* [1979] ECR 3045; Joined Cases 241, 242 and 245-250/78 *DGV v. Council and Commission* [1979] ECR 3017; Joined Cases 64 and 113/76, 167 and 239/78, 27, 28 and 47/79 *Dumortier Frères v. Council* [1979] ECR 3091.
119. Joined Cases 124/76 and 20/77 *Moulins Pont-à-Mousson v. Office Interprofessionel des Céréales* [1977] ECR 1795.

of the Council in respect of the limits on the exercise of its powers in matters of the Common Agricultural Policy. The Court based its conclusion on the findings that the principle of equality has:

> A particularly important place among the rules of Community law intended to protect the interests of the individual. Secondly, the disregard of that principle in this case affected a limited and clearly defined group of commercial operators.... Further, the damage alleged by the applicants goes beyond the bounds of the economic risks inherent in the activities in the sector concerned.[120]

Compensation claims based on a breach of legitimate expectation also arose in the *Mulder* cases. In an attempt to curb the over-production of milk within the Community, the Commission introduced a scheme under which dairy farmers were paid a premium for agreeing not to market milk for a period of five years. Around 100 dairy farmers took up the offer. During the subsequent five-year period, the Commission introduced new measures, one of which was a system of milk quotas under which farmers were required to pay a special levy on milk produced over and above their quota. The quotas were based on the amount of milk marketed during a year specified in the regulation. The regulation however, did not make special provision for the farmers who had agreed not to market their milk. When the five-year period came to an end, the farmers applied for quotas so as to be able to begin marketing milk again. When applying the normal rules under the regulation, their milk quota production was zero, as in the specified year they had not produced any milk. As such, the farmers were left in a position where they were no longer receiving a premium, and were unable to start marketing milk again because their quota was set at nothing.

In proceedings on a preliminary reference under Article 234 EC, the Court held that the imposition of a quota system that did not take into account the farmers who had previously agreed to refrain from marketing milk, infringed the farmers' legitimate expectations, and was therefore invalid.[121] The Court observed that where a producer 'has been encouraged by a Community measure to suspend marketing for a limited period in the general interest and against payment of a premium he may legitimately expect not to be subject, upon the expiry of his undertaking, to restrictions which specifically affect him precisely because he availed himself of the possibilities offered by the Community provisions'.[122] As a result, the Council adopted another regulation granting the farmers who had ceased production a special reference quantity equal to 60% of the quantity of milk marketed in the twelve months immediately preceding the period in which they had given their undertaking.

---

120. Joined Cases 64 and 113/76, 167 and 239/78, 27, 28 and 47/79 *Dumortier Frères v. Council* [1979] ECR 3091, para. 11.
121. Case 120/86 *Mulder v. Minister van Landbouw en Vissereij (Mulder I)* [1988] ECR 2321.
122. Ibid., para. 24.

In *Spagl*,[123] another case arising out of the same facts as *Mulder I*, the Court found that the reduction of 40% for those producers who had agreed not to market their milk, substantially exceeded the reductions applied to those farmers who had continued to produce milk during the previous five years. Ruling that the application of such a high rate of reduction amounted to a restriction which specifically affected producers who had availed themselves of a Community measure, the Court concluded that 'the contested 60% rule likewise infringes the legitimate expectations which the producers concerned were entitled to entertain as to the limited nature of their undertakings'.[124] The Council regulation was therefore declared void.

The outcome in *Spagl* resulted in a number of claims being brought by farmers seeking compensation from the Community under Article 288(2). The first to be decided were those brought by the applicants in *Mulder II*.[125] The fact that the previous cases stated above had already established that the Community had infringed on the principle of legitimate expectation, which was a superior rule of law for the protection of individuals, meant that the case hinged on whether the breach was sufficiently serious as to be characterized as manifest and grave. In relation to the first regulation which established the quota system and left the applicants in a position where they could not market milk after the end of the five-year period, the Court ruled that:

> In so far as it failed completely, without invoking any higher public interest, to take account of the specific situation of a clearly defined group of economic agents . . . the Community legislature manifestly and gravely disregarded the limits of its discretionary power, thereby committing a sufficiently serious breach of a superior rule of law. That breach is all the more obvious because the total and permanent exclusion of the producers concerned from the allocation of a reference quantity, which in fact prevented them from resuming the marketing of milk when their non-marketing . . . undertaking expired, cannot be regarded as being foreseeable or as falling within the bounds of the normal economic risks inherent in the activities of a milk producer.[126]

The Court continued, however, by ruling that the applicants were not entitled to compensation in respect of the subsequent regulation introducing the 60% rule. While admitting that the rule infringed on the legitimate expectations of the

123. Case 189/89 *Spagl v. Hauptzollamt Rosenheim* [1990] ECR I-4585.
124. Ibid., para. 29.
125. Joined Cases C-104/89 and C-37/90 *Mulder and Others v. Council and Commission (Mulder II)* [1992] ECR I-3061; See A. Arnull, 'Liability for Legislative Acts under Article 215(2) EC', in *The Action for Damages in Community Law*, eds T. Heukels and A. McDonnell (The Hague: Assert Institute, 1997), 129.
126. Joined Cases C-104/89 and C-37/90 *Mulder and Others v. Council and Commission (Mulder II)* [1992] ECR I-3061, paras 16-17.

producers, it concluded that the breach was not sufficiently serious to claim compensation under Article 288(2) EC:

> It must be borne in mind first that, unlike the 1984 rules, which made it impossible for the producers concerned to market milk, the 60% rule enabled those traders to resume their activities as milk producers. Consequently, in the amending regulation . . . the Council did not fail to take the situation of the producers concerned into account. Secondly, it must be observed that, by adopting [the] Regulation . . . the Community legislature made an economic policy choice with regard to the manner in which it was necessary to implement the principles set out in [previous judgments of the Court of Justice]. . . . The Council made that choice in such a way as to maintain the level of other producers' reference quantities unchanged while increasing the Community reserve by 600,000 tonnes, or 60% of aggregate foreseeable applications. . . . Accordingly, the Council took account of a higher public interest, without gravely and manifestly disregarding the limits of its discretionary power in this area.[127]

The applicants consequently were only entitled to damages for the period between the end of the non-marketing undertaking and the entry into force of Regulation 764/89 EC which entitled them to a quota of 60% of the quantity of their reference period. These damages were to compensate them for the loss of profit based on the difference between what they might reasonably have expected to earn if their quotas had not been set at zero, and what they actually earned by selling milk outside the quota system together with what they actually or potentially could have earned by carrying on alternative activities.

In its reasoning the Court made scant mention of the requirement set out in *HNL* and the *Quellmehl and Gritz* cases that the Community would only be liable where those affected by the measure constituted only a clear and limited group. In his Opinion, Advocate General Van Gerven considered in detail the scope and requirements of this criterion. In doing so, the Advocate General drew a distinction between a 'clearly defined group' and a 'limited group'. In expanding on the term 'clearly defined', Van Gerven opined that a group would be clearly defined where the number of persons affected is capable of being determined at the time when the ruling is given on the compensation. In applying this definition to the facts of *Mulder II*, the Advocate General concluded that this criterion was clearly met on the basis that the circle of potential persons affected is established *a priori*. Only non-marketers were eligible for compensation and their number and identities were known.[128] He then went on to compare the situation in *Mulder II* to that of *HNL*:

> The Court referred in [the HNL] judgment to the very large categories of traders affected, 'in other words, all buyers of compound feeding-stuffs

127. Ibid., paras 20-21.
128. Joined Cases C-104/89 and C-37/90 *Mulder and Others v. Council and Commission (Mulder II)* [1992] ECR I-3061, AG Van Gerven's Opinion, 116, para. 28.

> containing protein'.... In [Mulder II], not all non-marketers can actually be regarded as having been adversely affected, but only those who, on the expiry of their non-marketing undertaking, had not definitively abandoned milk production and suffered damage as a result because [they were] prevented from resuming production.[129]

In respect of a 'limited group' the Advocate General found nothing in the case law of the Court of Justice to support the claim that the Community's liability was dependant on the (absolute) number of persons adversely affected. Even if one overlooks the fact that it would be impossible for the Court to set a figure for the maximum number of individuals to be affected, Advocate General Van Gerven argued that the words 'limited group' should be construed as referring to 'a group of undertakings on which the unlawful act imposed a specific disadvantage in comparison with other groups of undertakings, which those other groups did not have to bear'.[130] This was clearly the case in *Mulder II* in respect of the first regulation excluding the farmers from the quota system. Once again the Advocate General highlighted the differences between the situation in *Mulder II* and that of *HNL*:

> That condition is clearly satisfied in [Mulder II]: compared with milk producers who did not interrupt their milk production, the non-marketers concerned were affected by the levy system specifically – and moreover, seriously – since they alone were prevented by the contested rules from producing milk and, as a result, could not resume milk deliveries. In HNL, the position in that respect was also different. The Court determined that the effect of the unlawful measure at issue in that case on the individual undertakings concerned was small, since the price increase caused by the measure was definitely modest and the resultant burden was spread over the whole economic sector, since essentially all poultry farmers and egg producers were affected.[131]

The Advocate General's reasoning is, in the authors' view, correct. The fact that the loss was caused to a large number of traders is indicative of, rather than contrary to, the seriousness of the breach. Further, to hold that a breach will only be serious when it affects a small (absolute) number of individuals, would seem counter-intuitive to the first requirement under the *Schöppenstedt* formula, that a legislative measure is general in nature. The characteristic of generality clearly envisages, and even demands, that the measure be such that it has an impact on a large variety of individuals. As stated above, the Court made no mention of this aspect of the case in its ruling in *Mulder II*. It can be assumed that the Court agreed, however, given the fact that it granted compensation to the farmers (albeit only with respect to the first regulation), despite the size of the group, and the serious financial implications that this would have.

129. Ibid.
130. Ibid., para 29.
131. Ibid.

In summarizing the factors that contribute to the Court's finding of a sufficiently serious breach, it is helpful once again to follow the approach adopted by Van Gerven, this time writing extra-judicially.[132] The Advocate General identifies three clear elements that the Court will take into consideration: Whether the institution exercised its power in the way it did because of a higher public interest which justified the harm caused to individual interests; whether the harm caused by the exercise of discretionary power concerned a clearly defined group of individuals; and whether the individuals who have been harmed are expected to support the harm they suffered within reasonable limits. Of these three factors, only the first relates to the concept of breach properly so-called. The other two factors relate to the Court's intention to restrict the drain on public funds resulting from liability on account of legislative measures. In so doing, they refer to the number of applicants and the nature of the harm opposed to the breach itself.[133] The effect of the first element is that an institution does not, or at least does not seriously, exceed its powers where it seeks to strike a balance in a reasonable and not disproportionate way, between the individual interests at stake and an overriding public interest. This was clearly illustrated by the Court in *Mulder II*, where it denied compensation in respect of the second regulation. In setting the quota at 60% of the special reference period for non-marketing farmers, the Council was indeed taking their interests into consideration, while at the same time seeking to satisfy the overriding public aim of controlling the level of milk being marketed in the Community. In respect of the second element listed by Van Gerven, an applicant's claim will be reinforced where it can be shown that the measure only caused loss to a clearly defined and limited group of traders. While it was originally thought that failure to show that only a small number of people could potentially bring an action for compensation would be fatal to the applicant's claim, the success of the applicants in *Mulder II* shows that this is not the case. Instead, emphasis is placed on the need to be able to determine the number of people – be that a large or small number – affected by the measure when the ruling on liability is given. The third element finds its roots in the Court's judgment in *HNL*, and is justified on the basis that traders, who knowingly enter into a highly regulated marketplace, must be prepared to accept that there are certain economic risks inherent to operating in that sector. Compensation will only be available where the Community act has exceeded the bounds of that risk. This approach was clearly confirmed by the Court in *Mulder* where it stated that the applicants were not entitled to expect to be able to return to the market after five years on the same terms as when they left. This did not however, prevent them from receiving compensation in respect of the losses that they had suffered as a result of the Commission's failure to take their situation into account.

132. W. Van Gerven, *Non-contractual Liability of Member States, Community Institutions and Individuals for Breaches of Community Law with a view to a Common Law for Europe*, [1994] 1 MJ 6, at 27-28.

133. Ibid., at 28.

3.4. Justifications

Where the Court sets the barrier to success as high as it has in relation to Article 288(2) EC, it is inevitable that the defences open to the institutions become intrinsically linked to the need for the applicant to satisfy the threshold set by the Court. As such, many of the issues arising as regards justifications or defences available to the Community institutions have already been touched on in the previous section. By looking at justifications we are really only seeking to address the same question – what factors will influence the Court in its decision to either award or deny compensation? This time, however, the question is being tackled from the point of view of the institutions. As such, rather than being specific, definable defences, the justifications relate more closely to factors that can be used by the institutions to tip the balance away from the applicants, and in favour of a ruling that, despite there having been a breach, that breach was not 'sufficiently serious' to warrant compensation being paid by the Community. With this in mind, the subsequent paragraphs deal with three specific justifications that may be used to prevent a breach from being 'serious': the existence of an important general interest that takes precedence over the individual interest of the injured party; a breach that was the result of an erroneous, but excusable, approach to an unresolved legal question; and the complexity of the situation and the difficulty in the application or interpretation of the texts.

3.4.1. Overriding General Interest

One example of where the Court has been willing to accept that a Community act did not constitute a sufficiently serious breach on the basis that it sought to serve an important general interest is *Merkur*.[134] This case was one of many such cases concerned with Monetary Compensatory Amounts (MCAs), which constituted payments made to individuals by the Community in an attempt to minimize the effects of fluctuating currencies. Merkur was a barley producer. Barley was mistakenly excluded from the MCA regime, but was later added by way of a Commission Regulation. Merkur claimed that he was entitled to payments of MCAs on his exports for a three-month period prior to the implementation of the correcting Regulation, and brought proceedings against the Commission under Article 288(2) EC. In setting out the standard against which the Community act would be measured to determine whether there had been a serious breach, the Court reasoned that:

> In those circumstances, although the possibility of protecting the legitimate interests of the trader cannot be excluded, nevertheless the Community could only be rendered liable for the damage suffered by such traders as a result of the adoption of legislative measures governing the above system if in the absence of any overriding public interest the Commission were to abolish

134. Case 43/72 *Merkur Außenhandel-GmbH & Co. KG v. Commission* [1973] ECR 1055.

> or modify the compensatory amount applicable in a specific sector with immediate effect and without warning and in the absence of any appropriate transitional measures and if such abolition or modification was not foreseeable by a prudent trader.[135]

The effect of the Court's ruling is that where there is an overriding public interest – in this instance guaranteeing monetary stability and the proper functioning of the market – an individual will only be entitled to compensation where it can be shown that the Commission, in its adoption of the act, has infringed on a fundamental, general principle of EC law – in this instance the principle of legitimate expectations. A further example of the weight attributed to the principle of legitimate expectation can be seen in the context of the *Sofrimport* case.[136] The applicant, a fresh fruit wholesaler and importer, sought compensation for loss suffered as a result of three Commission regulations suspending import licenses for Chilean dessert apples and fixing import quotas on dessert apples coming from third countries. Prior to the implementation of the contested Commission regulations the applicant shipped a cargo of dessert apples from Chile to the Community. The national authority in the Member State where the apples were to be imported refused to grant import licenses on the basis of the newly implemented Commission Regulations. All three Commission Regulations were subsequently declared void, as they failed to provide protective measures for goods in transit as required by Article 3(3) of Council Regulation 2707/72 EEC.[137] Sofrimport later brought proceedings under Article 288(2) EC seeking compensation for the losses suffered on the cargo of apples that it could not import. In respect of the serious breach criterion, the Court made it clear in that case that the Community incurred liability on the basis of its failure to take account of the position of importers, like the applicant, who had goods in transit, which it was the specific purpose of the relevant legislation to protect.[138] That legislation therefore created a legitimate expectation in favour of the applicant, disregard of which, caused loss beyond the economic risks inherent in the business concerned.[139] Even where the principle of legitimate expectation has been breached, however, this does not automatically render the Community liable where there is an overriding interest. As Advocate General Van Gerven observed in his Opinion in *Mulder II*, 'to fail completely to take account of the particular situation of traders, without invoking any overriding public interest, constitutes a serious, inexcusable breach'.[140]

135. Ibid., para. 6.
136. Case 152/88 *Sofrimport v. Commission* [1990] ECR 2477.
137. O.J., English Special Edition, 1972 (28 to 30 Dec.), at 3.
138. Case 152/88 *Sofrimport v. Commission* [1990] ECR 2477, paras 27-29.
139. Ibid., para. 31.
140. AG Van Gerven's Opinion in Joined Cases C-104/89 and C-37/90 *Mulder and Others v. Council and Commission (Mulder II)* [1992] ECR I-3061, para. 45.

3.4.2. An Excusable Error

Where an error can be said to be excusable, it cannot, by definition, be a manifest breach. For a breach to be manifest, it requires an obvious error of judgment. The extent to which an error will be excusable, depends on, for example, whether the decision is clearly unreasonable, whether the institution has properly taken account of relevant facts, whether it was put on notice before committing the breach, or whether the error was merely technical.[141] Referring once again to Advocate General Van Gerven's Opinion in *Mulder II*, 'only where the public authority's error is inexcusable, that is to say where it could not reasonably have been committed, have its powers been manifestly and gravely disregarded'.[142] The Court's reasoning in the case seems to embody the principle of reasonableness to the extent that, despite the Council having made an error by setting the quota at 60% of the reference period sales, it did not constitute a serious breach, as the Council had reasonably attempted to take account of the farmers' interests when striking a balance between the producers and the needs of the milk sector.

Failures to take into account relevant considerations arose in the Court's rulings in *Dumortier Frères* and *Sofrimport*, where the Community institutions committed serious breaches by failing to consider the interests of relevant traders. This should, however, be contrasted with the case of *HNL*, where, despite failing to take into consideration the interests of the applicants, the breach was not sufficiently serious due to the very wide category of traders adversely affected by the measure.

Where a technical error has been made which has led to de facto discrimination between producers of similar products, it is unlikely that there will be a manifest breach. This was the case in *Roquette Frères*[143] where the Commission had made errors in its calculations of fixing Monetary Compensation Amounts, which resulted in amounts for starch products being fixed much higher than those for other basic products. Despite those errors, the Court held that the breach was not sufficiently serious so as to show a manifest disregard by the Commission of the limits of its discretion, and so dismissed the case.

3.4.3. Complexity

The complexity of the issues surrounding a Community act may also play a significant role in whether or not the measure can be said to constitute a sufficiently serious breach. This point was well illustrated by the CFI in its ruling in *Holcim.*[144]

141. M. Brealey & M. Hoskins, *Remedies in EC Law*, 2nd edn (London: Sweet & Maxwell, 1998), 365.
142. AG Van Gerven's Opinion in Joined Cases C-104/89 and C-37/90 *Mulder and Others v. Council and Commission (Mulder II)* [1992] ECR I-3061, para. 30.
143. Case 20/88 *Roquette Frères v. Commission* [1989] ECR 1553, para. 26.
144. Case T-28/03 *Holcim (Deutschland) AG v. Commission of the European Communities* [2005] ECR II-1357.

The case arose out of an appeal by the applicants, who were manufacturers of construction materials, against a Decision of the Commission ordering them to pay fines of over 5 million euros (EUR), for a breach of Article 81(1) EC. The Decision was subsequently annulled and the applicants brought an action against the Commission under Article 288(2) EC seeking to reclaim the costs incurred in bringing the annulment action. In assessing whether the Commission's Decision amounted to a sufficiently serious breach of Community law, the CFI held that regard must be had to the fact that the context in which the decision was taken and the subsequent annulment action was particularly complex. Both the initial decision and the annulment action involved a very large number of undertakings and almost the entire European cement industry, and it was necessary to analyze a great number of documents. Further, it was necessary to take account of the difficulties in applying the provisions of the EC Treaty in matters relating to cartels. The result of these factors was that, despite having been annulled, the Commission's decision could not be regarded as amounting to a serious breach for the purposes of Article 288(2) EC.

4. THE JUDGMENT IN *BERGADERM*

The somewhat artificial distinction between legislative and administrative acts, and the problems that this causes, could not be maintained indefinitely. The first signs of reform came – not in a case brought for damages against the Community, however, but rather in an action brought against Member States. As has been seen in relation to Member State liability, the Court in the case of *Brasserie du Pêcheur/Factortame* ruled that, on the basis that the protection of individual rights deriving from Community law cannot vary depending on whether a national authority or a Community authority is responsible for the damage, there was no reason why the conditions under which a Member State could be liable for a breach of Community law should, in the absence of particular justifications, be any different from the conditions of liability applicable to Community institutions in like circumstances.[145] Not only is this basic premise undoubtedly correct, but in the case of *Brasserie du Pêcheur/Factortame*, it also served two further purposes by underlining the affinity between State liability and the rule of law, and legitimized the Court's recognition of the right to reparation against Member States.[146] Furthermore, the fact that the Court's ruling on the issue of Member State liability could be directly influenced by the rules governing Community liability opened the door to the possibility that rules on Community liability could be equally influenced by the Court's decision in *Brasserie du Pêcheur/Factortame* on Member State liability.

145. Case 46/93 *Brasserie du Pêcheur v. Bundesrepublik Deutschland and The Queen v. Secretary of State for Transport, ex parte Factortame and others* [1996] ECR I-1029.
146. T. Tridimas, *The General Principles of EC Law*, 3rd edn (Oxford: OUP, 2006), 486.

This possibility came into fruition several years later in the Court's ruling in *Bergaderm.*[147]

Bergaderm, a pharmaceuticals company, sought damages from the Community on the basis of losses suffered as a result of the Cosmetics Directive,[148] which prohibited the use of certain substances in cosmetic products. Chief among the prohibited substances was a carcinogenic molecule that Bergaderm used in the production of its sun oil, Bergasol. Bergaderm argued that the Commission had infringed procedural requirements in the adoption of the Cosmetics Directive and that it had breached Bergaderm's right to a defence. Further, Bergaderm maintained that the directive was administrative as opposed to legislative in nature, in that the directive concerned Bergasol exclusively, and they should not therefore be required to satisfy the test of sufficiently serious breach. The CFI disagreed,holding that the directive was of general application, and therefore of a legislative nature, and that liability would only ensue where it could be shown that there had been a serious breach of a superior norm for the protection of the individual. The CFI held that it was not necessary to establish whether or not the procedural rules governing the adoption of the Directive were such rules, as the Commission had not infringed them in any event, and went on to dismiss the case. On appeal to the ECJ, Bergaderm argued that the CFI had erred in its assessment of the Directive as a measure of a legislative nature, and second that there had been no breach of a superior rule of law. While the ECJ rejected the appeal, the point of interest is the way in which it reached that decision. Rather than relying on the traditional distinction of legislative and administrative acts, the Court shifted the focus of its analysis to concentrate on the amount of discretion enjoyed by the Community institutions, and drew on the conditions it had set down in *Brasserie du Pêcheur/ Factortame* in the context of Member State liability:

> The Court has stated that the conditions under which the State may incur liability for damage caused to individuals by a breach of Community law cannot, in the absence of particular justification, differ from those governing the liability of the Community in like circumstances. The protection of the rights which individuals derive from Community law cannot vary depending on whether a national authority or a Community authority is responsible for the damage. As regards Member State liability for damage caused to individuals, the Court has held that Community law confers a right to reparation where three conditions are met: the rule of law infringed must be intended to confer rights on individuals; the breach must be sufficiently serious; and there must be a direct causal link between the breach of the obligation resting on the State and the damage sustained by the injured parties. As to the second condition, as regards both Community liability under Article 215 [now Article 288(2) EC] of

---

147. Case C-352/98 P *Laboratoires Phramaceutiques Bergaderm and Groupil v. Commission* [2000] ECR I-5291.
148. Directive 76/768 on the approximation of the laws of the Member States relating to cosmetic products (O.J. 1976 L 262, p. 169). The directive was subsequently amended by Directive 93/ 35/EEC, O.J. 1993 L 151, p. 32.

> the Treaty and Member State liability for breaches of Community law, the decisive test for finding that a breach of Community law is sufficiently serious is whether the Member State or the Community institution concerned manifestly and gravely disregarded the limits of its discretion. Where the Member State or the institution in question has only considerably reduced, or even no, discretion, the mere infringement of Community law may be sufficient to establish the existence of a sufficiently serious breach.... The Court finds that the general or individual nature of a measure taken by an institution is not a decisive criterion for identifying the limits of the discretion enjoyed by the institution in question. It follows that the first ground of appeal, which is based exclusively on the categorisation of the Adaptation Directive as an individual measure, has in any event no bearing on the issue and must be rejected.[149]

In order to succeed in an action for damages against a Community institution, therefore, the ECJ ruled that it is neither necessary nor relevant to determine whether the measure is legislative or administrative in nature. The applicant must instead show that the rule of law infringed conferred rights on individuals; that the breach was sufficiently serious; and that there is a direct causal link between the breach of the obligation and the damage suffered by the applicant. In respect of the seriousness of the breach, the ECJ maintained that this was to be determined with reference to the criteria of manifest and grave disregard by the institution for the limits of its discretion. In doing so, however, the Court cites paragraph 56 of its judgment in *Brasserie du Pêcheur/Factortame* and rules that these are the criteria that need to be taken into account when assessing whether a Community institution has committed a seriously breach of a Community rule.[150] While this certainly shifts the determination of whether a breach is serious onto the basis of discretion, it is, as of yet, unclear how the reformulation of the sufficiently serious breach test will affect the factors which have traditionally been taken into consideration in determining whether an institution has gravely and manifestly disregarded the limits of its discretion. In concrete terms, it is likely that the Court will continue to give credence to its previous case law on the subject, but will assess the weight of each aspect of the case in light of the factors listed in *Brasserie du Pêcheur/Factortame*. Where the institution has considerably reduced or no discretion, however, then any breach will be illegal per se. In the subsequent case of *Fresh Marine*,[151] Advocate General Stix-Hackl noted that the use of the phrase 'considerably reduced' discretion was significant in that it broadened the range of acts, breach of which will be illegal per se:

> Even if it should be found that that provision confers discretion on the Commission that does not necessarily mean that the strict condition for liability will

149. Case C-352/98 P *Laboratoires Phramaceutiques Bergaderm and Groupil v. Commission* [2000] ECR I-5291, paras 41-47.
150. Case 46/93 *Brasserie du Pêcheur v. Bundesrepublik Deutschland and The Queen v. Secretary of State for Transport, ex parte Factortame and others* [1996] ECR I-1029, paras 56-57.
151. Case C-472/00 *P Commission v. Fresh Marine* [2003] ECR I-7541.

> apply, as it did under the traditional case law. The less stringent condition of a 'mere infringement of Community law' requires only 'considerably reduced discretion'.[152]

The Advocate General also drew attention to the fact that it was necessary to examine the specific provision of a measure rather than generalizing about the degree of discretion enjoyed in a particular policy area, when assessing whether an institution's discretion is 'considerably reduced':[153]

> The argument that the Community institutions always have a broad discretion in anti-dumping matters is based on an impermissible generalisation of the judgments of the Community judicature, which each concerned specific individual provisions and, in the majority of cases, dealt with the competence of the Council and not that of the Commission.[154]

In removing the legislative/administrative distinction, the Court is recognizing that the Community administration may enjoy ample discretion and may be required to make choices that are equally difficult, complex and sensitive to those of the legislature, and that its liability should therefore be governed by the same conditions.[155] The test of manifest and grave breach may therefore be applied to the administration as well as the legislature. It is submitted that this change was not intended to make it more difficult to bring an action in damages against the Community institution, but rather to harmonize the law relating to liability not only as between Community institutions and Member States, but also as between the institutions themselves and the functions that they perform. As Tridimas argues,[156] the few pre-*Bergaderm* cases that have been successful under the *Schöppenstedt* formula would almost certainly have been successful under the *Bergaderm* formula. The application of the State liability criteria for determining the seriousness of a breach may, in fact, make it easier to bring a successful claim against the Community. Rather than having to rely on inconsistently applied factors, such as the number of undertakings affected, the degree of harm suffered and the extent of the breach, applicants may rely on the potentially more generous factors listed in *Brasserie du Pêcheur/Factortame*.

5. COMMUNITY LIABILITY POST-*BERGADERM*

Despite the Court of Justice's rather categorical ruling in *Bergaderm* that the administrative/legislative distinction was no longer relevant, the case law that has followed it is not so unequivocal. While broadly adhering to the three-part

152. Ibid., para. 79.
153. See further C. Hilson, 'Role of Discretion in EC Law on Non-contractual Liability', *CMLRev.* 42 (2005): 677, at 684.
154. Case C-472/00 *P Commission v. Fresh Marine* [2003] ECR I-7541, para. 78.
155. T. Tridimas, *The General Principles of EC Law*, 3rd edn (Oxford: OUP, 2006), 488.
156. Ibid.

unitary test favoured in *Brasserie du Pêcheur/Factortame* and *Bergaderm*, recent case law has sent contradictory signals in respect of how the test should be applied. Many post-*Bergaderm* cases have concentrated on the interpretation of 'serious breach'. Before entering into a discussion of serious breach, however, it might be useful to mention a series of decisions dealing with the issue of individual rights and liability arising from international agreements binding on the Community.

The Community Courts have so far rejected compensation actions on the basis of a breach of an agreement related to WTO law provisions. As is well known, the Court of Justice, through its case law, has ruled that provisions of the WTO agreement are capable of having direct effect.[157] Relying on such case law, the Courts held that WTO rules are 'not in principle intended to confer rights on individuals' and 'the Community [can not] incur non-contractual liability as a result of infringement of them'.[158] Despite some strong criticisms[159] the Courts have adopted the same approach in cases where a ruling of the WTO Dispute Settlement Body has already identified a breach of WTO law and the implementation period has already expired. The Court's reasoning being that WTO Members were nonetheless in a position to negotiate and reach a settlement even if only on a temporary basis and this flexibility would not allow the enforcement of WTO obligations in Community Courts.[160]

As far as serious breach is concerned, following the Court of Justice's reformulation of the criteria for liability under Article 288(2) EC in *Bergaderm*, depending on the circumstances of the case, a Community institution may be found to have committed a serious breach even though it enjoys broad discretion, while a breach may not be serious even though the institution has committed an error in a field where it enjoyed only a limited amount of discretion.[161]

The Court's ruling in *Camar and Tico*,[162] the first case in which the ECJ applied the test of manifest and grave disregard to an administrative error post-*Bergaderm*, concerned a claim by Italian banana importers who claimed to have suffered losses in the transition from a national to a common market.

157. See for instance Case C-149/96 *Portugal v. Council* [1999] ECR I-8395.
158. See T-18/99 *Cordis Obst und Gemüse Großhandel v. Commission* [2001] ECR II-913, paras 46, 51; Case T-174/00 *Biret International SA v. Council* [2002] ECR II-17, paras 60-64; T-69/00 *FIAMM and FIAMM Technologies* [2005] ECR II-5393, paras 108-115.
159. See Advocate General Tizzano in C-377/02 *Léon Van Parys NV v. Belgisch Interventie- en Restitutiebureau (BIRB)* [2005] ECR I-1465 at paras 74-97. See further A. Thies, 'Biret and Beyond: The Status of WTO Rulings in EC Law' *CMLRev.* 41 (2004): 1661-1682 and M. Bronckers, 'The Relationship of the EC Courts with Other International Tribunals: Non-committal, Respectful or Submissive?', *CMLRev.* 44 (2007): 601-627, at 611.
160. Case T-19/01 *Chiquita Brands and others* [2005] ECR II-315 and C-377/02 *Van Parys* [2005] ECR I-1465. Despite the Court's rulings in these cases, there are indications that the ECJ, especially in a non-WTO context, might be willing to enter into a more careful analysis if the international agreement could be intended to confer specific rights. See Case C-308/06 *Intertanko and others v. Secretary of transport*, nyr.
161. T. Tridimas, *The General Principles of EC Law*, 3rd edn (Oxford: OUP, 2006), 489.
162. Joined Cases T-79/96, T-260/97 and T-117/98 *Camar and Tico v. Commission and Council* [2000] ECR II-2193.

Regulation 404/93 EC provided for a common quota regime for the importation of bananas from third countries. Article 30 of the regulation obliged the Commission to implement transitional measures to aid importers with the shift from national regimes to a Community regulated market. The applicants imported the majority of their bananas from Somalia. When the civil war broke out in 1990, it became impossible for them to continue their normal supplies. They appealed to the Commission to increase their quotas for bananas coming from other third countries so as to offset the loss of Somalian bananas. The Commission, however, refused to do so. In an action before the CFI, the Court ruled that the Commission's refusal was a breach of Article 30 of the Regulation, and proceeded to assess whether the applicants were entitled to compensation.

The proceedings in the CFI took place prior to the ECJ's ruling in *Bergaderm*, and, as such, in deciding whether the applicants were entitled to compensation, the CFI based its decision on the *Schöppenstedt* formula. The CFI found that despite the broad discretionary power conferred on the Commission under Article 30 of the Regulation, the Commission's decision was essentially individual in nature and its decision should therefore be considered as administrative. It followed that the mere breach of Article 30 was sufficient to allow the applicants to recover compensation from the Community. Upon appeal to the ECJ, however, the Court applied the conditions for liability as they had been set out in *Bergaderm*. After outlining the three conditions formulated in *Brasserie du Pêcheur/Factortame* for conferring a right on individuals to reparation, the Court confirmed the importance of discretion by holding that the CFI had indeed committed an error in law by ruling that the Commission's liability could arise from the mere illegality of its decision without first evaluating the amount of discretion that it enjoyed.[163] It is important to note, however, the pragmatic way in which the ECJ proceeded to deal with the issue. Rather than upholding the Commission's appeal on the basis of the CFI's error, the ECJ ruled that the appeal must nevertheless be dismissed on the basis that, had the CFI assessed the amount of discretion enjoyed by the Commission, then the result would still have been the same as the Commission's conduct amounted to a grave and manifest disregard for that discretion. The Court's ruling in *Camar and Tico* stands in stark contrast, however, to the subsequent ruling of the CFI in *Dieckmann & Hansen*, where the CFI refused to grant compensation on the basis that the Commission enjoyed wide, general discretion when dealing with public health matters.[164] The action stemmed from a decision of the Commission prohibiting the import of fish products from Kazakhstan on the grounds of public health. Following the prohibition, importers who had contracted to import caviar from Kazakhstan shortly before the introduction of the ban, brought a claim arguing that the Commission had breached its duty to take into consideration the rights of importers, by failing to adopt transitional measures for importers who had already entered into import contracts. The CFI dismissed the claim on the basis that public health, as an overriding public interest, may preclude the adoption of transitional

163. Ibid., para. 59.
164. Case T-155/99 *Dieckmann & Hansen v. Commission* [2001] ECR II-3143.

measures. Furthermore, the CFI held that the Commission was entitled to impose a ban on the basis of the general risk posed by imports from third countries without being required to prove that such products constitute an actual risk. The CFI's ruling is a clear illustration that even where a breach may be sufficiently serious to allow an individual to claim compensation where the institution enjoys wide powers of discretion, the Court will not allow such recovery where overriding public interests are concerned. Similarly, the simple fact that the institution does not enjoy wide discretionary powers does not mean that a breach will automatically entitle an individual to a claim in damages. The post-*Bergaderm* case law of the CFI suggests that in the field of administrative action, an error on the part of an institution will only give rise to liability where it is the result of a lack of due diligence.[165] The CFI's ruling in *Comafrica*[166] once again arose out of a claim brought by importers of bananas. The importers sought the annulment of a number of Commission Regulations fixing the annual reduction coefficients for the determination of the number of bananas that each trader could import. They also sought compensation for the losses they claimed to have suffered as a result of the regulations fixing the coefficients. The CFI concluded that the measures adopted by the Commission were of an administrative nature, adopted in the course of its exercising only a limited discretion. The Court continued:

> The finding of an error or irregularity on the part of an institution is not sufficient in itself to attract the non-contractual liability of the Community unless that error or irregularity is characterised by a lack of due diligence or care.[167]

This conclusion appears to be at odds with the ECJ's decision in *Bergaderm* for a number of reasons. First, the CFI continues to place importance on the administrative/legislative distinction despite its having been expressly rejected by the ECJ as irrelevant for the purposes of actions for damages. Not only this, but the CFI's determination of the nature of the measures in question is not consistent. In the citation above, it is clear that the CFI considers the Regulations to be of an administrative character, while earlier in the judgment, for the purposes of annulment, it had rejected the applicant's contention that they were bundles of individual decisions and found that they were measures of general application.[168] Second, in establishing the seriousness of the Commission's breach, the CFI focuses on the degree of care shown by the Commission rather than the degree of discretion that it enjoyed. Exactly where the CFI drew its inspiration from for this line of reasoning is not entirely clear.

A third prominent case on the issue of non-contractual liability of the Community to come before the European Courts since *Bergaderm* was *Fresh*

165. T. Tridimas, *The General Principles of EC Law*, (Oxford: OUP, 2006), 490.
166. Joined Cases T-198/95, T-171/96, T-230/97, T-174/98 and T-225/99 *Comafrica and Dole Fresh Fruit Europe v. Commission* [2001] ECR II-1975.
167. Ibid., para. 144.
168. T. Tridimas, *The General Principles of EC Law*, 3rd edn (Oxford: OUP, 2006), 490.

Marine.[169] The case involved a Norwegian company, which, in an attempt to avoid anti-dumping and anti-subsidy duties, agreed with the Commission not to sell its salmon in the Community below a minimum price. During 1997, based on a report submitted to it by the applicant, the Commission came to the conclusion that the applicant had failed to honour this agreement and adopted a regulation imposing provisional anti-dumping duties on the applicant. Subsequent clarifications provided by the applicant convinced the Commission that it had not in fact breached the terms of the agreement, and the Commission repealed the anti-dumping duties. The applicants then brought an action before the CFI seeking to recover compensation for the losses it claimed to have suffered as a result of the wrongly imposed anti-dumping duties.

The CFI began its reasoning in relation to the substance of the claim by establishing that the Commission regulation was administrative in nature.[170] Although admitting that the measure of the Commission should, in principle, be regarded as constituting legislative action involving choices of economic policy, the Commission's act was based on the sole fact that the Commission believed that the applicant had broken its undertaking, and the resulting measure was in fact an administrative operation which specifically and exclusively concerned the applicant. The adoption of the measure in itself did not involve any choices of economic policy and conferred on the Commission only very little or no discretion. Citing the ECJ's ruling in *Bergaderm*, the CFI concluded, therefore, that the mere infringement of Community law would be sufficient to lead to the non-contractual liability of the Community. Despite referring to the ECJ's ruling in *Bergaderm*, the CFI continued in a similar vein to its ruling in *Comafrica*, by finding that an error which, in analogous circumstances, an administrative authority exercising ordinary care and diligence would not have committed, would support the conclusion that the conduct of the Community institution was unlawful in such a way as to render the Community liable under Article 288(2) EC.[171] While the CFI did, at least, make reference to the ECJ's ruling in *Bergaderm* and thereby give the appearance that it was following the ECJ's lead, in reality the CFI continued to rely on the administrative/legislative distinction, and grounded its reasoning on a duty of diligence rather than discretion as is prescribed by *Bergaderm.* In doing so, the CFI concluded that the Commission had indeed breached its duty of diligence and allowed the applicants to recover compensation for their loss – although their award was reduced on the grounds of contributory negligence. On appeal to the ECJ,[172] the Court, this time couching its words in terms of individual and general measures, reiterated that the administrative/legislative distinction was irrelevant, and continued to follow the discretion-based approach laid down in *Bergaderm.*

169. Case C-472/00 *P Commission v. Fresh Marine* [2003] ECR I-7541.
170. Ibid., para. 57.
171. Ibid., para. 61.
172. Case C-472/00 *P Commission v. Fresh Marine* [2003] ECR I-7541.

Despite applying a different test to that utilized by the CFI, the ECJ once again upheld the CFI's decision:

> It follows that the Commission clearly did not comply with its obligation to impose provisional duties only where there is reason to believe that the undertaking has been breached. In the circumstances of the present case, such conduct must be regarded as a sufficiently serious breach of a rule of Community law satisfying one of the conditions for the incurring of non-contractual liability by the Community. Accordingly, the first two grounds of appeal must be rejected.[173]

The decisions discussed above illustrate that there is a clear difference between the approaches adopted by the ECJ and the CFI in deciding whether an individual has a right to compensation from the Community. While both approaches focus on the amount of discretion enjoyed by the institution in question, the criterion is granted different weight according to the court judging the action. The ECJ has attributed greater importance to the criteria of discretion, while CFI rulings continue to focus on the legislative or administrative nature of the breach and are dominated by the concepts of duty of care and diligence. While, as has been seen above, these two different methodologies do not necessarily lead to different outcomes, they do serve to inject a certain level of uncertainty into an already opaque area of law. Furthermore, the divergence of methodologies appears to undermine the underlying aim of *Bergaderm* – the harmonization of criteria establishing non-contractual liability against the Community or a Member State.

Tridimas maintains that, in the case of purely administrative, as opposed to policy measures, the CFI's approach is preferable, and that an error or irregularity on the part of an institution should not give rise to liability, unless it is the result of a lack of diligence or care. In contrast, Tridimas considers that the ECJ's approach lacks structure and principle, as it is based on an ad hoc evaluation of the limits of discretion.[174] While this is undoubtedly a strong and valid critique of the approaches adopted by the two Courts, and there is no logical reason why a test of due diligence should not be introduced in situations where the institution does not enjoy a wide discretion, this does not, however, serve to justify the departure by the CFI from the case law of the ECJ by its continued insistence on distinguishing between administrative and legislative acts. Despite offering a less abstract framework for determining the test to be applied in a given situation, this artificial categorization of measures continues to be used inconsistently, and, on a fundamental level, is subject to the same ad hoc evaluation of discretion as the ECJ's approach. The advantage of the ECJ's approach is that the true focus of the investigation – the discretion of the institution – is emphasized, rather than being obscured by the art of arbitrary categorization.

Needless to say, the divergence between in Courts in their application of the serious breach test could not be sustained indefinitely, and matters eventually came

173. Ibid., paras 31-32.
174. T. Tridimas, *The General Principles of EC Law*, 3rd edn (Oxford: OUP, 2006), 492.

to a head in the *CEVA* litigation. CEVA Santé animale SA was a pharmaceutical company that marketed a veterinary medicinal product containing the active ingredient progesterone. In veterinary medicine, progesterone is used in cows and mares to treat disorders of the reproductive system. In May 2000, the Commission adopted a proposal for a directive amending Directive 96/22 EC concerning the prohibition on the use in stock farming of certain substances. The proposal required Member States inter alia provisionally to prohibit the administration of progesterone to animals reared for human consumption, while maintaining the derogation for therapeutic and zootechnical purposes. In July 2000, the applicants applied to the Commission to include progesterone on a list of exceptions so that it could be used on farm animals. The Commission failed to take any action and in November 2000, the respondents brought proceedings before the Court of First Instance seeking principally a declaration pursuant to Article 232 EC that the Commission had failed to comply with its obligations under Community law and an order pursuant to Article 288 EC that the Community repair the damage suffered by the respondents as a result of the Commission's unlawful failure to act. The applicant explained that it had suffered damage due to the fact that it had been unable to market its products to farmers of food-producing animals and several competent national authorities had withdrawn or not extended marketing authorizations for their products. In establishing whether, through its failure to act, the Commission had committed a serious breach of a superior rule, the CFI reasoned simply that the inaction of the Commission constituted a clear and serious breach of the principle of sound administration giving rise, in principle, to liability on the Community's part and that there was therefore no need to establish whether the Commission's inaction was administrative or legislative in nature, or to determine the exact scope of its discretion. The CFI made no mention of *Bergaderm* in its ruling, and failed to apply any relevant test that either the ECJ or the CFI had previously established in the context of rulings on Article 288(2) EC. The CFI did not even seek to apply the administrative/legislative distinction.[175] Needless to say, the ECJ showed little mercy to the CFI when the case came before it on appeal:

> The Court of First Instance did not at any point in the judgment under appeal explain in detail the discretion which the Commission enjoys.... Nor did the Court of First Instance set out adequately for legal purposes the reasons or circumstances which might exceptionally have explained why such an analysis would serve no purpose. It must for those reasons be concluded that the Court of First Instance erred in law in holding in paragraph 103 of the judgment under appeal, without having established the scope of the discretion enjoyed by the Commission, that the Commission's inaction ... constituted

175. Joined Cases T-344/00 and T-345/00 *CEVA* and *Pharmacia Enterprises v. Commission* [2003] ECR II-229.

> a clear and serious breach of Community law giving rise to liability on the part of the Community. The ground of appeal must therefore be upheld.[176]

If the Court of Justice wished for the harshness of its words in *CEVA* to act as a wake up call for the CFI, it appears to have worked. The next time the CFI had the opportunity to rule on Community liability, its reasoning was a flawless application of the test set out in *Bergaderm*. The case of *Holcim*[177] arose in the context of competition law and an investigation by the Commission into a cartel of German cement producers in breach of Article 81 EC. The Commission concluded that the practices of the cement producers was contrary to Article 81 EC and imposed fines of EUR3.841 million and EUR1.85 million on Alsen Breitenburg Zement und Kalkwerke GmbH ('ABZK') and Nordcement AG, who, during the proceedings, merged with Alsen AG to form Holcim AG – the applicant. Holcim challenged that decision before the Court of First Instance. After having commenced proceedings, and upon prompting from the Commission, Holcim made arrangements for a bank guarantee to be provided to the Commission, thus avoiding the need to pay the fines immediately. In its ruling, the Court of First Instance, amongst other things, annulled the Commission's Decision. Holcim then asked the Commission to reimburse the costs incurred by it in setting up the bank guarantees. The Commission declined to do so and so Holcim brought proceedings under Article 288(2) EC to recover the losses that it had suffered as a result of setting up the guarantee.

Holcim argued that had the Commission not erred in its Decision that Holcim had breached Article 81 EC, it would not have been required to set up the guarantee. In a textbook application of the ECJ's ruling in *Bergaderm*, the CFI commenced its analysis with an examination of the Commission's discretion in deciding that the appellant's actions had breached Article 81 EC.[178] The CFI held that, despite the fact that the Commission had only limited discretion in determining whether or not there had been a breach of Article 81 EC, this did not automatically result in the Commission being liable in damages. Discretion, while being the principal criterion in determining the seriousness of breach, is not the only element that needs to be considered. The factual complexity of the case and difficulties of application and interpretation also had a role to play.

> Regard being had to the fact that [the case annulling the Commission's decision] was a particularly complex case, involving a very large number of undertakings and almost the entire European cement industry . . . and to the fact that it was necessary to analyse a great number of documents, including in the applicant's specific situation, it must be held that the defendant was faced with complex situations to be regulated.

176. Case C-198/03 P *Commission v. CEVA and Pfizer* [2005] ECR I-6357, paras 67-70.
177. Case T-28/03 *Holcim (Deutschland) v. Commission* [2005] ECR II-1357.
178. Ibid., para. 87.

> On all of those grounds, it must be held that the breach of Community law found in the Cement judgment as regards the part of the decision concerning the applicant is not sufficiently serious.[179]

On appeal, the ECJ upheld the CFI's reasoning in its entirety.[180] It appeared, therefore, that through its faultless application of the *Bergaderm* test, the ECJ's approach to serious breach had won out, and the pre-*Bergaderm* distinction between legislative and administrative acts had truly been assigned to the annals of judicial history. Any celebrations that may have taken place in chambers at the ECJ were, however, short-lived. It was not long before the CFI changed tack once more.

The cases of *Abad Pérez v. Council*[181] and *É.R. and Others v. Council and Commission*[182] concerned actions brought by Spanish cattle breeders, by indirect victims and by the next of kin of five people who died in France from Creutzfeldt-Jakob disease (CJD) – the human form of mad cow disease. The applicants sought reparation for the harm allegedly suffered as a result of acts and omissions on the part of the Council and the Commission in relation to the spread in Europe of mad cow disease and the new human variant. In addressing the applicants' case, the CFI began its reasoning in the standard way. The Court reiterated that a successful claim of non-contractual liability required the applicants to prove the unlawfulness of the conduct of which the institutions are accused; the reality of the damage; and the existence of a causal connection between the conduct and the damage in question. The Court then went on to cite *Bergaderm* and the role that discretion plays in determining breaches of superior rules. The normal approach of the Court, post-*Bergaderm*, is then to assess the amount of discretion exercised by the institution and whether or not its conduct amounted to a serious breach of a superior norm. The CFI in *Abad Pérez* took a different approach however, and instead chose to decide the case on the basis of causation. Causation is dealt with in-depth in the next section of this chapter. Suffice it to say at this point that, in order to be awarded compensation, the applicant needs to prove that the damage suffered was the direct result of the alleged unlawful act of the Community institution. After having examined whether or not the loss suffered by the applicants was a direct cause of the Community's failure to take action in relation to CJD, the CFI held that it had not been established that the allegedly unlawful actions and omissions on the part of the Council and the Commission could be regarded as certain and direct causes of the damage alleged. The applicants had failed to show that if the Council or Commission had adopted – or had adopted earlier – the measures that the applicants criticized them for not adopting, the damage in question would not have occurred.[183] While neither the reasoning nor the conclusion of the CFI is in doubt, the prominence and emphasis that the Court placed on the causation element is

179. Ibid., paras 114-116.
180. Case C-282/05 P *Holcim (Deutschland) v. Commission* [2007] ECR I-2941.
181. Case T-304/01 *Abad Pérez and others v. Council and Commission* [2006] ECR II-4857.
182. Case T-138/03 *É.R. and others v. Council and Commission* [2006] ECR II-4923.
183. The CFI also applied a similar style of causation-based reasoning in the following Joined cases T-3/00 and T-337/04 *Athanasios Pitsiorlas v. Council of the European Union and European Central Bank* [2007] II-4779.

worthy of discussion. In structuring its judgment by first setting out the criteria necessary for non-contractual liability to exist, and then citing the seminal case of *Bergaderm*, the CFI followed standard judicial protocol and the methodology of the Court of Justice. By then concentrating solely on causation, however, the CFI evades either having to follow or apply *Bergaderm*. While such failure on the part of the CFI to follow *Bergaderm* has in the past met with swift rebukes from the ECJ, on appeal, the new approach, provided that the CFI correctly applies the test of causation, does not provide grounds for an appeal and cannot therefore be struck down by the ECJ. The Court of First Instance therefore relegated *Bergaderm* and the opaque, contradictory, and unpredictable case law that surrounds the question of breach to the status of a secondary issue, only to be addressed in the event that the applicant can prove causation.

Such an approach is not without its advantages. It avoids the thorny issue of breach and debates over the appropriateness and the effectiveness of situation specific tests of discretion or arbitral categorizations such as the administrative/legislative distinction. Furthermore, given that the criteria for recovering damages are cumulative, it cannot be said that the CFI's causation-based approach will alter the results in the cases before it. Regardless of whether or not a case does involve a serious breach, an applicant could not recover compensation unless it satisfied the causation test. What may change, however, is the status of the applicant in relation to that of the defendant institution. At least in the first instance, the Court's causation-based approach places the applicant in a position of considerable strength in comparison to the traditional approach. The strength of the applicant is increased by virtue of the fact that traditionally the test of causation is only relevant once a breach has been established. By examining causation first, the Court suspends reality and adopts a 'best-case scenario' approach in favour of the applicant by assuming that there has been a breach. This offers both psychological and tactical advantages to the applicant that do not exist under the *Bergaderm* approach which requires applicants to fight an uphill battle to prove, not only that the institution breached a superior rule, but that the breach in question was serious. Despite such hypothetical advantages, however, it is doubtful that the causation-based test will result in a greater number of applicants being awarded damages. In the three prominent cases in which the CFI has applied the causation test, none of the applicants were successful. Even if an applicant does satisfy the causation test, due to the cumulative nature of the liability criteria, the applicant has only delayed, rather than avoided, being required to prove breach.

While it was hoped that subsequent case law would clarify the situation, the case of *Schneider II* has only served to exacerbate an already convoluted line of authority. The case formed part of a series of litigation that started with a Commission decision declaring that a merger between Schneider and Legrand was incompatible with the common market. In *Schneider I*,[184] the applicant

184. Case T-310/01 *SchneiderElectric v. Commission (Schneider I)* [2002] ECR II-4071.

successfully had the Commission Decision annulled. *Schneider II*[185] concerned a subsequent claim by the applicant to recover compensation for losses caused by the Commission's erroneous decision. In contrast to *Holcim*, where the CFI clearly held that the Commission had only limited discretion in its application of Article 81 EC, in *Schneider II*, the Court ruled that in its task as competition regulator, the Commission was entrusted with a considerable degree of discretion and that it would be inhibited in the performance of those duties, contrary to the general Community interest, if the concept of a serious breach was construed as comprising all errors or mistakes which, even if of some gravity, were not by their nature or extent alien to the normal conduct of an institution with the task of overseeing the application of the competition rules.[186] In making such determinations it was the Court's duty to set the threshold at such a level as to balance the interests of both the individuals that had suffered loss and the need for the Commission to be able to effectively fulfil its duties:

> A sufficiently serious breach of Community law, for the purposes of establishing the non-contractual liability of the Community, cannot be constituted by failure to fulfil a legal obligation, which, regrettable though it may be, can be explained by the objective constraints to which the institution and its officials are subject as a result of the provisions governing the control of concentrations.
>
> On the other hand, the right to compensation for damage resulting from the conduct of the institution becomes available where such conduct takes the form of action manifestly contrary to the rule of law and seriously detrimental to the interests of persons outside the institution and cannot be justified or accounted for by the particular constraints to which the staff of the institution, operating normally, is objectively subject.
>
> Such a definition of the threshold for the establishment of non-contractual liability of the Community is conducive to protection of the room for manoeuvre and freedom of assessment which must, in the general interest, be enjoyed by the Community regulator of competition, both in its discretionary decisions and in its interpretation and application of the relevant provisions of primary and secondary Community law, without thereby leaving third parties to bear the consequences of flagrant and inexcusable misconduct.[187]

The Court proceeded to conduct an in-depth investigation into the defects of the economic analysis that the Commission had undertaken in reaching its decision that the merger between Schneider and Legrand inhibited competition. The Court emphasized that such economic analysis generally involves, as regards both the facts and the reasoning employed, complex intellectual propositions into which certain inadequacies may creep, in view of the time constraints to which the Commission was subject.[188]

185. Case T-351/03 *SchneiderElectric v. Commission (Schneider II)*, [2007] ECR II-2237.
186. Ibid., para. 122.
187. Ibid., paras 123-125.
188. Ibid., paras 127-139.

In response to the applicants claim that the Commission had breached its rights of defence, the Court held that there had been a manifest and serious infringement in so far as the Commission had omitted in the statement of objections a reference to a matter that was essential to the operative part of the incompatibility decision. That breach of the rights of the defence was neither justified nor accounted for by the particular constraints to which the Commission staff was objectively subject.[189]

The CFI therefore went back to the traditional *Bergaderm*-style of reasoning – looking first at serious breach before turning to causation. The Court itself offers nothing in the way of explanation for reverting back to this approach, and there is little to suggest why the Court was motivated to decide *Schneider II* in this way. One possible explanation is that *Schneider II*, like *Holcim*, derived from an annulled Commission measure that had been adopted in the context of competition law. It is possible, therefore, that the Court, rather than seeing *Schneider II* as a run-of-the-mill Community liability case subject to the same approach as every other case brought under Article 288(2) EC, preferred to follow the approach in *Holcim*, the facts of which are most closely analogous to those of *Schneider II*. The possibility of this being true is bolstered by the fact that at no point in its ruling does the CFI make reference either to *Bergaderm* or *Abad Pérez* or any of its more recent Article 288(2) EC judgments. Instead, the CFI relies predominantly on the *Holcim* ruling.

While it is understandable that the CFI would rely heavily on *Holcim* when making it ruling in *Schneider II*, in doing so, the Court has once again injected yet another element of complexity and uncertainty into the area of Community liability. As the situation currently stands, the CFI appears to be applying two different strategies for dealing with claims under Article 288(2) EC: The *Bergaderm/Holcim* reasoning in competition law cases and a causation-based approach in all other cases. Only time will tell whether this was the Court's intention or whether it is simply an unfortunate result of the CFI seeking to flex its political muscle by deciding cases without recourse to the ECJ's ruling in *Bergaderm*. Regardless of the approach adopted by the Court, the applicant will still need to satisfy the tests of both serious breach and causation, no matter the emphasis that the Court places upon each criteria or the order in which it decides to treat them. As always, a successful applicant must be prepared for whatever the Court decides to throw at it.

6. LIABILITY FOR LAWFUL ACTS

Once an applicant had shown that its claim is admissible, the starting point of the Court in its rulings is to investigate whether or not the Community institution, through its conduct, has breached its duties. Although a measure need not have been formally declared illegal under Article 230 EC for an applicant to be

189. Ibid., paras 256-259.

successful,[190] illegality is, in practice, nonetheless, a pre-condition to compensation. The Court, however, has never expressly excluded the possibility that, in exceptional circumstances, liability might arise out of a lawful legislative act. In some cases, the Court rather ambiguously appears to have deliberately left open the possibility of liability for lawful acts, while at the same time rejecting all applications for compensation.

Holding the Community liable in damages caused by a lawful act does not require the applicant to show fault on the part of the Community, and thereby amounts to the imposition of the concept of strict liability – a concept that is not unknown to many Member States. Recovery by individuals in strict liability claims often requires the applicant to demonstrate that he has suffered special or abnormal damages. On a national level, this is based on the notions of 'special sacrifice' or 'equality before the public burden', which have their roots in German and French law.[191] These concepts require the State to compensate individuals if, as a result of a lawfully valid act taken in the public interest, they have suffered harm in a distinct and disproportionate way in comparison to other affected individuals.

Before addressing the substantive issues associated with a claim for damages arising from lawful acts, a small note should be made as to procedure. Liability for a lawful act is a new plea in law which must be raised in the application. In accordance with both Article 42(2) of the *Rules of Procedure of the Court of Justice* and Article 48(2) of the *Rules of Procedure of the Court of First Instance*, no new plea in law may be introduced in the course of the proceedings unless it is based on matters of law or of fact that come to light in the course of the proceedings.[192] Therefore, if the action was initially brought on the basis of damages resulting from an unlawful act of the Community, a submission based on the legality of an act cannot be raised once proceedings have started.

With regard to the substantive elements of a claim based on lawful acts, Advocate General Mayras addressed the principle of special damage in *Compagnie d'Approvisionement v. Commission.*[193] The claim arose out of the devaluation of the French franc in 1969, which caused the Council to decree that France should grant subsidies for imports of cereal products from the Member States and third countries. It was then up to the Commission to fix the amount of those subsidies. The applicants, who were French traders and producers of cereals, brought an action for damages on the basis that they had suffered losses. The devaluation of the French franc meant that the subsidy did not precisely compensate for the resulting price increases. They claimed that the Community should incur liability, even though the amount of the subsidies had been legally fixed, because they had

190. An action for damages under Art. 288(2) EC is an autonomous action, and not dependant upon the Court having first annulled the measure under Art. 230 EC. See Case 5/71 *Aktien-Zuckerfabrik Schöppenstedt v. Council* [1971] ECR 975.

191. In German law the concept is that of a '*Sonderopfer*', while under French law it is referred to as '*rupture de l'égalité devant les charges publiques*'.

192. Case C-104/97 P *Atlanta AG and others v. Commission of the European Communities and Council of the European Union* [1999] ECR I-6983, paras 27-29.

193. Joined Cases 9 and 11/71 *Compagnie d'Approvisionnement v. Commission* [1972] ECR 391.

suffered unusual and special damage by being treated less favourably than importers from other Member States. In his Opinion, Advocate General Mayras, drawing inspiration from Advocate General Roemer's Opinion in *Plaumann*,[194] considered that the abnormal or special nature of damages manifested itself in two elements: The damage must be particular to one or more persons; and it must be so serious as to exceed the duties imposed on each citizen by the requirements of life in a Community.[195] The Advocate General concluded that the applicants in their submissions had not satisfied either of those conditions, as the system of subsidies affected all French millers and dealers in cereals, and that damage affecting a whole branch of industry and trade did not constitute special damage. In the case itself, while not denying, in principle, the possibility of liability arising out of a lawful act, the Court tersely dismissed the applicant's claim without reference to Advocate General Mayras' Opinion. The ECJ stated that any liability for a valid legislative measure was inconceivable in the present situation, as the measures adopted by the Commission were only intended to alleviate, in the general economic interest, the consequences that resulted from the devaluation of the franc.[196] The Court did not, however, rule out the possibility of an award of damages in other, narrower situations that were not concerned with measures adopted in the general economic interest.

In *Biovilac*,[197] the applicants brought an action for compensation on the basis of lost revenue allegedly caused by the introduction of Community Regulations on the sale of skimmed-milk powder for use in feed for pigs and poultry. In reference to the applicant's submission that they were entitled to compensation, despite the fact that the Community Regulations were lawful, Advocate General Slynn in his Opinion reiterated that the applicants could only succeed in such a claim where it could be shown that they had suffered particularly severe losses as a result of the act. The Advocate General then drew parallels between the requirement to pay compensation for the expropriation of property and the notion of special sacrifice, by opining that a claim for compensation could exist if, in the Community interest steps are taken which caused a business to suffer financial loss or to be run down. According to the Advocate General, such a situation is equivalent to the confiscation of a business and there can be no confiscation without compensation.

After having recognized in principle the existence of a claim for compensation of damage resulting from a valid act, Advocate General Slynn continued that such a right to compensation must be construed narrowly. In particular, compensation should not be awarded where the applicant knew or ought to have known of the risk involved when he first began to market his products. He concluded that the applicants had been operating in the market for a sufficient period of time to be aware of the commercial risks involved, and that the loss suffered was within the

194. Case 25/62 *Plaumann & Co. v. Commission* [1963] ECR 199.

195. AG Mayras' Opinion in Joined Cases 9 and 11/71 *Compagnie d'Approvisionnement v. Commission* [1972] ECR 391, 423.

196. Ibid.

197. Case 59/83 *Biovilac v. EEC* [1984] ECR 4057.

commercial risk of an undertaking operating in the existing market conditions. The Court appeared to follow the reasoning of its Advocate General when it concluded:

> An action for damages brought under Article 215 [now Article 288 EC] of the Treaty for unlawful legislative action cannot succeed unless the damage alleged by the applicant exceeds the limits of economic risks inherent in operating in the sector concerned. That principle would have to be applied a fortiori if the concept of liability without fault were accepted in Community law.[198]

The Court therefore, expressly left open the possibility of liability arising without the need for an illegal act, provided that the applicant could show that it had suffered special damage which was not foreseeable, and which exceeded the limits of economic risk inherent in the sector concerned. While the ECJ may have left the door open to possible claims against lawful acts, it is the CFI that has come closest to walking through it. Despite eventually rejecting the claim for compensation, the CFI, in its ruling in *Dorsch Consult*,[199] went so far as to lay down the conditions that would need to be satisfied for a claim to succeed. The applicant was a German firm of consultant engineers, which had been contracted to perform services for the Ministry of Works Housing in Iraq. Following the Iraqi invasion of Kuwait in 1990, the United Nations Security Council adopted Resolution No. 660 (1990) to the effect that there had been a breach of international peace and that Iraqi forces should withdraw immediately from Kuwait. Following Iraq's failure to comply with the Resolution, a second resolution – Resolution No. 661 (1990) – was passed, imposing an embargo on trade with Iraq and Kuwait. In compliance with this second resolution, the Council adopted Regulation 2340/90 EC preventing trade by the Community with Iraq and Kuwait. In retaliation to the UN Resolution, the Iraqi government passed, with retroactive effect, Law No. 57, which froze all property and assets and income held by them at the material time, and owed to the governments, undertakings, companies and banks of those States that had adopted the embargo. The result was that Dorsch Consult, which still had outstanding debts with the Iraqi authorities, was unable to recover the money owed to it. The applicants therefore brought an action against the Community alleging that its loss was the result of the trade embargo, and more specifically, the result of Council Regulation 2340/90 EC. The CFI rejected the action on the grounds that there was no causal link, and that the applicant had failed to prove actual and certain damage. Before doing so, however, the CFI examined in some detail the conditions of liability for lawful acts.

On analyzing the Court's previous case law on the possibility of liability arising from valid acts, the CFI concluded that compensation would only be granted where the applicant satisfied three criteria: The applicant must have suffered both 'special' and 'unusual' damage. Once the applicant had demonstrated both of these elements, it would still only be able to claim compensation where the

198. Ibid., para. 28.
199. Case T-184/95 *Dorsch Consult Ingenieurgesellschaft mbH v. Council of the European Union and Commission of the European Communities* [1998] ECR II-667.

legislative measure giving rise to the alleged damage could not be justified by a general economic interest.[200] The Court defined unusual damage as that which constitutes a 'still subsisting injury', affecting a particular circle of economic operators in a disproportionate manner in comparison with others. Damage would be 'special' if the applicant could show that the loss exceeded the limits of economic risks inherent in operating in the sector concerned. After having defined the limits of the conditions to be satisfied, the Court then went on to assess whether and how the applicants could show that they had suffered special and unusual loss.

In respect of the unusual nature of the alleged damage, the Court noted that the adoption of Law No. 57 was designed to freeze the 'assets' held in Iraq by undertakings established in the Community. It followed, therefore, that it was not only the applicant's claims that were affected, but also those of all the other Community undertakings which, when the embargo on trade with Iraq was imposed by Regulation No. 2340/90 EC, had not been paid. As was noted by the applicant during the hearing, the claims of Community undertakings against Iraq which, following the imposition of the Community embargo on trade with that country became irrecoverable and which had to be covered by State guarantees, amounted to USD 18 000 million. As such, the applicant could not be regarded as forming part of a category of economic operators whose property interests were affected in a manner that set them apart from all other economic operators. The applicant had not, therefore, suffered special damage or made an exceptional sacrifice.

As regards the special nature of the alleged damage, the Court considered that the limits of the economic risk inherent in operating in Iraq had not been exceeded by the adoption of Regulation 2340/90 EC and the resulting imposition of Law No. 57. It was common ground that Iraq, by reason of its involvement in a war with Iran long before its invasion of Kuwait on 2 August 1990, was already regarded as a 'high-risk country'. In those circumstances, the economic and commercial risks deriving from the possible involvement of Iraq in renewed warfare with neighbouring countries and the suspension of payment of its debts for reasons associated with its foreign policy constituted foreseeable risks inherent in any provision of services in Iraq and the resulting damage was not, for the purposes of Article 288(2) EC, special.

The third element – that the measure cannot be justified on the grounds of general economic interest – allows the Court to balance the conflicting interests of, firstly, international organizations such as the UN and more often the EU itself, and the needs of individual undertakings. In seeking to address that balance, the CFI reasoned that:

> Whilst it is true that rules intended, by the imposition of a trade embargo against a non-member country, to maintain international peace and security have, by definition, effects which affect the freedom to pursue a trade or business, thereby causing harm to persons who are in no way responsible for the situation which led to the adoption of the sanctions, the fact

200. Ibid., para. 80.

> nevertheless remains that the importance of the aims pursued by such rules is such as to justify negative consequences, even of a substantial nature, for some operators. Consequently, having regard to the objective of general interest so fundamental for the international community of bringing to an end the invasion and occupation of Kuwait by Iraq and maintaining international peace and security in the region, the damage alleged by the applicant, even if it were capable of being classified as substantial, within the meaning of the *Bosphorus* judgment,[201] cannot render the Community liable in this case.[202]

Despite the CFI's initial specification when originally outlining the conditions to be applied that the measure must not be justifiable on general economic grounds, the word 'economic' was conspicuously absent when the Court applied a test to the facts in *Dorsch Consult*. It appears, therefore, that the same interpretation of 'economic' should be used in relation to legal acts as has been used in respect to a 'measure of economic policy' in the context of *Schöppenstedt*,[203] where the formula is used so as to limit the amount of control that can be exercised where the decision-makers have to make policy choices. Indeed, the CFI sought to justify the measure not on any economic basis, but rather on the aims to be achieved by the UN measures – namely to safeguard international peace and security.

The high thresholds required by special and unusual damage establish a normative framework that makes it virtually impossible for liability to arise, and serves to underscore the exceptional character of liability.[204] There is yet to be a case that has satisfied the three-stage test set out by the CFI. Often, a claim will fail at the hurdle of special damage without the need for the Court to evaluate whether or not the damage was usual and whether the measure can be justified.

One example where the CFI has decided a case on the basis of 'unusual damage' arose in the *FIAMM* case, which involved the EU's relationship with the WTO. The CFI acknowledged the principle of liability in the absence of unlawfulness but denied the right to compensation on the basis that the applicant had not suffered 'unusual damage' since retaliatory measures imposed by other WTO members were an 'inherent risk' in any international traders export operations.[205]

201. Case C-84/95 *Bosphorus Hava Yollari Turizm ve Ticaret AS v. Minister for Transport, Energy and Communications Ireland and the Attorney General* [1996] ECR I-3953. The case dealt with substantial losses suffered by an airline operator, which, as a result of UN Sanctions against the Former State of Yugoslavia, had its airplanes impounded. The Court ruled that, even though the losses suffered by the operator were substantial, the impounding of aircraft could not be regarded as either inappropriate or disproportionate, when considered in light of the aims of the sanction, which consisted in putting an end to the state of war in the Former State of Yugoslavia, and to the massive violations of human rights and humanitarian international law in the Republic of Bosnia-Hezegovina. The disproportionateness of the loss must therefore be considered in light of the aims to be achieved by the legal act.
202. Case T-184/95 *Dorsch Consult Ingenieurgesellschaft mbH v. Council of the European Union and Commission of the European Communities* [1998] ECR II-667, paras 87-88.
203. See discussion above, at 106 ff.
204. T. Tridimas, *The General Principles of EC Law*, 3rd edn (Oxford: OUP, 2006), 495.
205. Case T-69/00 *FIAMM and FIAMM Technologies* [2005] ECR II-5393, para. 205.

The applicant has since appealed to the ECJ. Advocate General Maduro has already expressed his disagreement with the CFI's findings. The ECJ has yet to rule on the issue.[206]

A good example of the CFI's reasoning in respect of 'special damage' arose in the case of *Area Cova v. Council and Commission*.[207] The case concerned a group of fishermen who claimed compensation for losses resulting from Community legislation fixing the quota for halibut. The CFI rejected the application on the basis that the reduction in fishing quotas was neither unforeseeable, nor did it totally prevent the pursuit of such fishing. Moreover, the alleged loss rested on the premise that the applicants enjoyed a right to exploit the shoal of fish in question, which, despite the sustained length of time that they had been fishing in those waters, they had not acquired. The Court continued that, in any event, economic operators cannot rely on an acquired right to the maintenance of an advantage arising from Community legislation, especially legislation worked out in the context of an international organization in which the Community participates.[208]

An example of the lengths that the Court is willing to go in its reasoning when considering whether the loss suffered by the applicant amounted to unusual damage arose in the *Galileo* case.[209] The applicants were a group of companies that offered and supplied electronic services to the air transport, travel, leisure and hotel industry sectors as regards access to data relating to offers, timetables and prices. In carrying out that activity, they had registered a number of trademarks and company names containing the word 'Galileo'. The Commission subsequently adopted the name Galileo for the Community project on the European satellite radio navigation system. The applicants brought a claim seeking damages against the Community for an alleged infringement of their intellectual property rights. After having failed to show that the Commission had acted illegally, the applicants sought to argue that they were nevertheless entitled to damages as they satisfied the criteria set out by the CFI in *Dorsch Consult*. The applicant claimed that the use of the word 'Galileo' had affected and would affect their rights in a completely unique way because the applicants were the only undertakings whose rights had been affected by the measure in question (unusual damage). Furthermore, the likelihood of a public authority disregarding trademark law by using the word Galileo for a project, when that breach could easily have been avoided, was not at all inherent in the fact of operating in a particular economic sector (special damage). Lastly, the applicant claimed that the Commission's choice of the word Galileo was not

206. Joined Cases C-120 and 121/06 *FIAMM*, Opinion of AG Maduro of 20 Feb. 2008, nyr in the ECR. For a comment on this case see A. Thies, 'Case Note' *CMLRev*. 43 (2006): 1145-1168.
207. Case T-196/99 *Area Cova v. Council and Commission* [2001] ECR II-3597.
208. Ibid., paras 174-177; See also T-69/00 *FIAMM and FIAMM Technologies* [2005] ECR II-5393, paras 108-115.
209. Case T-279/03 *Galileo International Technology a.o. v. Commission* [2006] ECR II-1291.

justified by any general economic interest (lack of justification). The CFI took a different view however, and reasoned that:

> Even if the applicants had been able to demonstrate that they suffered real damage which was caused by the Commission's use of the word 'Galileo', that damage could not be regarded as exceeding the limits of the risks inherent in the use by the applicants of the same term in respect of their trade marks.
>
> By choosing the name 'Galileo' to designate their trade marks, products and services, the applicants could not deny that they were inspired by the first name of the renowned Italian mathematician, physicist and astronomer, born in Pisa in 1564, who is one of the great names in European culture and scientific history. Thus, the applicants voluntarily exposed themselves to the risk that someone else (in this case, the Commission) could legally – that is to say, without infringing their trademark rights – give the same famous name to their satellite radio navigation research programme. Furthermore, in 1989, the National Aeronautics and Space Administration (NASA) had already chosen the word 'Galileo' to designate a space mission, namely the launch of an observation satellite to the planet Jupiter.
>
> It is not appropriate, therefore, in the circumstances of this case, to describe the damage allegedly suffered by the applicants as unusual.[210]

Questions should undoubtedly be raised as to the soundness of any judgment that seeks to limit liability for the infringement of a trademark on the basis that the right holder was inspired by a figure of historical importance. The circumstances that inspired registration of a trademark are not relevant to the question of infringement and should not influence a decision as to whether damages should be awarded. Setting high thresholds to recovery in cases concerning public bodies is clearly justifiable. Acknowledging that a potential claim can exist, but setting thresholds that cannot be satisfied by even the most meritorious of claims, is not.

The ambivalence of the CFI on this issue is further demonstrated by its ruling in *Masdar.*[211] The Court expanded the scope of claims based on lawful acts by recognizing the possibility of an applicant relying on unjust enrichment to establish the non-contractual liability of Community institutions, yet, still denied recovery because the applicant failed to demonstrate unusual and special damage. The case arose over a sub-contract concluded by the applicant, Masdar, with a Commission contractor, Helmico. After falling behind in its contractual payments to Masdar, Helmco became insolvent. Masdar then sought to recover the money from the Commission, which refused to pay it directly. The applicant then brought an action for damages claiming that the Commission had breached certain principles of non-contractual liability recognized in many of the Member States. It cited inter alia the civil law action based on the principle of the prohibition of unjust enrichment. The CFI began its reasoning by establishing firstly, that the wording of Article 288(2) EC does not prevent claims in damages being brought in the absence of unlawful

210. Ibid., para. 150.
211. Case T-333/03 *Masdar v. Commission* [2006] ECR II-4377.

conduct, and secondly, in relying on principles common to the Member States, that a claim for damages could be brought on the grounds of unjust enrichment. Although the CFI was willing to extend the grounds upon which a claim in damages in the absence of unlawful conduct could be based, the Court went on to dismiss the claim due to the applicant's failure to prove unusual and special damage:

> It has not been established that the applicant suffered unusual and special damage going beyond the limits of the economic and commercial risks inherent in its operations. In all contractual relationships there is a certain risk that a party will not perform the contract satisfactorily or will even become insolvent. It is for the contracting parties to mitigate that risk in a suitable manner in the contract itself.[212]

Despite the apparent willingness of the CFI to accept, at least in principle, the possibility of a claim for compensation based on a legal act, it remains to be seen whether the ECJ will ever formally accept such an action. It is clear at least from the high thresholds that it has set, that the Court is fearful that the relaxation of the conditions will lead to a host of spurious claims. Given the low number of actions that have been brought, and the fact that none of them has been successful, it is debatable whether this fear is fully justified. Who can say, however, that there would not have been more claims had either the ECJ or the CFI allowed any of the applicants in the above cases to recover compensation? The high thresholds for recovery are at least consistent with the Court's traditional approach to EU public law, and the caution with which it has treated any application by individuals that calls the validity of an act of the Community into question. While certain commentators may feel that, doctrinally, the setting out of the conditions that need to be satisfied in order to bring a claim, before formally admitting that such a claim can in fact be brought, is unsatisfactory and, by putting the cart before the horse, is liable to maintain uncertainty,[213] it does not, in any event, worsen a situation already riddled with obscurity. For those applicants brave (or desperate) enough to attempt a claim for compensation on this basis, they, at least, have a clear idea of the path to be taken, and the obstacles to be overcome – even if it not clear that they will ever achieve their goal.

7. CAUSATION

As the section on the elements of serious breach has illustrated, the test of causation, whilst always having been a fundamental element of the liability test, has come into prominence in recent cases.[214] The underlying premise of the causation

212. Ibid., para. 103.
213. See T. Tridimas, *The General Principles of EC Law*, 3rd edn (Oxford: OUP, 2006), 495.
214. See Case T-304/01 *Abad Pérez and others v. Council and Commission* [2006] ECR II-4857; Case T-138/03 *É.R. and others v. Council and Commission* [2006] ECR II-4923; Joined cases T-3/00 and T-337/04 *Athanasios Pitsiorlas v. Council of the European Union and European Central Bank* [2007] II-4779.

test is, that when assessing whether an applicant is entitled to receive compensation under Article 288(2) EC, the Community will only be liable to make good losses or injuries that have been *caused* by the Community.[215] Where causation cannot be proved, an applicant will not be entitled to compensation regardless of the losses suffered. The question of causation contains two elements and arises at two points during the proceedings. The first element relates to the admissibility of the claim, and ordinarily poses a problem where the damage has been caused by a Community measure which has been implemented by the national authorities. The second element is one of substance and requires an applicant to establish a sufficiently direct link of causality between the alleged wrongdoing and the damage suffered by the applicant.[216] The first element relates to concurrent and joint liability of the Community and the Member States and is addressed at length in a separate chapter. The following paragraphs concentrate on the substantive test of causation which consists of both a legal and factual test.

7.1. Factual Causation and Acts of the Applicant

The principle that the Community will only be liable for damage arising directly out of its own actions is reflected in the wording of Article 288(2) EC, according to which the Community is liable to make good any damage caused by its institutions or by its servants in the performance of their duties. Whether the damage has been caused directly by one of the Community institutions for the purposes of Article 288(2) EC is, to a large extent, a question of fact to be determined on a case-by-case basis, having regard to the relevant circumstances of the case. In an attempt to offer more concrete guidance, however, Advocate General Trabucchi, in his Opinion in *Compagnie Continentale*, offered a helpful definition, opining that:

> Direct damages are those which derive from the unlawful act of the subject responsible and which do not depend on the intervention of other causes, whether positive or negative.... In this connexion the conduct or attitude of the victim is relevant in two respects:
> (1)in relation to the very existence of the unlawful act, which is only considered as such where the false feeling of confidence was engendered in persons who are responsibly mindful of their duty to keep themselves informed of matters affecting them; and
> (2)in relation to negligence, which even the victim of false information may have shown by failing to limit the production of future damage.[217]

---

215. Case 4/69 *Alfons Lütticke GmbH v. Commission* [1971] ECR 325, para. 10.
216. Case T-149/96 *Confederazione Nazionale Coltivatori Diretti (Coldiretti) and 110 farmers v. Council and Commission* [1998] ECR II-3841, para. 101; Case C-472/00 *P Commission v. Fresh Marine* [2003] ECR I-7541, para. 118.
217. AG Trabucchi's Opinion in Case 169/73 *Compagnie Continentale France v. Council of the European Communities* [1975] ECR 117, para. 4.

The *Compagnie Continentale* case concerned a French exporter of cereals who claimed that the Council had acted in breach of its duty to safeguard the position of exporters by lowering the amount of the compensatory amounts payable on the amount of wheat exported, without taking account of those exporters who had already entered into export contracts. The comments of the Advocate General highlight, firstly, that, in order for damage to be considered direct, the way in which the damage arose must not be dependant on an intervening outside cause. It must be the acts or omissions of the Community institution that caused the damage. Therefore, the Community will not be liable where the damage would not have arisen but for the occurrence of a subsequent event. The second part of Advocate General Trabucchi's definition relates to the effect that the applicant's own conduct may have on causation. This part of the Advocate General's definition concerns the applicant's knowledge at the time of the breach, and involves assessing whether, upon having suffered a loss, the applicant took sufficient steps to mitigate that loss.

7.1.1. Direct Damage

In *Schneider II*, the CFI was faced with a claim arising out of a Commission decision declaring a merger between Schneider and Legrand to be incompatible with the common market. In *Schneider I*,[218] the applicant successfully had the Commission decision annulled, while *Schneider II* dealt with a resulting claim under Article 288(2) EC to recover losses suffered as a result of the Commission's decision. In respect of the test of causation, the Court began its ruling by setting out how the question of causation should be approached:

> The analysis of the causal link cannot start from the incorrect premise that, in the absence of an unlawful measure, the institution would have refrained from acting or would have adopted a contrary measure, which could also amount to unlawful conduct on its part, but must be based on a comparison between the situation arising, for the third party concerned, from the wrongful measure and the situation which would have arisen for that third party if the institution's conduct had been in conformity with the law.
>
> Where the unlawful circumstance on which the claim for compensation is based is associated with a decision whose effect is to withhold from an applicant an authorisation or other favourable measure, it cannot be presumed, for the purpose of analysing the effects of the wrongful measure and the comparison between the real situation and the reconstructed legal situation, that, in the absence of the defect identified, the applicant would necessarily have been granted the authorisation or other favourable measure sought by it.[219]

The Court starts from the premise that, in assessing causation a comparison needs to be made between the situation brought about by the unlawful decision in

218. Case T-310/01 *SchneiderElectric v. Commission (Schneider I)* [2002] ECR II-4071.
219. Case T-351/03 *Schneider Electric SA v. Commission of the European Communities* [2007] ECR II-2237, paras 264-265.

question, and the situation as it would have existed had the decision been adopted legally. In order for the applicants to succeed, therefore, they had to prove that had the Commission not committed a serious breach in its decision, it would have cleared the merger. The Court then clarified the evidential burden on the applicant by ruling that the mere fact that the Commission's decision was in breach of a superior rule did not necessarily mean that it was the wrong decision. It could not be assumed that had the Commission not committed a breach, it would have cleared the merger. It was up to the applicant to prove that this was the case. Where it failed to discharge this evidential burden the link between the breach and the loss would be too tenuous to be considered direct, and the applicant would not be able to recover. In carrying out the comparison on the facts of the case before it, the Court reasoned that:

> It is difficult to determine the nature and amount of the divestiture which would have been necessary to render the transaction compatible with the common market and obtain the Commission's agreement that it should proceed. It is even more difficult to determine the impact on the total value of the assets held by the applicant of the transfers and transactions which those corrective measures would have involved.
>
> It follows that an assessment of the changes to the economic parameters which would necessarily have accompanied any decision of compatibility is too uncertain to be a basis for a useful comparison with the situation resulting from the incompatibility decision. Even if it is accepted that Schneider may have lost a real opportunity to secure a decision of compatibility, the materialisation of that opportunity is linked to parameters that are too uncertain to be the subject of any convincing quantification.[220]

The Court therefore concluded that, despite the breach committed by the Commission in adopting the decision, and given that it was not possible to accurately determine the extent to which Schneider would have needed to divest part of its interest in Legrand for the merger to be cleared, and whether or not Schneider could, in fact, have made such a divestiture, the applicant had failed to prove that in the absence of the Commission's breach the merger would have been cleared. As such, a comparison could not be made between the loss suffered as a result of the breach and the situation that the applicant would have been in had the breach not occurred, because it was not clear whether or not the merger would have been cleared even where the breach had not been committed. Despite failing to prove that the entirety of the loss suffered had been caused by the Commission's breach, the applicant did convince the Court that there was a link between the wrongful act committed and two types of damage, namely the costs incurred by the undertaking in participating in the resumed investigation of the transaction after the judgment annulling the decision;[221] and the reduction of the transfer price which the

220. Ibid., paras 282-283.
221. Ibid., para. 300.

applicant had to grant to the purchaser of the assets in Legrand.[222] With regard to the latter aspect, however, the Court reduced the damages awarded on the basis of Schneider's own actions. The effect of the CFI's ruling is to place yet another heavy evidential burden on the applicant and in many ways requires it to second guess the approach that the Court will adopt. The applicant is required not only to illustrate the way in which the institution's breach caused it to suffer loss, but also to accurately determine the situation that would have existed had the institution not committed a breach. This requires the applicant to prove a hypothetical. In *Schneider II*, for example, the applicant had to show that had the Commission not committed a breach, it would have cleared the merger. The likelihood of proving such a claim will be dependant upon the amount of discretion available to the institution. Where the institution has only limited discretion and a limited number of options in the way it comes to a decision, it will be reasonably straightforward for the applicant to show what would have happened had the breach not occurred. Where the institution enjoys a greater level of discretion, however, it can implement a measure in numerous different ways, and take into consideration various different factors, making it almost impossible for the applicant to prove what would have happened had there not been a breach. Even the applicants in *Schneider II*, who *prima facie* had a strong claim, could only prove that had the Commission not breached its duties, the applicant would not have had to come before the Court.

7.1.2. The Applicant's Conduct

The second part of Advocate General Trabucchi's definition of causation establishes that the conduct or attitude of the applicant is relevant in two ways. First, in relation to the existence of the unlawful act and the duty on individuals to keep themselves informed of matters affecting them; and second, in relation to negligence, which even the victim of false information may have shown by failing to limit the production of future damage. This part of the Advocate General's definition clearly concerns the applicant's knowledge at the time of the breach, and involves assessing whether, upon having suffered a loss, the applicant took sufficient steps to mitigate his loss. It appears from the Advocate General's Opinion that the test used when assessing the applicant's actual knowledge is subjective in nature, taking into account the actual knowledge of the particular applicant in the case. The Court of Justice in *Compagnie Continentale* applied both a subjective and objective test, holding that:

> One must ask not only whether the conduct [of the Community institution] in fact caused the wrong impression on the applicant's part . . . but also whether it could and should have caused such an error in the mind of a prudent person.

In applying the test to the facts of the case, the Court reasoned that:

> The applicant, as a prudent exporter, fully informed of the conditions of the market, was not unaware and in any event could not be unaware that such was

222. Ibid., para. 311.

> the position at the time the contracts were concluded, and of the consequences which would result therefrom as regards the compensatory amounts.... The applicant was effectively in a position to appreciate the effect which an alteration in the conditions of the market could have on the application of the Articles referred to. Accordingly the damage alleged has not been caused by the conduct of the Council. The application must therefore be dismissed.[223]

In assessing whether the actions of the Community institutions caused damage therefore, one needs to show that not only did the conduct of the institution cause the applicant to act in a manner which caused him to suffer a loss, but also that any prudent person would also have acted in the same way as the applicant. One must therefore first evaluate the initial conduct of the applicant so as to establish whether a causal link exists between the institution's act and the damage suffered. Once this has been ascertained, one must appraise the applicant's continuing conduct to assess whether this corresponds to how the prudent person would have acted. It is assumed that the prudent person will mitigate the loss suffered. Where the applicant has failed to do this, the Court will hold that his acts have contributed to the loss suffered, and reduce the amount of compensation accordingly. This approach falls in line with the Court's judgment in *Brasserie du Pêcheur/Factortame*, on the need for the injured person to show reasonable diligence.[224]

Therefore, while the first stage of Advocate General Trabucchi's test goes to establishing causation, the second part concerns the degree of liability of both the Community and the applicant, and will cause the Court to reduce the award of compensation accordingly. The possible negligence on the part of the applicant may even be such as to break the chain of causation altogether, leaving the applicant without any compensation – as was the effect of the Court's ruling in *Odrigitria*.[225] The case arose from a dispute over the exact demarcation of marine territories between the Republic of Senegal and the Republic of Guinea-Bissau, which had been continuing since the 1960s. A Greek ship owner, fishing with a license granted under an agreement between the Senegalese Government and the Community, had his vessel seized by Guinea-Bissau authorities for fishing in their marine territories without a valid fishing license. The ship owner claimed damages from the Community for breach of its duty to inform those fishermen to whom it had granted licenses of the dispute. In its ruling the Court concluded that even if one assumes that the Community had breached its duty, and could be liable to compensate the applicant, the chain of causation was broken by the applicant himself choosing deliberately, and at his own risk, to fish in those waters. Alternatively, where this was not the case, the vessel could only have been in that area through navigational error, which amounted to an external intervening cause, and

223. AG Trabucchi's Opinion in Case 169-73 *Compagnie Continentale France v. Council of the European Communities* [1975] ECR 117, paras 23-33.
224. Case 46/93 *Brasserie du Pêcheur v. Bundesrepublik Deutschland and The Queen v. Secretary of State for Transport, ex parte Factortame and others* [1996] ECR I-1029, paras 82-85.
225. Case T-572/93 *Odrigitria v. Council and Commission* [1995] ECR II-2025.

served to break the chain of causation. The damage could not, therefore, be said to have been caused by the actions of a Community institution, and the applicant was not entitled to compensation.

A more recent example of an instance where the Court has reduced an award of damages on the basis of the applicant's conduct is the *Schneider II* judgment. It will be recalled from the discussion above that the Commission committed a serious breach of a superior rule in its decision that a proposed merger between Schneider and Legrand was incompatible with the common market. Schneider successfully had the decision annulled, and was subsequently awarded damages in respect of the expenses it had incurred and the reduced price it had to charge in order to sell Legrand within the time period of divestiture set down by the Commission. In respect of this second award, the CFI determined that Schneider's conduct had contributed to its own loss and accordingly reduced the award of damages by one-third. In coming to this conclusion the CFI reasoned that:

> Schneider could not have been unaware that the merger at the very least entailed the risk of creating or strengthening a dominant position in a substantial part of the common market and that, accordingly, the transaction would be prohibited by the Commission on the basis of Article 2(3) of the regulation.... It may thus be inferred that Schneider itself contributed to its own loss by assuming the real risk of a subsequent declaration of incompatibility of a concentration that had been brought about legally and, consequently, the possibility of a forced sale of the assets acquired.... It follows from all the foregoing considerations that the Commission must be ordered to make good... two-thirds of the loss suffered by Schneider as a result of the reduction of the Legrand transfer price.[226]

It is clear, therefore, that the CFI followed the approach of the ECJ in *Compagnie Continentale* when it concluded that Schneider, as a prudent supplier of low-voltage electric equipment in France, fully informed of the conditions of the market, could not have been unaware of the risk that the Commission would require it to divest from Legrand within a specified period. The CFI's decision to reduce its award of damages appears to be correct, especially when one considers that Schneider had acquired shares in Legrand prior to the Commission's decision on the merger. While there is an exception to the standstill provisions in the EC Merger Regulation in respect to public bids, standard market practice prescribes that undertakings make their offers conditional upon regulatory clearance being given before proceeding with an acquisition of this type. Failure to follow such practice clearly opens the applicant up to increased risks that should not be borne by the Community institutions.

226. Case T-351/03 *Schneider Electric SA v. Commission of the European Communities* [2007] ECR II-2237, paras 330-335.

7.2. Legal Causation: Foreseeability

The evolution of the Court's case law in relation to Article 288(2) EC has seen the introduction of a more pronounced role for the legal test of foreseeability when assessing whether or not there is a causal link between the Community action and the damage. This was illustrated by the CFI in *Dorsch Consult.*[227] The case concerned a German firm of consultant engineers which had been contracted to perform services for the Ministry of Works Housing in Iraq. Following the Iraqi invasion of Kuwait in 1990, the United Nations Security Council imposed an embargo on trade with Iraq and Kuwait. In compliance with this resolution, the Council adopted Regulation 2340/90 EC, preventing trade by the Community with Iraq and Kuwait. In retaliation, the Iraqi government passed, with retroactive effect, Law No. 57 which froze all property and assets owed to the governments, undertakings, companies and banks of those States that had adopted the embargo. The result was that Dorsch Consult, which still had outstanding debts with the Iraqi authorities, was unable to recover the money owed to them. The applicants brought an action against the Community alleging that its loss was the result of the trade embargo, and, more specifically, the result of Council Regulation 2340/90 EC. In respect of the question of foreseeability, the CFI held that even if it were appropriate to see the adoption by the Council of Regulation 2340/90 EC as an 'arbitrary decision' taken by 'certain governments' within the meaning of Law No. 57, it was the applicant that bore the burden of proof for establishing a causal link between the act and the damage caused. The CFI considered that the applicants had failed to establish to the requisite legal standard that the adoption of Law No. 57 constituted, as a retaliatory measure, an objectively foreseeable consequence in the normal course of events of the adoption of Council Regulation 2340/90 EC, and, as such, the applicant was not entitled to recover damages.[228] This falls in line with the rationale that has dominated and justified the restrictions that the Court has placed on the recovery of damages against Community action: The Community institutions should be protected so that their ability to make difficult policy choices is not compromised. The Community is responsible for the creation, execution and implementation of a vast range of legislation, the effects of which are immeasurably broad. It is impossible for the Community institutions to be able to take into consideration every possible effect that a piece of legislation has, and it would be severely handicapped in its work if it was required to do so. The Court, drawing on a concept familiar to many Member States, affords protection to the institutions by ruling that the institutions will only be responsible for objectively foreseeable consequences which arise in the normal course of events from the adoption of a specific piece of legislation.

In applying the test in *Dorsch Consult*, the CFI first ruled that the adoption by the Iraqi government of a Rule freezing all assets and income from enemy country firms in retaliation to a UN embargo, and thereby making debts owed to the

227. Case T-184/95 *Dorsch Consult Ingenieurgesellschaft mbH v. Council of the European Union and Commission of the European Communities* [1998] ECR II-667.
228. Ibid., para. 72.

applicants irrecoverable, was not a foreseeable consequence of the adoption of Regulation 2340/90 EC which sought to implement the embargo. The Court then went further, reasoning that even if it were appropriate to consider that Law No. 57 was a foreseeable consequence of the adoption of Regulation No. 2340/90 EC, it was still by way of retaliation for the maintenance of the Community embargo that the Iraqi authorities were refusing to pay that applicant's claims. The Court considered that the alleged damage could not, in the final analysis, be attributed to Regulation 2340/90 EC, but must be attributed to United Nations Security Council Resolution No. 661 (1990), which imposed the embargo on trade with Iraq. This suggests that even if the adoption of the Iraqi Rule was foreseeable, the applicants could not have recovered damages as the chain of causation would have been broken because the Community had simply acted in pursuance of a direction under the United Nations Charter.[229]

It should be borne in mind, however, that in *Dorsch*, the claim was based on liability for a lawful act. It is unclear whether the Court would take the same view where the measure was adopted in breach of Community law. That having been said, the Court's reasoning is consistent with previous rulings of the Court establishing that Member States will not be responsible for damage caused to an individual where the national authorities merely implemented a Community measure and had no discretion.[230] The lack of discretion on the part of the Community in implementing the UN Resolution, by analogy, could not, therefore, be seen to break the chain of causation between the UN Resolution and the loss suffered by the applicant. While one may debate the wisdom of the Court's decision in respect of the absence of justice offered to the individual, the Court's approach, through its consistency, at least serves to uphold the principle of legal certainty.

8. DAMAGES

Once an applicant has satisfied the Court that all the conditions for liability exist, it is up to the Court to assess whether damages should be awarded, and, if so, how much the applicant should receive. In its evaluation, the Court will scrutinize whether the applicant has successfully proved the existence and extent of the damages claimed. The damages must be quantifiable in financial terms, since under Articles 235 and 288(2) EC the Court is only empowered to make a monetary award,[231] payable

229. Tridimas suggests that this might also extend to other international laws, *The General Principles of EC Law*, 3rd edn (Oxford: OUP, 2006), 496.
230. See in particular Case 133/79 *Sucrimex v. Commission* [1980] ECR 1299; and Case 175/84 *Krohn v. Commission* [1986] ECR 753.
231. A. Toth, 'The Concepts of Damages and Causality as Elements of Non-contractual Liability', in *The Action for Damages in Community Law*, eds T. Heukels and A. McDonnell (The Hague: Assert Institute, 1997), 27.

either in euros or in national currency.[232] In accordance with Article 19 of the Statute of the Court of Justice of the European Communities and Article 38(1)(c) of the Rules of Procedure of the Court of Justice, the application must contain, *inter alia*, the subject-matter of the dispute and a brief statement of the grounds on which the application is based.

8.1. Submitting a Claim

In order to meet the requirements set out in the Court's procedural rules, an application seeking compensation for damage caused by a Community institution must state the evidence from which the conduct alleged against the institution by the applicant may be identified, the reasons for which the applicant considers there to be a causal link between the conduct and the damage that he claims to have suffered, and the nature and extent of that damage.[233] Failure to submit sufficient details in the application will amount to an infringement of Article 19 of the Statute and Article 38(1)(c) of the Rules of Procedure of the Court of Justice and constitutes an absolute bar to proceeding with a case. The Court may consider at any time, and of its own motion, in accordance with Article 92(2) of the Rules of Procedure, whether an application contains sufficient information for it to proceed with the claim.[234] A general claim for unspecified damages will not, under normal circumstances, be sufficiently concrete for an application to be valid and the claim is therefore liable to be dismissed as inadmissible.[235] This rule is not, however, without exception. In *Granaria v. Council*, the applicant had merely stated that it had sustained pecuniary damage as a result of the Regulation in question, reserving its right to give details of the extent of the loss at a later stage. The ECJ held that, while ordinarily such an abridged form of application would be insufficient to comply with the rules of procedure, in the present case, the incomplete nature of the application did not necessarily render it inadmissible. The Court reasoned that when an action for damages is brought before the Court under Article 288 EC and the legal basis of the Community's liability is disputed, the desirability of making the procedure more economical can lead the Court to give a decision early in the proceedings on the question whether the conduct of the institutions has been such as to entail the liability of the Community, while reserving consideration of questions relating to causality, as well as those concerning the nature and extent of the damage, for a later stage.[236] The ability of an applicant to rely on this ruling is, however, limited. The admissibility of a claim which does not satisfy all of the

232. When converting the award into the applicant's national currency, the rate to be applied is that prevailing at the date of the judgment. Joined Cases 64 and 113/76, 167 and 239/78, 27, 28 and 47/79 *Dumortier Frères v. Council* [1979] ECR 3091, paras 8-13.
233. Case T-64/89 *Automec Srl v. Commission* [1990] ECR II-367, para. 73.
234. Case 3/66 *Alfieri v. Parliament* [1966] ECR 437, at 447.
235. Case 5/71 *Aktien-Zuckerfabrik Schöppenstedt v. Council* [1971] ECR 975, 984.
236. Case 90/78 *Granaria BV v. Council and Commission*, [1979] ECR 1081, paras 5-6.

Court's procedural rules is exceptional, and the Court has interpreted the margins governing when such a claim will be acceptable narrowly.

One example of where the Court did admit a claim brought on the basis of unspecified damages was in *Coldiretti*.[237] The applicants were a group of farmers claiming for damages as a result of a Decision adopted by the Community in an attempt to control the outbreak of BSE in the UK. The CFI admitted the applicants' claim for unspecified damages on the basis that, although the pleadings did not definitively quantify the damage suffered by each farmer, they nonetheless contained, in annexes to the application, detailed estimates of the losses allegedly sustained by the beef industry generally, and the criteria and parameters applied in arriving at those estimates. The Court recognized the difficulties encountered by the applicants in attempting to evaluate the loss correctly and quantify the damage suffered by each farmer, and acknowledged their request that the complex computation be carried out by a group of experts.

The CFI concluded that, although exact quantification of the damages had not been given, the information supplied by the applicants was sufficiently precise to identify the nature and character of the damage pleaded, and the approximate extent of the alleged damage. Consequently, the defendants were able to prepare their defence without any other information in support, and the Court was in a position to rule on the action, subject to the need arising for further details concerning the precise scope of the damage suffered by each of the applicants.[238] It appears, therefore, that provided that the applicants can demonstrate that the exact quantification of damages would require a complex computation of damages requiring experts; that they have gone to reasonable lengths to give an accurate approximation of the amount of damages claimed; that sufficient information is available so that the defendants to the action are not unreasonably hindered in making their defence; and the Court can still rule on the substance of the claim, then the application will be admissible.[239]

8.2. The Existence and Extent of the Damage

Proving the existence of damage is a question of admissibility. Where the applicant fails to show that the existence of the alleged damages is actual and sufficiently certain, in a form recognized as recoverable by the Court, the claim will be

237. Case T-149/96 *Confederazione Nazionale Coltivatori Diretti (Coldiretti) and 110 farmers v. Council of the European Union and Commission of the European Communities* [1998] ECR II-3841.
238. Ibid., paras 49-50.
239. See also Joined Cases 29, 31, 36, 39-47, 50 and 51/63 *SA des Laminoirs, Hauts Fourneaux, Forges, Fonderies et Usines de la Providence and Others v. High Authority* [1965] ECR 911, at 939, where the ECJ held that an 'exact assessment' of the damage sustained is needed, but an approximate determination based on sufficiently reliable facts, preferably collected by an expert, will suffice if it is not possible to make an exact assessment.

dismissed as inadmissible.[240] Conversely, the extent of the damage is a substantive question going to the merits of the case, which needs to be demonstrated once the Court is satisfied that a form of admissible damage exists.[241]

8.2.1. Sufficiently Certain: The Existence of Damage

The existence of recognizable damage may manifest itself in damages arising from a loss of profit, future loss of earnings or non-material damage. In respect to loss of profit, in *Kampffmeyer*,[242] which concerned a Commission Decision, the effect of which was to wrongfully impose levies on grain importers, the Court concluded that the applicants were entitled to recover compensation not only for the levy that had been wrongfully imposed on them, but also for lost profits in cases where importers had cancelled their import contracts as a result of the levy. The ECJ was only willing, however, to allow the applicants to recover damages to the extent that the applicant could show that he was legitimately entitled in all the circumstances to make the profit and that he was only prevented from doing so by an unlawful act of the Community. On the facts of the case, given the speculative nature of the applicants' purchases, the Court estimated their indemnification to be 10% of the amount that they would have paid in levies had they continued to perform the import contracts rather than cancelling them.

A further example arose in *CNTA*, which concerned the withdrawal of compensatory amounts on exports of oil seed.[243] The Court ruled that, in fixing the level of compensation to be paid to exporters, consideration needed to be had for the fact that the maintenance of the compensatory amounts was not guaranteed and that the applicants could not legitimately expect to recover the full amount of profits that would have accrued from the contracts. The protection afforded to the applicants by Article 288(2) EC extended to the exporters in so far as their legitimate expectations required that they not suffer loss by reason of the withdrawal of the compensatory amounts. It was therefore only the loss flowing directly from the Community act – in this case the withdrawal of the compensatory amounts – and not the total sum of projected profits that could be recovered by the applicant. The applicants were therefore not entitled to recover the profits that it would have made had the disputed action of the Commission not occurred.

In respect of claims for future damages, the ECJ's original position was to reject them as inadmissible.[244] The Court altered its stance in relation to

240. Joined Cases 19-20, 25 and 30/69 *Richez-Parise a.o. v. Commission* [1970] ECR 325 para. 31; Case T-285/03 *Agraz and Others v. Commission* [2005] ECR II-1063, paras 70-78.
241. Case 51-81 *De Franceschi* [1982] ECR 117, para. 9; Joined Cases 256, 257, 265, 267/80, 5 and 51/81 and 282/82 *Birra Wührer SpA and others v. Council and Commission* [1984] ECR 3693, para. 9; Case T-478/93 *Wafer Zoo* [1995] ECR II-1479, para. 49. See also H.G. Schermers & D.F. Waelbroeck, *Judicial Protection in the European Union*, 6th edn (The Hague: Kluwer International, 2001), 1126.
242. Joined Cases 5, 7, 13-24/66 *Kampffmeyer and others v. Commission* [1967] ECR 317.
243. Case 74/74 *CNTA v. Commission* [1975] ECR 533, paras 45-47.
244. Joined Cases 9 and 25/64 *FERAM a.o. v. High Authority* [1965] ECR 311, at 320-321.

Article 288(2) EC, however, when it held in *Kampffmeyer* that Article 235 EC does not prevent the Court from declaring the Community liable for imminent damage, provided that such damage is foreseeable with sufficient certainty. This is the case even where the damage claimed cannot be precisely quantified.[245] The ECJ's reasoned firstly, that it may be necessary to admit such a claim where to do so would prevent even greater damage, and secondly, that the majority of the Member States of the Community recognized a declaration of liability for future damages that are sufficiently certain. The Court will not allow a claim for future damages, however, where the damage 'appears to be possible' or 'might ensue in the future.' Such a claim will be too doubtful and insufficiently precise.[246]

The Court has not only been willing to grant compensation for financial loss, but also for non-material losses. In *Algera*, the Court awarded Miss Algera, a Community employee whose appointment had been wrongfully withdrawn, 100 EPU (European Payments Union) in respect to the upheaval and discomfort that the Community action had caused her.[247] In another staff case, Miss De Bruyn received equitable (*ex aequo et bono*) damages of BEF 40,000, for being dismissed without sufficient reason.[248] The Court has also been willing to accept a claim in damages as a result of damage caused to the applicant's reputation;[249] damage caused by a five-year delay in handling a request for recognition of a professional illness;[250] and erroneous exclusion from an internal competition.[251] In many cases, however, the Court has simply ruled that the annulment of the contested decision sufficiently repaired any injury to the applicant and therefore did not grant damages.[252]

8.3. Quantifying Damages: The Extent of the Loss

The underlying principle in quantifying an award of compensation is to put the applicant in, or as close to, the position that he would have been in, had the unlawful act not been adopted.[253] The quantum of the damage is therefore determined by comparing the actual assets of the person concerned with his notional assets in the event that he had not been affected by the wrongful act.[254]

245. Joined Cases 5, 7, 13-24/66 *Kampffmeyer and others v. Commission* [1967] ECR 317, paras 6-8.
246. Case 147/83 *Münchener Import-Weinkellerei Herold Binderer GmbH v. Commission of the European Communities* [1985] ECR 257, paras 19-20.
247. Joined Cases 7/56, 3-7/57 *Dineke Algera a.o. v. Common Assembly* [1957-58] ECR 39.
248. Case 25/60 *De Bruyn v. Common Assembly* [1962] ECR 39.
249. Case T-231/97 *New Europe Consulting and Brown v. Commission* [1999] ECR II-2403.
250. Case T-165/89 *Plug v. Commission* [1992] ECR II-367.
251. Case T-84/91 *Meskens v. Parliament* [1992] ECR 2335.
252. *See*, Joined Cases 59/80 and 129/80 *Mariette Turner, née Krecké, v. Commission of the European Communities* [1981] ECR 1883, paras 73-74.
253. Case 238/78 *Ireks-Arkady GmbH v. Council and Commission* [1979] ECR 2955, para. 5, at 2999.
254. K. Lenaerts, D. Arts & I. Maselis, *Procedural Law of the European Union*, 2nd edn (Sweet & Maxwell, London, 2006), 11-48.

Determining what amounts to adequate reparation to put the applicant in a position he would have been in, but for the wrongful act, is not always straight forward, and cannot always be done immediately by the Court. Where the applicant has successfully made a plea for unspecified damages, or for future loss of profits, the Court's common practice is to require the parties to come to an agreement as to an appropriate award of damages. Where the parties are incapable of reaching agreement, the Court will step in to fix the amount of the award.[255] The Court will only fix the amount, however, where it has sufficient information to do so. If the parties have failed to reach an agreement, and the applicant has failed to adduce sufficiently precise evidence to prove the extent of the loss, the Court will not award damages, but dismiss the application.[256]

When called upon to fix the amount of an award, the Court will take into consideration both the acts of the applicant and commercial practices. An award may therefore be altered to take account of interest to be awarded on the sum, and whether the sum should be reduced to take account of any losses that the applicant has passed on to consumers.

Where an applicant has wrongfully been obliged to pay a levy, and he has, or could have, increased prices to customers so as to offset the amount charged on the goods, his losses will have been 'passed on', and he will not be entitled to an award of damages.[257] The price increase takes the place of the compensation. As Lenaerts, Arts and Maselis observe, there appears from the Court's ruling, to be an obligation on the prudent vendor to pass on the loss brought about by an unlawful act of a public authority in his or her selling prices if market conditions so allow.[258] This is clearly in line with the national rules on mitigation of loss, and the Court's rulings on reduced liability in the context of causation, due to acts on the part of the applicant. As with causation, the burden lies on the institution to prove that the applicant has, or could have, passed the loss on to consumers.[259]

Default interest, constituting a legal evaluation and determination of the loss suffered by reason of the delay in complying with an obligation, is calculated from the date of judgment, and not from the date on which the damage was caused.[260] The principle behind this is that the extent of the damage is only determined on the date of the judgment. As such, the Court has already taken all claims in interest, up to that date, into consideration.[261] Interest is only due, therefore, for the period between the date of judgment by the Court and the date on which the compensation

255. See for example Case 74/74 *CNTA v. Commission* [1975] ECR 533, para. 47.
256. Ibid.
257. Case 238/78 *Ireks-Arkady GmbH v. Council and Commission* [1979] ECR 2955, para. 14; See further C. Rudden & W. Bishop, 'Gritz and Quellmehl: Pass It On', *ELRev.* 6 (1981): 243.
258. K. Lenaerts, D. Arts & I. Maselis, *Procedural Law of the European Union*, 2nd edn (London: Sweet & Maxwell, 2006), 11-50.
259. H.G. Schermers & D.F. Waelbroeck, *Judicial Protection in the European Union*, 6th edn (The Hague: Kluwer International, 2001), 1131.
260. Case 27/59 and 39/59 *Alberto Campolongo v. High Authority of the European Coal and Steel Community* [1960] ECR 795, paras 19-21.
261. Joined Cases 64 and 113/76, 167 and 239/78, 27, 28 and 47/79 *Dumortier Frères v. Council* [1979] ECR 3091, para. 11.

is transferred to the applicant. This is so without the applicant needing to prove actual loss or damage. Default interest rates are set by the Court so as to reflect approximately the current interest rates on the market.

8.4. Recovering Costs

The Court ordinarily awards a successful party expenses incurred in respect of bringing an action. Article 91(b) of the *Rules of Procedure* provides, however, that a successful party is only entitled to 'expenses necessarily incurred by the parties for the purposes of the proceedings, in particular the travel and subsistence expenses and the remuneration of agents, advisers or lawyers'. The CFI has ruled that Article 91(b) only provides for the recovery of costs incurred firstly, for the purposes of proceedings before the Court of First Instance and, secondly, to those necessary for those purposes.[262] Further, the Court of First Instance has held that even though, as a rule, substantial legal work is carried out in the course of the proceedings prior to the judicial phase, by 'proceedings' Article 91 of the *Rules of Procedure* refers only to proceedings before the Court of First Instance, to the exclusion of any prior stage.[263] As such, in its ruling in *Internationaler Hilfsfonds v. Commission*, the Court established that, while lawyers' fees can ordinarily be regarded as 'expenses', this is not the case when such fees are incurred in proceedings before the Ombudsman, because these are not expenses incurred in proceedings before the CFI and because a party has the option of applying to the Ombudsman without using a lawyer.[264] Similarly, in its order in *Ehcon v. Commission*, the Court held that the applicant had not managed to establish the existence of a direct causal relationship between the alleged costs incurred before the Ombudsman and the alleged illegalities, and that a citizen's free choice to refer a matter to the Ombudsman cannot appear to be the direct and necessary consequence of cases of improper administration which may be attributable to Community institutions or bodies.[265]

9. Conclusion

An applicant who wishes to embark upon an action to recover damages from the Community is advised to tread lightly. The journey is long and perilous, and there is little chance of success.

This chapter started from the premise that Article 288(2) EC worked together with the other judicial protection provisions under the Treaty, but that its aim was somewhat different. While Articles 230, 232 and 234 EC all seek to protect the

262. Case T-80/97 DEP *Starway v. Council* [2002] ECR II-1, para. 24.
263. Case T-38/95 DEP *Groupe Origny v. Commission* [2002] ECR II-217, para. 29.
264. Case T-294/04 *Inernationale Hilfsfonds v. Commission* [2005] ECR II-2719, para. 52.
265. Case T-140/04 *Adviesbureau Ehcon BV v. Commission of the European Communities* [2005] ECR II-3287.

individual by ensuring the effective running of the Community in accordance with the rule of law, Article 288(2) EC is more individual focused. It seeks to protect individuals from financial hardship suffered as a result of illegal Community action. In *Schöppenstedt*, by declaring Article 288(2) EC to be an independent form of action, the Court expressly acknowledged the importance of the right of individuals to be able to claim compensation from the Community. How then can the Court, on the one hand, proclaim the importance of Article 288(2) EC and yet, at the same time, deny effective protection to individuals by placing so many obstacles in the way of applicants seeking relief?

The issue is one of balance. At what point does the need to ensure justice for the individual outweigh the overarching need for certainty and institutional effectiveness? This is more a value judgment than it is a legal one and the answer reveals a great deal about the social underpinnings of the Community. Yet, a legal system only works where it reflects the values that it seeks to protect. The sometimes contradictory evolution of the case law belies the struggle of the ECJ and the CFI to marry the law with the principle and develop a set of rules which weigh the needs and interests of the citizen against the population.

From its earliest case law and the development of the administrative/legislative distinction, the Court has wrestled with different tests and techniques for striking a balance. While the distinction often seemed somewhat arbitrary, the underlying principle rings true: The right of the individual is more likely to outweigh the needs of society where the measure affects only a limited number of people. It follows, therefore, that the threshold of breach need not be as high where the measure is only of limited effect. The test was flawed only to the extent that it was based on the presumption that the limited effect of a measure would always justify the application of a lower threshold.

As it became apparent that the scope of a measure was not always determinative of whether or not the right of an individual to compensation outweighed the need for institutional efficiency, a new test was required. *Bergaderm* saw the Court shift its focus from formalistic distinctions to a more nuanced, graded test. It was institutional discretion that became important. The extent of breach that was necessary to claim compensation became directly proportionate to the amount of discretion enjoyed by the institution. By removing the legislative/administrative distinction, the Court recognized that the Community administration may enjoy ample discretion and may be required to make choices that are equally difficult, complex and sensitive to those of the legislature, and that its liability should be governed by the same conditions.

Although the ECJ's decision to abandon the artificial administrative/legislative distinction was generally well received, certain pockets of resistance, most notably the CFI, continued to prefer the pre-*Bergaderm* approach. A spate of judgments saw the CFI continue to apply the pre-*Bergaderm* distinction, despite explicit rulings from the ECJ that the outcome of cases could no longer be determined by whether or not the case dealt with an administrative or legislative measure. Only a judicial scolding from the ECJ in its judgment in *CEVA* seemed, at least temporarily, to put an end to the mounting confusion.

As is a feature of this area of law, the newfound clarity of approach, so impeccably displayed in *Holcim*, was short-lived. The CFI's recent rulings in *Abad Pérez* and *É.R. and Others* saw the CFI shift the test for liability away from breach and towards the test of causation. In a bold move, which, firstly, reduces the possibility of appeal to the ECJ, and secondly avoids (at least where there is no causal link) the need to address the complicated issue of breach, the CFI altered the dynamic of the liability test. The Court in effect now works in hypotheticals, where it rules that even if there is a breach – which is still to be proved – the applicant still would not succeed on the basis of causation.

It is yet to be seen whether the CFI's new approach means the end of the *Bergaderm* test, and with it the balance between individual protection and institutional efficiency which it embodied. The waters have been considerably muddied by the CFI's ruling in *Schneider II* where it returned to the *Bergaderm* approach. Does this signal a return to prominence for the criterion of breach and emphasis on discretion, or is the CFI seeking to adopt a different approach for competition cases opposed to all other matters? The answers to these questions are being awaited with interest.

In light of the number of potentially meritorious claims for damages that have been made under Article 288(2) EC, and the small number of cases in which applicants have succeeded, one may be led to conclude that the Court is, in effect, only paying lip service to its commitment to individual protection. A right cannot properly be called a right, and cannot, therefore, protect an individual, unless it is capable of being enforced. The right to compensation, and the individual protection that such a right provides, cannot be effective where the bar for success is set so high that even meritorious claims are doomed to fail. Where this is the case, the principle of institutional effectiveness no longer acts as a counter-balance but as a trump card to be played whenever the institutions are about to lose a hand.

It should be remembered, however, that it is much easier to destroy than to create. While it is the occupation of academics to critique (and often criticize) the work and ideas of others, and while there is much for which the European Courts can be criticized in relation to Article 288(2) EC, sight must never be lost of the enormity of the task facing the Court and the stoic way in which the judges of both the ECJ and the CFI approach their duty.

Chapter 4
Article 288(2) EC: The Appropriate Forum and Concurrent Liability

INTRODUCTION

The question of appropriate forum is one of the most important and most difficult criteria to analyze and apply in respect of admissibility of damages claims under Article 288(2) EC. The Court's case law in this area has become both complicated and somewhat contradictory, and numerous potentially meritorious claims have failed as a result of their being brought before the wrong court. The difficulty stems from the exclusive jurisdiction clauses found in Articles 235 and 240 EC. Article 235 EC confers exclusive jurisdiction on the Court of Justice (and now the Court of First Instance (CFI)) to hear cases falling within the ambit of Article 288(2) EC. Article 240 EC meanwhile asserts that

> [s]ave where jurisdiction is conferred on the Court of Justice by this Treaty, disputes to which the Community is a part shall not on that ground be excluded from the jurisdiction of the courts or tribunals of the Member States.

In theory, therefore, there exists a bright dividing line between situations which must be brought before the CFI – an admissible action under Article 288(2) EC – and those which must be brought before the national courts – any situation where exclusive jurisdiction has not been conferred on the Court of Justice. In reality, however, the situation is sadly not so straightforward. Complications arise when the above articles are read in conjunction with the wording of Article 288(2) EC. It is clear that the principle underlying non-contractual liability is that the financial loss must be made good by the authority that caused the loss through its unlawful action. Accordingly, the Community must make good financial losses caused by its institutions or its servants, while the Member State will be liable for any financial loss caused by national authorities. The Community institutions, for the most part, concern themselves with taking policy decisions and promulgating legal acts. The actual implementation of those policies, however, is often left to the agencies of the national governments acting on behalf of the Community.[1] The citizen often deals with a national authority, and it is as a direct result of this action that he or she suffers injury. This situation arises most commonly in the context of the Common Agricultural Policy (CAP), where individuals are often required to pay levies to the Community, or are entitled to receive Community subsidies. In such cases there exist two acts: the promulgation of the legal act by the Community institution, the rule determining whether a levy or a subsidy is due; and the implementation of that act by the national authority, the actual payment of a subsidy or the collection of a levy. Claimants may therefore be left wondering whether to bring an action against the Community institution or the national authority.

It is important to stress that when such a situation as that outlined above arises, the effect of the exclusive jurisdiction clause in Article 235 EC, when read together with Article 240 EC, is that it is not possible to bring a joint action against both the Community institutions and the national authorities. The CFI only has jurisdiction to decide on the liability of the Community institution, and the national courts may only determine the extent of liability on the part of the national institutions. Against whom, for which act, and where, therefore can an applicant bring an action? Can an applicant go directly to the CFI and seek Community damages against a Community institution under Article 288(2) EC, or must he or she first challenge the implementing act of the national authority under national law, before the national courts?

In an attempt to avoid the difficulties posed by concurrent liability, a claimant could attempt an indirect challenge for compensation from the Community institutions by first bringing an action under either Article 230 EC, which allows an individual to challenge the legality of a measure enacted by the Community, or under Article 232 EC, where an individual can challenge the Community's failure to act when it was under a duty to do so. Where the applicant alleges that he or she was wrongfully made to pay a sum of money to the Commission, he or she could apply directly to the Commission and request that it repay the money. If the Commission refuses to repay the money, then this refusal can be challenged under Article 230 EC. The applicant would be the addressee of the decision not to repay the money, and would therefore have standing under Article 230(4) EC. If the Commission fails to respond to the applicant's request, then action may be brought under Article 232 EC for the Commission's failure to act. In both instances, the Court of Justice will have to decide the validity of the Community measure, and whether the applicant has the right to be reimbursed.

Alternatively, where the Community has, by regulation, instructed the national authority to collect levies or distribute subsidies on the Community's behalf, then the measure will be directly applicable. The applicant may then

1. T.C. Hartley, 'Concurrent Liability in EEC Law: A Critical Review of the Cases', *ELRev.* 2 (1977): 249.

claim before the national court that the Regulation is in some way unlawful, and that the money has either been wrongfully collected, or wrongfully withheld.[2] The national court will then make a preliminary reference under Article 234 EC, questioning the validity of the Community measure. The result is that the applicant may indirectly challenge the Community measure, and seek a remedy against the national authority – to be decided by the national court – in accordance with the ruling of the European Court of Justice (ECJ). While an action before the national courts, coupled with a preliminary reference, may be the surest way of securing the admissibility of a claim, it may not be the most attractive route for an applicant. The applicant may be required to go through a long and expensive series of appeals before a reference is finally made. The time and expense will then only increase once the reference is received in Luxembourg, and then sent back to the national court for a final ruling.[3] A direct action, if brought correctly, may save both time and money for an applicant.

An analysis of the case law reveals that, as Oliver correctly identifies, the questions of before which court and against whom the applicant must bring his or her action are to be distinguished from the issue of who bears ultimate responsibility.[4] From its earliest case law, the Court of Justice has sought to limit the scope for bringing actions under Article 288(2) EC in the instance of concurrent liability by requiring the applicants first to commence proceedings before the national courts. As the doctrine has evolved, the case law of the Court of Justice has developed – sometimes inconsistently – to the point where certain claims under Article 288(2) EC will be admissible immediately, without recourse first having been had to national remedies, while others are only admissible once all other avenues have been exhausted. Before turning to examine the situations in which an applicant may or may not be required to exhaust all national remedies before bringing a claim, it is first necessary to outline the development of the doctrine of the exhaustion of national remedies, and thereby set the Court's reasoning in context.

1. THE EXHAUSTION OF NATIONAL REMEDIES

The evolution of case law regarding situations of concurrent liability has been based on the principle of exhaustion of national remedies. In its purest form, the exhaustion of national remedies rule requires that those who have suffered injury as a result of Community action first seek redress against national authorities before the national courts. It is only once this prerequisite has been complied with that the applicant may then bring proceedings under Article 288(2) EC. In the event that an

2. C. Harding, 'The Choice of Court Problem in Cases of Non-contractual Liability under EEC Law', *CMLRev.* 16 (1979): 389.
3. Ibid., at 391.
4. P. Oliver, 'Joint Liability of the Community and the Member States', in *The Action for Damages in Community Law*, eds T Heukels and A McDonnell (The Hague: Asser Institute, 1997), 285.

applicant fails to comply with the exhaustion rule, the CFI will declare an action under Article 288(2) EC as inadmissible. During the forty-year period over which the doctrine has developed, a lot of case law has been generated in an attempt to establish under which circumstances an applicant will have to first bring a national claim before being able to directly challenge the actions of the Community. With this in mind, the following paragraphs seek to outline the principal cases defining the scope of the exhaustion rule, before addressing the various circumstances in which those rules have since been applied.

The issue of concurrent liability and the development of the exhaustion rule first came before the European Court in 1967 in the *Kampffmeyer* case.[5] The case concerned a series of applicants, all of whom were grain dealers in Germany, who wanted to import maize from France. At the time, the relevant provisions of Community law specified that the applicants required import permits from the German Government in order to import maize. The permits were always to be granted, except in the case of special circumstances, in which case the national authorities needed to seek the consent of the Commission before refusing the import license. At the time, the importation of maize carried with it a levy, the rate of which was subject to fluctuation. The applicants applied for the import permits when the levy rate was zero, but the German authorities refused to grant the permits. The Commission consented to the refusal, and the ban was only lifted once the levy rate had been raised. The dealers were therefore required to make new applications for permits, and were required to pay a levy that they would not otherwise have been obliged to pay.

The Court of Justice had already annulled the Commission's decision permitting the German authorities to refuse to grant the import permits in the earlier case of *Toepfer*.[6] The applicants in *Kampffmeyer* sought to rely on the *Toepfer* ruling to bring a claim for compensation for the damages that they had suffered as a result of the refusal to grant import permits. In regard to the wrongful nature of the Commission's decision to allow the German authorities to refuse the permit applications, the Court ruled that

> [a]s it was aware of the existence of applications for licences, [the Commission] caused damage to the interests of importers who had acted in reliance on the information provided in accordance with Community rules. The Commission's conduct constituted a wrongful act or omission capable of giving rise to liability on the part of the Community. In trying to justify itself by the assertion that in view of the economic data at its disposal . . . a threat of serious disturbance was not to be excluded and that consequently its mistaken evaluation of the said data is excusable, the defendant misjudges the nature of the wrongful act or omission attributed to it, which is not founded on a mistaken evaluation

5. Judgments in Joined Cases 5, 7 and 13-24/66 *Kampffmeyer and Others v. Commission* [1967] ECR 245.
6. Joined Cases 106 and 107/63 *Alfred Toepfer and Getreide-Import Gesellschaft v Commission of the EEC* [1965] ECR 405.

> of the facts but in its general conduct.... The Commission's assertion that supervisory organisations cannot, under a general principle common to the laws of the Member States, be made liable, except in the case of gross malfeasance is equally irrelevant.[7]

After having established that the Community was, in principle, liable, the Court concluded that the loss suffered by the applicants fell into two categories: After the ban on imports was lifted, certain of the applicants continued to import the grain that they had bought, and subsequently pay the import levies. The other applicants, however, had cancelled their grain orders, and subsequently not imported the grain. The first group of applicants suffered loss equal to the levy paid, while the second group sought damages for the cancellation fees and the loss of profits suffered.

As regards the first group, the evidence put before the Court illustrated that the decision of the national authorities refusing to grant the permits was contrary to German law, and had been annulled by the national courts. Based on this, the ECJ ruled that

> [d]uring the oral procedure, the existence in the present case of the right to repayment was put in doubt by the applicants. The Court cannot, however... accept the conclusive nature of the alleged damage. It is proper, therefore, to ask the applicants concerned to prove that they have exhausted all methods of recourse both administrative and judicial under the relevant national law to obtain reimbursement of the sums improperly paid by way of levy. Only after production of such evidence would there be reason to consider whether any injury exists which the Community should make good.[8]

In a situation of concurrent liability, therefore, where the applicant had the possibility of a restitutionary claim against the national authorities, it must first exhaust that right under national law before seeking damages for non-contractual liability against the Community under Article 288(2) EC. Such proceedings had, in fact, already been instituted in the *Kampffmeyer* case. The national court had, however, stayed the national proceedings to await the outcome of the Community proceedings. In the same way, the Court of Justice decided to stay the Community proceedings in order to await a decision from the national court. As Hartley argues, the implicit effect of the Court's ruling was to establish that the German authorities were primarily responsible for the injury caused, while the Community institution remained only secondarily liable. The justification for this seems to be that under the provisions applicable at the time, such levies were not handed to the Community. If there was a right under national law to reclaim the levy therefore, it was not unreasonable to reclaim it from the national authorities, as it was they who were unjustly enriched. The Court could, however, have continued to award damages on the basis that it had already declared the Community act to be invalid, and then left it to the Commission to recover the money from the national government.

---

7. Joined Cases 5, 7 and 13-24/66 *Kampffmeyer and Others v. Commission* [1967] ECR 245, 263.
8. Ibid., 263-264.

As regards the second group of claimants claiming loss of profits and the cost of penalty fees on the contracts that they repudiated, the Court acknowledged that they had indeed suffered injury that could be claimed against the Community under Article 288(2). The ECJ went on to conclude, however, that

> [i]t is necessary to avoid the applicants being insufficiently or excessively compensated for the same damage by the different assessment of two different courts applying different rules of law. Before determining the damage for which the Community should be held liable, it is necessary for the national court to have the opportunity to give judgment on any liability on the part of the Federal Republic of Germany. This being the case, final judgment cannot be given before the applicants have produced the decision of the national court on this matter.[9]

While some justification may have existed for denying the restitutionary claim of the first group of applicants, the second group of applicants was claiming damages under tort law, falling squarely within the ambit of Article 288(2) EC. On a national level, the German court had stayed the proceedings to allow the Court of Justice to pass judgment, and the Court of Justice succeeded only in putting the ball back in the hands of the national court. While it is right that the applicants should be correctly compensated, given the fact that the national court had already stayed the proceedings before it, specifically so as to take into account any possible damages awarded by the Court of Justice, there was no risk of the applicants being incorrectly compensated. The effect of the ruling seemed to be, however, that no matter whether an applicant was claiming for damages in restitution or tort, where there was a possible claim against a national authority, the applicants had to first bring a claim before the national courts before an action under Article 288(2) EC would be admitted by the Court of Justice.

Five years passed before the ECJ could revisit its ruling in *Kampffmeyer*. The opportunity came when the importation of a consignment of wine from Greece by the Belgian firm Haegeman attracted a 'countervailing duty'.[10] The levy had been imposed under a Community regulation which the applicant firm then proceeded to challenge on the basis that it was contrary to the Accession Agreement between Greece and the Community. As in the *Kampffmeyer* case, the levy was collected on behalf of the Community by the Belgian authorities. The situation in *Haegeman* was distinguishable, however, on the basis that in the interim period between the judgment in *Kampffmeyer* and the action brought by Haegeman, the Council, by decision, had replaced contributions made by Member States with the Community's own resources. Thus, the payments in *Haegeman* went into the Community treasury, rather than being paid into national funds, as had been the case in *Kampffmeyer*. As such, the Court's justification for requiring that the first group of applicants in *Kampffmeyer* exhaust national remedies – on the basis that the Member

9. Ibid., 266.
10. Case 96/71 *R & V Haegeman v. Commission* [1972] ECR 1005.

State had been unjustly enriched, and was therefore primarily responsible – no longer applied. The Court was not, however, to be convinced:

> [T]he Community's own resources shall be collected by Member States on behalf of the Community 'in accordance with national provisions imposed by law, regulation or administrative action' and made available to the Commission . . . the establishment of these resources and the control of their collection is primarily the responsibility of the competent departments or agencies of the Member States. Disputes concerning the levying on individuals of the charges as levies . . . must be resolved, applying Community law, by the national authorities and following the practices laid down by the law of the Member States . . . It is therefore for the competent national authorities to rule on claims for the refund of that charge. The applicant's claim for a refund should therefore have been made to those authorities . . . Accordingly, at the present stage the claim for compensation for possible damage must be dismissed.[11]

The ambiguous concluding sentence of the judgment appears to be inviting the applicants to resubmit an application for tort damages once they have brought a claim under national law. With this ruling, the Court of Justice seems to be inexplicably increasing the risk of the applicants not being entitled to claim. While the limitation period for a claim under Article 288(2) EC is generously set at five years, this time could easily run out during the course of the proceedings before the national courts. As has been seen above, while Article 46 of the *Statute of the Court of Justice* provides for the limitation period to be interrupted by bringing a claim before the European Courts, there is no such interruption when proceedings are commenced in national courts. Therefore, even where the applicants successfully battle their way through the national courts, their claim against the Community may still be inadmissible on the grounds that the claim has been time-barred. This point has, however, since been addressed by the CFI, which concluded that the limitation period applicable to the action could begin to run only when the national courts had ascertained the existence of a patent infringement.[12]

While one would have thought the Court's ruling in *Kampffmeyer* was strict enough, as Hartley correctly acknowledges,[13] the Court's ruling in *Haegeman* is even more restrictive. The result of the *Haegeman* ruling is that the Community will not be liable to repay money which has been levied unlawfully on the basis of a Community measure, even where this money has been paid into the Community treasury rather than national funds. Furthermore, even where the applicant seeks damages in tort against the Community, such an action will not be admissible until the national courts have ruled on the legality of the acts undertaken by the national

11. Ibid., paras 5-17.
12. Case T-295/05 *Document Security Systems, Inc. v. European Central Bank* (ECB) [2007] ECR II-2835.
13. T.C. Hartley, 'Concurrent Liability in EEC Law: A Critical Review of the Cases', ELRev. 2 (1977): 255.

authority. At least in *Kampffmeyer*, the Court was willing to acknowledge, in principle at least, that the Community was partly liable.

The Court finally appeared to acknowledge the risk to applicants that they may suffer a denial of justice in concurrent liability cases when it handed down its judgment in *Merkur*.[14] The case was one of many such cases concerning Monetary Compensatory Amounts (MCAs), which constituted payments made to individuals by the Community in an attempt to minimize the effects of fluctuating currencies. In the case that a Member State's currency was strong, MCAs would be granted on exports of certain agricultural products, while levies would be charged on imports of the same products. Payments were made by, and to, national governments, as prescribed under the general provisions of Council Regulation 974/71 EEC. Originally, no provision was made for barley products. This omission was, however, subsequently rectified by Council Regulation 1687/71 EEC, which came into force three months after the MCA system was set in motion. Merkur, a German barley producer, claimed that he was entitled to payments of MCAs on his exports for the three-month period prior to the implementation of Regulation 1687/71 EEC. After the German authorities who were responsible for administering the MCAs refused to make the payments, Merkur brought proceedings against the Commission under Article 288(2) EC.

In its arguments before the Court, the Commission submitted, on the basis of *Haegeman*, that Merkur's claim was inadmissible, for he had failed to bring a claim against the national authorities before the German courts, and as such, had not exhausted all national remedies. The Commission argued that the applicant must bring an action before the national court, which could then refer a question to the ECJ under Article 234 EC. The Court rejected the Commission's reasoning, and instead held the claim to be admissible on the basis that

> [t]he Court already has the case before it and within its jurisdiction, and is therefore bound to see whether or not these regulations are tainted with the alleged irregularities. It would not be in keeping with the proper administration of justice and the requirements of procedural efficiency to compel the applicant to have recourse to national remedies and thus to wait for a considerable length of time before a final decision on his claim is made.[15]

The Court, therefore, takes a different approach to that previously seen, choosing to decide the issue of admissibility on the grounds of procedural efficiency and the proper administration of justice. While this was certainly welcome news for applicants, as it seemed to signal a slight opening by the Court of the scope for seeking damages against the Community, it left many questions unanswered, particularly as regards the status of the *Haegeman* ruling. Did the Court's decision signal an implicit rejection of the ruling in *Haegeman*, or was the Court simply following the forceful Opinion of Advocate General Mayras in his rejection of the Commission's argument in the case?

---

14. Case 43/72 *Merkur Außenhandel-GmbH & Co. KG v. Commission* [1973] ECR 1055.
15. Ibid., para. 6.

History shows that it appears to be the latter. In 1975, the Court gave a ruling that left no doubt that the *Haegeman* ruling was still good law, and it continued to play an important role in the context of concurrent liability. The case of *Grands Moulins*[16] saw an application from a company in Guadeloupe, a French overseas department, which claimed to be entitled to a series of grants, payments and export refunds from the Community. These payments were to be made by the French national authorities, which were in turn reimbursed by the Community out of the European Agricultural Guidance and Guarantee Fund (EAGGF). While the Community Regulations provided that the overseas departments were entitled to the grants, the Agricultural Fund did not provide for the reimbursement of Member States when making grants to overseas departments. The French authorities, therefore, refused to make the grant to the applicants, who in turn commenced proceedings against the Commission, claiming that the Commission's refusal to refund the French Government was the cause of the national authority's refusal to make the payments.

As Hartley argues,[17] the logical conclusion of the Court would have been to accept that the Commission's refusal to agree to reimburse the French Government was a breach of Community law, but then to dismiss the case on the substantive basis that it lacked causation. While one can envisage that the Commission's action was a principal reason for the French authority's refusal to grant the payments, one cannot say that it directly caused, in a legal sense, the national authorities to act in the manner in which they did. The Court, however, chose to dismiss the case on the grounds of admissibility, holding that

> [i]ts application is in fact for payment by the Community instead of by the competent authority of the State in question of the sums which it claims are payable to it under Community law. The provisions of Community law... leave no doubt that payment or refusal of payment are measures appropriate to the national authorities. It is thus for the national courts having jurisdiction in the matter to give a ruling on the legality of such measures, in pursuance of Community law, within the forms laid down by national law, following recourse, where necessary, to Article 177 [now Article 234 EC] of the Treaty.[18]

The fact that the Court dismissed the case on the grounds of admissibility, due to the applicant not having first brought a claim before the national courts, rather than on the substantive merits of the case, suggests the return to prominence of the *Haegeman* doctrine. This line of reasoning was then confirmed by

16. Case 99/74 *Société des grands moulins des Antilles v. Commission* [1975] ECR 1531.
17. T.C. Hartley, 'Concurrent Liability in EEC Law: A Critical Review of the Cases', *ELRev.* 2 (1977): 258.
18. Case 99/74 *Société des grands moulins des Antilles v. Commission* [1975] ECR 1531, paras 21-23.

the Court in its subsequent rulings in *IBC*[19] and *Cotelle*.[20] As in *Merkur*, the cases stemmed from the Community's introduction of MCAs in the field of agriculture. In *IBC*, the Court was faced with an application from an Italian company engaged in importing meat products from outside the Community. Due to the depreciation of the Italian Lira, MCAs were granted on imports into Italy, and in the case of imports coming from outside the Community, were deducted from the relevant import duties. While payments were still to be made by the national authorities, the introduction of Council Regulation 2746/72 EEC provided that the payments be financed out of the EAGGF. The Commission then passed a regulation reducing the level of payments. IBC claimed that the amount of MCAs payable was too small, and that the Commission had acted wrongfully in reducing them. It subsequently brought proceedings against the Commission for the difference between the amount it had been paid and the correct amount which it felt was due.

The case is distinguishable from *Grands Moulins* on the basis that in *IBC*, the applicants were correct in their claim that it was the Commission's act which directly caused the national authorities to reduce the MCAs payable to the applicant. The Court, however, refused to hear the case, concluding that the application was inadmissible on the basis that the applicants had not brought a claim against the national authorities to annul the Decision to pay the MCAs at the lower rate. This decision stands in direct conflict with *Merkur*, where the applicant failed to get MCAs because the Commission had failed to provide for them in its regulation. It is hard to see why in *Merkur* the Court was willing to admit the case, while in *IBC* it dismissed it, when for the purposes of admissibility there is no material difference between a failure on the part of the Commission to provide MCAs and a decision taken by it to reduce the level of MCAs to be paid.

The Court took a similar approach in *Cotelle*, another case based on the granting of subsidies and the abolition of MCAs. In this case, the applicants fell into two groups: those whose level of subsidies had been fixed before the abolition of MCAs, and those whose subsidies were fixed after the abolition of the MCAs. With regard to the first group, their subsidies were sufficient when fixed, but were insufficient when paid, due to the abolition of the MCAs. In the case of the second group, however, their subsidies were insufficient when fixed. The Court held that the claim for damages under Article 288(2) EC was inadmissible as regards those applicants whose subsidies had been fixed after the abolition of the MCAs. The Court came to this conclusion on the basis that the applicants were capable of bringing a claim before the national courts to challenge the decision of the national authorities to fix the subsidies at an insufficient level. For the first group, however, the Court ruled that their

19. Case 46/75 *Importazione Bestiame Carni srl v. Commission* [1976] ECR 65.
20. Joined Cases 67-85/75 *Lesieur Cotelle et Associés SA and Others v. Commission* [1976] ECR 391.

claim for non-contractual liability of the Community was valid, as they would not have been in a position to bring proceedings before the national courts. Sadly, the ECJ failed to make it clear exactly why no remedy would be available under national law. The case, therefore, created an ambiguous situation as to the circumstances when an applicant may bring a claim directly before the European Courts in the case of concurrent liability, and where it will first be required to exhaust national remedies.

The Court finally addressed this ambiguity in 1984 in its ruling in *Unifrex*.[21] Once again, the situation developed out of the payment of MCAs under the CAP. Unifrex exported cereals to Italy, and account of the MCAs was taken when agreeing on the purchase price, which was to be paid in lira. On 23 March 1981, the Italian lira was devalued by 6%. Under Article 3 of Regulation No. 974/71 EEC, the Commission was required to adjust the rate of MCAs in line with the devaluation of the Italian currency. It failed to do this, however, and the MCA rate only changed with the enactment of a Council Regulation on 6 April 1981. The applicant, therefore, brought an action before the Court of Justice for the injury it suffered for the period between 23 March and 6 April 1981, claiming that damages to the extent of nearly 3 million French francs (FF) were attributable to the Commission's failure to adjust the rate applicable to the MCAs. The Commission submitted that the claim should be dismissed as inadmissible on the grounds that the applicant had failed to exhaust all national remedies, as it could have brought an action against the national authorities annulling their decision to apply the disputed MCAs to Unifrex, and had not done so. The Court rejected the Commission's argument, and declared the action admissible on the following basis:

> An established body of the case-law of the Court of Justice shows that the action for damages, pursuant to Article 178 [now Article 235 EC] and 215 [now Article 288 EC] of the Treaty, was set up as an independent action, having its own particular place in the system of means of redress and subject to conditions for its use formulated in the light of its specific purpose. It must nevertheless be viewed in the context of the entire system established by the Treaty for the judicial protection of the individual. Where an individual considers that he has been injured by the application of a Community legislative measure that he considers illegal, he may, when the implementation of the measure is left to the national authority, contest the validity of the measure, when it is implemented, before a national court in an action against the national authorities. That court may, or even must, as provided for in Article 177 [now Article 234 EC], refer the question of the validity of the Community measure in dispute to the Court of Justice. However, the existence of such a means of redress will be capable of ensuring the effective protection of the individuals concerned only if it may result in making good the alleged

21. Case 281/82 *Société à responsabilité limitée Unifrex v. Commission and Council* [1984] ECR 1969.

> damage. That is not so in this case. The applicant has shown, without being contradicted by the Commission, that proceedings for annulment in the national administrative courts could not, in this case, have effectively protected the applicant. Even if the disputed Community rules were declared invalid by a preliminary ruling of the Court given in the context of such proceedings and the national decision were annulled, that annulment could not have required the national authorities to pay higher monetary compensatory amounts to the applicant, without the prior intervention of the Community legislature.[22]

The effect of this ruling is, therefore, that admissibility under Articles 235 and 288(2) EC will be conditional on the prior exhaustion of national remedies, only to the extent that those national remedies give effective protection to the individuals concerned, and are capable of leading to compensation for the damage alleged.[23] Thus, the Court appeared to overrule its previous judgments in *Haegeman* with regard to the claim for additional damages and *IBC*, and clarified the possibility of an immediate direct action before the European Courts, as provided for in *Cotelle*. The result of the case was to create a situation where, under certain procedures, the Court will deem national law to vest the applicant with remedies that are sufficient to compensate the injuries suffered, and other procedures where this is not the case. It is only with regard to this first group of procedures that the applicant will be required to exhaust all national remedies before embarking upon a claim against the Community. In the case of the latter procedures, the Court of Justice (and now the CFI) has been willing to admit direct claims against the Community without requiring that an action first be brought against the national authorities. Recent case law seems to confirm this approach. The CFI relied expressly on the *Unifrex* ruling in the case of *Cantina sociale di Dolianova*[24] when it rejected the Commission's argument that the Court should not admit the case. The case concerned a number of Italian wine producers. In conformity with Regulation 2499/82 EEC, concerning preventive distillation of table wine, the producers entered into contracts with Distilleria Agricola Industriale di Terralba (DAI) for the delivery of its wine. DAI subsequently became insolvent, with the result that the applicants did not receive the Community aid to which they were, in principle, entitled under the Regulation. Initially, the applicants brought proceedings before their national courts to recover their losses. Those proceedings were unsuccessful. The applicants then sought compensation from the Commission on the basis that the Commission, in drafting the Regulation, failed to create a scheme guaranteeing payment of the Community aid in the event of the distiller's insolvency. In respect of the admissibility of the claim, the CFI found that in the legal context of the case, the national

22. Ibid., paras 11-12.
23. W. Wils, *Concurrent Liability of the Community and a Member State*, ELRev. 17 (1992): 191, 199.
24. Case T-166/98 *Cantina sociale di Dolianova and Others v. Commission* [2004] ECR II-3991.

court was not authorized to order the Italian authority responsible to pay the applicants the Community aid in question, unless Regulation No. 2499/82 EEC was rectified retrospectively, which, if this were to be done, would require the Commission to adopt a regulation. As such, the national court did not have the power to grant a remedy that would sufficiently protect the applicants' interests. The CFI therefore concluded that the applicants were entitled to bring a direct claim for damages against the Community institutions without first exhausting all national remedies. *Cantina sociale di Dolianova* was not, however, the final word in respect of exhaustion of remedies. The waters have once again been somewhat muddied by the CFI. In *Danzer v. Council*, the applicants brought an action aimed at obtaining compensation for the loss allegedly suffered because of penalties imposed on them by the competent Austrian authorities on the basis of national law implementing two directives coordinating company law provisions. The CFI concluded that the applicants were seeking to obtain, through their action for damages, the result that would be obtained if the decisions were annulled under Article 230 EC. The CFI therefore rejected the claim as inadmissible on the basis that Articles 230 EC and 288(2) EC are independent actions and serve different purposes within the judicial framework.[25] To hold the claim as admissible would have the effect of circumventing the procedure under Article 230 EC, and amount to an abuse of process.

While the Court could have ended its ruling at that point, it chose instead to continue, and shed some much needed light on how applicants should proceed in similar situations. The CFI held that, in the system of legal remedies provided for by the Treaty, the appropriate legal remedy would have been to request that the national court annul the national decision in question by making a reference to the Court of Justice under Article 234 EC on the validity of the Community measures upon which the national decisions were based. When faced with submissions by the applicants that they had in fact followed this procedure, but that the national court had refused to make a reference, the CFI responded as follows:

> The mere fact that a party contends that the dispute gives rise to a question concerning the validity of Community law does not mean that the court concerned is compelled to consider that a question has been raised within the meaning of Article 234 EC. It may, in particular, find that there is no doubt as to the validity of the contested Community act and that, accordingly, it is not necessary to make a reference to the Court of Justice on that point...
>
> It is not for the Court of First Instance to assess, in the context of an action for damages, the appropriateness of that decision. To allow the present action as admissible would moreover enable the applicants to circumvent both the rejection of their applications for annulment of the national decisions imposing penalties by the national courts, which alone are competent to do so, and the refusal by those courts to grant their request for a reference to the Court of

25. Case 47/02 *Danzer v. Council* [2006] II-1779, para. 33.

> Justice for a preliminary ruling, which would undermine the very principle of judicial cooperation underlying the preliminary reference procedure.[26]

The Court, therefore, begins its reasoning from the well-established standpoint that only genuine damages claims will be admissible. Such claims will not be admissible where the true purpose behind them is to annul a measure for which the limitation period under Article 230(4) EC has expired. In its subsequent reasoning, it then states that the proper recourse in a situation where the applicant seeks to challenge national rules which it alleges are based on invalid Community measures lies before the national courts. It is then open to the national courts to make a reference under Article 234 EC to question the validity of the Community measures. Up to this point, the CFI's reasoning follows convention and precedent. What follows, however, sits, at the very least, uncomfortably with previous Article 288(2) EC rulings, particularly *Unifrex*.

In respect of the national court's failure to make a reference, the CFI relies on the ECJ's controversial ruling in *Köbler*.[27] The *Köbler* case also stemmed from the Austrian court of last instance's failure to make a reference to the ECJ. While the ECJ, in its ruling in *CILFIT*,[28] had established that national courts need not refer a question to the ECJ where the correct application of Community law is so obvious as to leave no scope for any reasonable doubt, up until *Köbler*, this had never been applied by a court of last instance, which, under a textual interpretation of Article 234(3) EC, is obliged to make a reference. In *Köbler*, the ECJ found that the Austrian court was within its rights not to refer the question to the ECJ. Through its reliance on *Köbler*, the CFI in *Danzer* showed the potential wide-ranging effects that the *Köbler* judgment could have. Not only did the CFI refuse to overturn the Austrian court's decision not to refer the question of the validity of the Community measures to the ECJ, but it also held that, because the possibility existed for the applicant to bring an action before the national court, following *Unifrex*, the applicant's claim under Article 288(2) EC was inadmissible. This reasoning meant that not only does *Köbler* have the effect of denying the applicant indirect recourse to the European Courts by means of Article 234 EC, but it also denies a secondary, direct recourse under Article 288(2) EC. The applicant has therefore twice been denied access to the European Courts.

Under *Unifrex*, an applicant's claim under Article 288(2) EC will be inadmissible where a claim exists against the national authorities and can be brought before the national courts. To that extent, it is true that the applicant in *Danzer* was able to bring a claim before the national courts requesting a preliminary reference under Article 234 EC. *Unifrex* goes further, however, and establishes that in order to render a claim under Article 288(2) EC inadmissible, any

26. Ibid., paras 37-39.
27. Case C-224/01 *Köbler v. Austria* [2003] ECR I-10239.
28. Case 283/81 *CILFIT v. Ministero della Sanità* [1982] ECR 3415.

available action before the national courts must afford the applicant effective protection, and be capable of leading to compensation for the damage alleged. In *Danzer*, an action for damages did exist against the national authorities. This right to compensation was, however, contingent upon a ruling from the ECJ on the validity of the Community measures underpinning the national rules. It is a well-established tenet of European Law that national courts are not empowered to rule on the validity of Community measures[29] and as such, a claim for compensation could only exist at national level once the case had been sent to Luxembourg. Where the national court refuses to make a reference, the applicant is denied access to the European Courts, and as such, no effective remedy exists at a national level to compensate the individual. The national court was not in a position to effectively protect individual rights, and a claim before the CFI under Article 288(2) EC should be admissible. Supporters of the ECJ's reasoning in *Köbler* may still, not unreasonably, argue that the CFI's reasoning in *Danzer* was correct. While national courts are not empowered to question the validity of Community measures, they are entitled to confirm it, as the Austrian court did. Furthermore, the ECJ's ruling in *CILFIT* permits national courts to determine whether or not it is necessary for a reference to be made, and the national court was well within its rights to exercise that discretion. Such decisions cannot be made without an appraisal of the substantive issues in the case, and as such, the applicant had its day in court and its grievances were heard. The mere fact that it was not successful does not mean that the national court was not effectively protecting its interests, and this should not, therefore, entitle the applicant to a claim under Article 288(2) EC that would otherwise be inadmissible, and thereby take up more judicial time and ink.

While the reasoning and ultimate conclusion of the CFI is questionable, the Court's underlying aim is far less contentious. While the *Danzer* ruling may not sit easily with other individual pieces of case law, it does follow the general trend that the European Courts have been working towards since *Unifrex*. Furthermore, the CFI's wide-angled, contextual approach is clearly correct. The Court does not view Article 288(2) EC in the abstract, but rather seeks to place it within the overarching system of judicial protection and judicial cooperation. The price of granting greater freedom to national courts to decide issues of European law is that inconsistencies have to be tolerated. If this leads to greater overall coherency and efficiency, particularly in areas as obtuse as concurrent liability, then it is a cost that should be borne, even if it leads to individual instances of uncertainty and inconsistency.

The remainder of this section seeks to distinguish the procedures according to which the Court will require the exhaustion of national remedies, and those where such exhaustion will not be so required.

29. Case 314/85 *Foto-Frost v. Hauptzollamt Lübeck-Ost* [1987] ECR 4199.

2. RESTITUTION

The Court of Justice will consider a claim to be one that is restitutionary in nature where the aim of the proceedings is to recover an amount that the applicant considers it was wrongly obliged to pay. Such a situation can be exemplified by the facts arising in the *Haegeman* case.[30] It will be remembered that the applicants sought repayment of a levy that they were obliged to pay on a consignment of wine imported from Greece. The levies were collected by the Belgian authorities on behalf of the Community. Similarly, in *Roquette*,[31] the applicants were required to pay Monetary Compensatory Amounts (MCAs) on their exports. Under the provisions then in force, the payments were collected by the French authorities and then handed over to the Community. Roquette claimed that the payments had been wrongfully imposed, and commenced proceedings before both the French courts, against the national authorities, and against the Community, before the Court of Justice, for the repayment of the levies that it had been obliged to pay. In both cases, the Court ruled that the applicants must first bring proceedings in the national court before the ECJ would rule on whether a claim existed against the Community institutions. To this end, the Court dismissed the claim in *Haegeman* and stayed its ruling in *Roquette* until the French court had given a ruling.

It is clear, therefore, that restitutionary claims fall within the group of procedures that the Court considers should first be brought before the national courts. As such, the exhaustion of national remedies doctrine will apply, because, in the language of *Unifrex*, such a means of redress will be capable of ensuring the effective protection of the individual. The question remains, however, as to whether the Court is justified in its assumption that national law will provide an adequate remedy. As Wils comments,[32] in a situation where a Member State has acted in accordance with a Community measure, which is subsequently considered to be unlawful, it is doubtful whether national law would in fact provide a remedy. If the levy goes into the Community treasury, which, since the establishment of the Community own resources is usually the case, the Member State can probably not be considered as having been unjustly enriched. Where this is indeed the case, the *Unifrex* condition should apply, to the extent that where the applicant can show that a claim does not exist under national law against the national authority, then the application for damages against the Community under Article 288(2) EC should be admissible. The effect of the Court's case law, therefore, appears to be that in the interests of preventing a denial of justice to applicants with a meritorious claim, Community law implicitly requires Member States to make an action against national authorities available in the instance that duties have been levied on the basis of an unlawful Community measure.[33] The Court of Justice will

30. Case 96/71 *R & V Haegeman v. Commission* [1972] ECR 1005.
31. Case 26/74 *SA Roquette frères v. Commission No. 2* [1976] ECR 677.
32. W. Wils, *Concurrent Liability of the Community and a Member State*, ELRev. 17 (1992): 196.
33. See further, A. Tatham, 'Restitution of Charges and Duties Levied by the Public Administration in Breach of Community Law: A Comparative Analysis', *ELRev.* 19 (1994): 146.

presume that the Member States have complied with this duty unless and until the applicant can prove otherwise. Where the applicant can discharge this burden of proof without having recourse to commencing national proceedings, then he or she may bring a direct action in damages before the CFI under Article 288(2) EC. Alternatively, the applicant will continue to be required to exhaust all national remedies before bringing a damages claim against the Community. As the national courts have no jurisdiction to declare that the Community act, on the basis of which payment was made, is invalid, they must make a reference to the Court of Justice under the preliminary ruling procedure provided for under Article 234 EC.[34] If the Court of Justice considers the Community measure to be invalid, then this should prove sufficient for the national court to order restitution of the undue amount to the applicant.

The only instance where a claimant may be able to recover restitutionary damages directly before the Court of Justice is in the exceptional case where the Court of Justice has limited the effects of its judgment in a preliminary ruling declaring a Community measure invalid. This was illustrated during the course of the *Roquette* litigation. As stated above, the litigation stemmed from the payment by Roquette of MCAs on its exports. After *Roquette* had been before the Court of Justice on a number of occasions on the basis of the same set of facts, on 15 October 1980 the Court handed down a ruling on a series of questions that had been referred to it by means of Article 234 EC concerning the validity of Regulation 652/76 EEC.[35] After having replied that the Regulation was indeed invalid, the Court went on to examine the effect of its ruling:

> [T]he invalidity of the regulation in this case might give rise to the recovery of sums paid but not owed by the undertakings concerned in countries with depreciated currencies and by the national authorities in question in countries with hard currencies which, in view of the lack of uniformity of the relevant legislation, would be capable of causing considerable differences in treatment, thereby causing further distortion in competition . . . For these reasons it must be held that the fact that the provisions of the regulations in question have been found invalid does not enable the charging or the payment of monetary compensatory amounts by the national authorities on the basis of those provisions to be challenged as regards the period prior to the date of this judgment.[36]

Following the judgment of the Court of Justice, Roquette returned to the *Tribunal d'instance*, which upheld Roquette's claim. This judgment was then upheld by the *Cour d'appel*, but later quashed by the *Cour de cassation*. The *Cour de cassation* took the view that only the Court of Justice had jurisdiction to limit the effects in time of the invalidity of the Regulations in question, and that the *Cour d'appel* had not given due effect to the judgment of the Court of Justice. The applicants then

34. K. Lenaerts, D. Arts & I. Maselis, *Procedural Law of the European Union*, 2nd edn (London: Sweet & Maxwell, 2006), 11-020.
35. Case 145/79 *SA Roquette Frères v. French State – Customs Administration* [1980] ECR 2917.
36. Ibid., paras 52-53.

brought proceedings directly against the Community, seeking compensation for the damage suffered as a result of the application of the invalid provisions. Roquette was therefore seeking restitution of the monies it had been wrongfully obliged to pay as MCAs. While the Court of Justice eventually dismissed the claim on its merits, it did agree to hear the proceedings. On the question of admissibility, the Court ruled:

> In the present case, the remedies provided for by domestic law for obtaining reimbursement of excessive monetary compensatory amounts are unavailable to the applicant for the very reason that the Court's judgment . . . applied by the French courts, ruled that the invalidity of the regulations fixing those amounts could not enable the charging thereof to be challenged as regards the period prior to the date of that judgment. Accordingly, no remedy under national law can effectively ensure reparation for any damage suffered. The action is therefore admissible.[37]

It can be concluded, therefore, that where an applicant seeks to recover an amount paid under an allegedly unlawful Community measure which has been collected by the national authorities on behalf of the Community, then he or she must first bring an action against the national authorities in the national courts. Only if the applicant can prove, either directly, or after having received a declaration from the national court to the same effect, that national law does not provide sufficient redress to cover the applicant's loss, can a claim be brought before the Community Courts under Article 288(2) EC.[38] Furthermore, a claimant will be able to bring a claim directly before the Community courts in the exceptional instance that he or she is relying on a previous ruling of the Court of Justice annulling the relevant Community measure, the effect of which has been restricted.

3. UNLAWFUL FAILURE TO ACT

This situation arises where, in instances such as those in *IBC* and *Cotelle*, outlined above, the Member State, acting on allegedly invalid Community legislation, refuses to make a payment allegedly owed to the applicant, or fails to grant import/export licenses when they should have been granted.[39] On a national level, the only remedy available to the applicants would be the annulment of the decision by the national authorities to refuse to grant the subsidy. Where the

37. Case 20/88 *SA Roquette Frères v. Commission* [1989] ECR 1553, paras 16-17.
38. This conclusion was recently confirmed by the CFI in Case T-91/05 *Sinara Handel v. Council and Commission* [2007] ECR II-245, where the Court considered that it had no jurisdiction to hear a claim for compensation for loss of profit corresponding to the amount of anti-dumping duties. The Court considered that the damage had arisen exclusively from the payment of the sum owed in respect of the anti-dumping duties imposed, with the result that the action was, in fact, a claim for repayment of the duties. The duties were collected by the national authorities and, as such, the national courts alone had jurisdiction to deal with such a claim.
39. See Joined Cases 5, 7 and 13-24/66 *Kampffmeyer and Others v. Commission* [1967] ECR 245.

national authorities, in their refusal, have correctly followed the procedure provided for by the Community measure in assessing whether an action for annulment exists, the national court would be required to assess the validity of the Community measure. This is clearly outside of the national court's jurisdiction,[40] and as such, it would be required to make a preliminary reference to the ECJ under Article 234 EC to rule on the validity of the relevant Community measure.[41] If, upon the preliminary ruling, the Court of Justice declares the Community measure to be invalid, one of two possible situations arises.

The first possibility is that once the Court has declared the Community measure to be invalid, there exists a legal basis under national law for the applicant to recover damages from the national authorities. Where such damages are sufficient to cover the applicant's loss, a claim against the Community institutions under Article 288(2) EC will be inadmissible. This was the situation that arose in *Grands Moulins* (outlined above) and *AERPO*.[42] In *AERPO*, the applicants claimed that a Commission Regulation which sought to alter the conversion factors for calculating the basis upon which certain grants would be awarded, was invalid. The effect of this on the applicants was that the provisions of the allegedly unlawful Regulation reduced the amount of subsidies that they were entitled to. The applicants claimed under Article 288(2) EC, first, to recover the difference between the amounts received and the amounts to which the applicants considered that they were entitled, and second, to recover compensation for damage derived from the fall in prices resulting from the adoption of the contested Regulation. The Court ruled that the second head of damage was admissible. It went on to hear the case without addressing the admissibility of the first head of damage, on the basis that the applicant was relying on the same set of facts in both instances, and the Court would have to look to the substance of the case in any event. The Court dismissed the entire application based on the substance of the second head of damages. Had the applicants only sought to recover the first head of damage, given the strong arguments put forward by the Commission, it is likely that the Court would have declared the action inadmissible, following the *Haegeman* and *Roquette* line of case law, on the basis that, in reality, the applicant's claim was one of restitution, and should therefore have been brought before the national court.

Before turning to assess the second situation that may arise after a preliminary ruling declaring a Community measure to be invalid, it should be noted that the first possibility above is subject to the same exception, mentioned in relation to restitutionary claims, where the Court of Justice limits the effect of its preliminary ruling.

---

40. Case 314/85 *Foto-Frost v. Hauptzollamt Lübeck-Ost* [1987] ECR 4199.
41. In light of the ruling in *Kampffmeyer*, where the Court of Justice stayed its proceedings to await the judgment of the German court, one can argue that, where injury is suffered as a result of a joint decision of the Community institutions and the national authorities, the national judge will not be required to submit a preliminary reference where he or she is entitled, by reason of national law, to annul the national part of the decision, and base, at least a proportion of the award of damages, on this annulment. See W. Wils, 'Concurrent Liability of the Community and a Member State', *ELRev.* 17 (1992): 200.
42. Case C-119/88 *AERPO v. Commission* [1990] ECR 2189.

This situation arose in the *Quellmehl and Gritz* cases,[43] where the Court had previously declared a regulation granting subsidies for starch to be invalid. In response to the Commission's submission that the applicants should have first brought an action against the national authorities in the national courts, the Court of Justice held that:

> The Council and the Commission, the defendants, also object that in order to obtain the refunds claimed the applicant should have brought an action for payment of the refunds against the competent national bodies in the national courts. However, that objection cannot be upheld. Although it is true that an action for the payment of amounts due under Community regulations may not be brought under Article 178 [now Article 235 EC] and the second paragraph of Article 215 [now Article 288 EC] of the EEC Treaty, the claims submitted by the applicant in this case cannot be classed as claims for the payment of amounts due, but rather as claims for compensation for the alleged damage resulting from the unlawfulness established by the judgment of the Court. In the circumstances of the case, moreover, it is clear that, pursuant to the judgment of the Court, a national court could not have upheld such an action in the absence of any provision of Community law authorising the national bodies to pay the amounts claimed.[44]

The second possibility is that once the ECJ has declared the Community act invalid, there exists no legal basis upon which the national authorities may be obliged to make a payment to the applicants. In that case the ruling in *Unifrex* applies, and the applicant would be entitled to bring an action before the CFI against the relevant Community institution because the exhaustion of national remedies could not lead to the applicant receiving adequate redress for the injury caused. Such a situation has arisen in several cases concerning the alleged unlawfulness of the omission of certain products in a regulation for the granting of subsidies on exports,[45] the fixing of subsidies at too low a level,[46] and the failure to raise the level of MCAs where the monetary market conditions had changed.[47]

In establishing whether an applicant may, therefore, bring an action directly before the CFI without first having recourse to the national courts, the question to be asked is whether the declaration by preliminary ruling of the Court of Justice that the Community measure is invalid is sufficient *in itself* to provide the legal basis needed by the national court to grant the repayment requested.[48] If the

43. Case 238/78 *Ireks-Arkady v. Council and Commission* [1979] ECR 2955; Joined Cases 241, 242, 245-250/78 *DGV v. Council and Commission* [1979] ECR 3017; Joined Cases 261 and 262/78 *Interquell v. Council and Commission* [1979] ECR 3045.
44. Ibid., para. 6.
45. Case 43/72 *Merkur Außenhandel-GmbH & Co. KG v. Commission* [1973] ECR 1055.
46. Joined Cases 9 and 11/71 *Compagnie d'Approvisionnement v. Commission* [1972] ECR 391.
47. Case 281/82 *Société à responsabilité limitée Unifrex v. Commission and Council* [1984] ECR 1969.
48. K. Lenaerts, D. Arts & I. Maselis, *Procedural Law of the European Union*, 2nd edn (London: Sweet & Maxwell, 2006), 11-021.

preliminary ruling of the ECJ does afford the national court with such a basis, then, following the rule in *Unifrex*, an action under Article 288(2) EC would be inadmissible. Where no such legal basis exists, the applicant will be entitled to bring a claim of non-contractual liability before the CFI.

One further situation exists, however, whereby an applicant may bring an action directly before the CFI without having recourse to the national courts. This situation arises where, for example, a Community regulation provides that exporters of product (A) are entitled to a subsidy on their exports, but exporters of product (a) are not so entitled. Where products (A) and (a) are materially the same and there exists no reason to distinguish between them, exporters of product (a) may feel that the Commission has given their competitors a significant competitive advantage which cannot be justified, and seek compensation for their losses. In such a case, even if one were to go before the national court and bring an action against the national authorities charged with administering the subsidies, there would be little that the national courts could do. As Harding points out,[49] it is for the Court of Justice to say whether payment ought to be made to exporters of product (a), or ought not to have been made to exporters of product (A). This requires an assessment of Community legislative action, and falls outside the jurisdiction of the national court. Only the Court of Justice is in a position to evaluate the policy decisions of the Commission, and not the national courts. As such, the applicant should not be required to first go before the national court. Support for this proposition can be found implicitly within the *Merkur* ruling,[50] where the Court, relying on the principles of administrative effectiveness, admitted a claim under Article 288(2) EC, where the applicant brought an action against an omission on the part of the Commission to provide subsidies for the export of barley products, while provision was made for subsidies on the export of other types of cereal.

While the distinction may be fine, and sometimes artificial, the case of *Dietz*[51] exemplifies the importance of distinguishing between situations where the applicant is claiming that it is entitled to a subsidy that it has not received, and the situation where the applicant is claiming that its competitor should not be entitled to a subsidy that has already been paid to it. The applicants were German exporters of sugar. They had concluded a contract for the sale of sugar with an Italian undertaking. In fixing the price for the sale, the parties had taken account of the compensatory payments to which the applicant was entitled by Community regulation, upon the export of the sugar to Italy. Between the time at which the contract was made and the point at which it was carried out, the Commission introduced a further regulation placing duties on imports into Italy. The effect of this was to reduce the amount that the applicants would receive from the German authorities upon exporting the consignment of sugar. Dietz first brought an action

49. C. Harding, 'The Choice of Court Problem in Cases of Non-contractual Liability under EEC Law', *CMLRev.* 16 (1979): 394.
50. Case 43/72 *Merkur Außenhandel-GmbH & Co. KG v. Commission* [1973] ECR 1055.
51. Case 126/76 *Firma Gebrüder Dietz v. Commission* [1977] ECR 2431.

against the German authorities under national law. Fearing the possibility that the German courts might not make a reference to the ECJ under Article 234 EC, and not wishing to be time-barred from an application under Article 288(2) EC, the applicant commenced proceedings before the Court of Justice. While in its claim against the national authorities Dietz had requested that it be paid the difference between the subsidies it had received and those to which it was entitled at the time that it signed the contract of sale, the formal statement of claim submitted under Article 288(2) EC was subtly different. In its direct action claim, the applicant sought damages for the loss caused to it by the Commission's failure to take transitional measures for the protection of persons in the applicant's position. This shifted the basis of the claim from one in restitution deriving from the German authority's refusal to pay a specific sum, to a claim in tort for the Commission's failure to take measures to avoid the applicant's loss. Despite strong objections from the Commission, the Court declared the action admissible:

> The Court has only stated that it has no jurisdiction in cases in which the application was in fact directed against measures adopted by the national authorities for the purpose of applying provisions of Community law. Even if the Court, within the context of proceedings for a preliminary ruling, considered that the rules applicable were such as to cause damage because of the absence of appropriate transitional measures, the national court would not be empowered to adopt those measures itself, with the result that a direct application to the Court on the basis of Article 215 [now Article 288 EC] of the Treaty would still be necessary. The matter has been brought before the Court within the bounds of its jurisdiction and it is therefore under a duty to examine whether the alleged omission . . . constitutes an infringement of the law such as to incur the liability of the Community. The application is therefore admissible.[52]

The principle can, therefore, be summarized as being that where the applicant is bringing a claim on the basis that it has not received payments that were due to it, the damage sought is a restitutionary claim for a liquidated sum – that is, the amount that would have been paid to the applicant if the national authorities had not relied on the unlawful Community act. In the second case, however, the applicant is claiming against a Community measure which unlawfully entitles *someone else* – that is, the applicant's competitor – to a subsidy. The claim here is one of unliquidated damages in tort, brought on the basis that the Community has discriminated against the applicant. While a direct action under Article 288(2) EC will not be admissible in the first case, such an action will be admissible in the second case.

One final point should be noted as regards injury caused by a refusal on the part of a national authority to act. While the majority of the above discussion has focused primarily on a refusal to grant subsidies, the discussion is equally relevant

52. Ibid., paras 5-7.

to the refusal to grant a license. With special regard to licenses, however, the issue of time plays an enhanced role. Even if a declaration of invalidity in preliminary ruling proceedings results in the national court's annulling the refusal to grant a license, the loss of years can no longer be made good. Consequently, an action in damages brought against the Community institution from which the act declared invalid originated would be admissible.[53] This point was evidenced in *Krohn*, where the applicant sought damages under Article 288(2) EC after the German authorities refused to grant it import licenses.[54] On the issue of admissibility, the Court, after having restated the common position that Article 288(2) EC is an independent measure, went on to rule that

> [t]here is nothing to suggest that the annulment of the Bundesanstalt's decision and the issue, after the lapse of several years, of the import licences claimed in 1982 would compensate Krohn for the damage suffered by it at that time; such an annulment would therefore not remove the need for the applicant, if it is to obtain compensation, to bring an action before the Court under Article 178 [now Article 235 EC] and the second paragraph of Article 215 [now Article 288 EC] of the Treaty. In those circumstances, the admissibility of this action cannot be made dependent on the exhaustion of the national rights of action available against the Bundesanstalt's decision.[55]

This is clearly in line with the *Unifrex* case law, whereby the applicant's claim will be admissible, without the need for prior exhaustion of national remedies, where it can prove that there does not exist, under national law, a satisfactory form of redress. This will be so even if the events giving rise to the claim (i.e., the refusal to grant a license) would normally be challengeable before the national courts. It is clear, therefore, that applicants must take care when drafting statements of claim that they are indeed seeking a form of compensation that falls within the jurisdiction of the CFI.

4. TORT

The conclusion to be drawn from the above discussion is that where the action is not a mere restitutionary claim designed to obtain a payment or reimbursement from a national authority, but is a true tort claim in respect of damage caused by an illegal Community measure, then this falls squarely within the text of Article 288(2) EC, and a claim may be brought directly before the CFI. The justification for this is that it is not the role of the national court to decide how a Community institution ought to have exercised its legislative powers. Cases falling within the scope of 'true tort' claims often arise where one can show that the applicant has

53. K. Lenaerts, D. Arts & I. Maselis, *Procedural Law of the European Union*, 2nd edn (London: Sweet & Maxwell, 2006), 11-021.
54. Case 175/84 *Krohn & Co Import-Export v. Commission* [1986] ECR 753.
55. Ibid., paras 27-29.

suffered an actual 'injury' – often alongside the financial loss resulting from an undue payment or a failure to grant a subsidy or a license.[56] This 'actual' injury often manifests itself in events such as the applicant becoming the subject of insolvency proceedings, a weakening of the undertaking's competitive position,[57] or the price of having, at short notice, to obtain credit.[58]

For the claim to be admitted, it is not sufficient, however, to illustrate simply that the damages sought fall within the category of tort damages, as opposed to restitution. The underlying principle, which runs throughout the area of non-contractual liability, is that financial loss must be made good by the authority that caused the injury by its actions. Accordingly, the Community must make good only the financial loss that can be said to flow from its institutions or its servants, and the national authorities will only be responsible for losses caused by their own actions. Similarly, the Community cannot be held responsible for losses attributable to the national authorities, just as the national authorities cannot be responsible for losses stemming from the Community. With the Community and national legal systems only being able to assess the liability of their respective institutions, it stands to reason that a single joint action against both the Community and national authorities in liability cannot exist. A determination must therefore be made: against which institution may the applicant claim? The decisive criterion appears to be the respective decision-making powers of the Community and the Member States.[59] The relevance of the decision-making powers of the institutions was well illustrated in the *Mulder* case.[60] In accordance with Council Regulation 1078/77 EEC, a group of Dutch and German dairy farmers had abstained from delivering milk and dairy products for a period of five years. During this period, pursuant to Council Regulation 857/84 EEC concerning the creation of an additional levy system, the Dutch and German authorities set up a quota system to limit the amount of milk and dairy products that could be delivered. The quotas were determined on the basis of the amount of milk and dairy produce delivered by farmers during the previous calendar year. Once the five-year non-marketing period was over, the applicants sought to apply for quotas under the new system. Their applications were refused on the basis that during the reference period – which fell during the non-marketing period – the applicants had not delivered any milk or dairy products. The effect of the Council Regulations was to turn a temporary non-marketing agreement into a permanent obligation on the applicants not to deliver milk or dairy products. In preliminary reference proceedings before

56. K. Lenaerts, D. Arts & I. Maselis, *Procedural Law of the European Union*, 2nd edn (London: Sweet & Maxwell, 2006), 11-022.
57. *See*, the discussion on Case 126/76 *Firma Gebrüder Dietz v. Commission of the European Communities* [1977] ECR 2431.
58. Joined Cases 116 and 124/77 *G.R. Amylum N.V. and Tunnel Refineries Ltd v. Council and Commission* [1979] ECR 3497; and Case T-167/94 *Detlef Nölle v. Council and Commission* [1995] ECR II-2589, para. 42.
59. K. Lenaerts, D. Arts & I. Maselis, *Procedural Law of the European Union*, 2nd edn (London: Sweet & Maxwell, 2006), 11-016.
60. 120/86 *J. Mulder v. Minister van Landbouw en Visserij* [1988] ECR 2321, paras 24-26.

the Court of Justice, the applicants secured a ruling that the Community rules were invalid on the grounds that they were in breach of the principle of legitimate expectation. In its judgment the Court held:

> [W]here such a producer has been encouraged by a Community measure to suspend marketing for a limited period in the general interest and against payment of a premium he may legitimately expect not to be subject, upon the expiry of his undertaking, to restrictions which specifically affect him precisely because he availed himself of the possibilities offered by the Community provisions.... Contrary to the Commission's contention, total and continuous exclusion of that kind for the entire period of application of the regulations on the additional levy, preventing the producers concerned from resuming the marketing of milk at the end of the five-year period, was not an occurrence which those producers could have foreseen when they entered into an undertaking, for a limited period, not to deliver milk.... Such an effect therefore frustrates those producers' legitimate expectation that the effects of the system to which they had rendered themselves subject would be limited.[61]

The applicants then instituted further proceedings before the European Courts under Article 288(2) EC, claiming damages against the Council and Commission for the earnings lost (unliquidated damages) as a result of the delay in granting the milk quotas. As regards admissibility, the Council and the Commission argued that the action was inadmissible on the grounds that the true cause of the injury was the national authorities' refusal to allocate reference quantities to the applicants. The Court held the claim to be admissible and rejected the defendants' argument on the basis that

> [t]he defendant institutions do not claim that it was for the Member States to allocate reference quantities to the applicants using powers which were not provided or appropriate for dealing with cases of farmers who entered into non-marketing undertakings. Accordingly, the unlawfulness alleged in support of the claim for damages must be regarded as issuing, not from a national body, but from the Community legislature; hence any damages ensuing from the implementation of the Community rules by national bodies is attributable to the Community legislature.[62]

The Court of Justice admitted the direct action under Article 288(2) EC on the basis that, under the Community law in force at the time of the refusal, the Member State did not have the power to carry out the act sought by the applicants – namely the allocation of a milk quota. The refusal to perform the act sought could not therefore be attributable to them.[63] The financial loss stemmed, therefore, from the illegality

61. Ibid.
62. Ibid., para. 9.
63. K. Lenaerts, D. Arts & I. Maselis, *Procedural Law of the European Union*, 2nd edn (London: Sweet & Maxwell, 2006), 11-022.

of the Community act in its failure to provide a milk quota for farmers in the same position as the applicants. This was so even though implementation of the act was left to the Member States. The loss of earnings, which resulted from the delay in being granted the quotas, was therefore attributable to the Community.

By contrast, in its ruling in *CNTA*,[64] the Court of Justice considered that the sole cause of the damage resulted from the actions of the national authorities. The case arose from the grant of subsidies to oil seed farmers under Council Regulation 136/66 EEC. The regulation provided that national authorities were obliged to pay subsidies to oil seed farmers who were in possession of subsidy certificates granted by the Community. The Member States would then be reimbursed from the EAGGF. In certain previous cases, the French national authorities Société interprofessionnelle des oléagineux (SIDO) had decided that the fact that farmers did not apply for the subsidy certificate until after having processed the seeds, did not preclude the grant of subsidies, since this would constitute an excessive penalty for a mere administrative error. The national authorities were aware that the Commission did not share this view. Having failed to apply for a certificate before processing their seeds, the applicants were granted the subsidy on the condition that they agreed to reimburse the French authorities the sum of FF 8.5 million, in the case that the Commission decided that the applicants were not eligible for the grants. The Commission considered that the applicants were not eligible for subsidies, as they had not applied for the certificates before processing the seeds as prescribed by Community law, and therefore refused to reimburse the French authorities from the EAGGF. The French authorities, in turn, sought to claim the FF 8.5 million from the applicants. The applicants brought a direct action challenging the Commission decision to refuse to reimburse the French authorities, and claimed damage in respect of the loss they had suffered. After stating that the Court only has jurisdiction to award compensation for damage caused by the Community institutions, and that it must be determined whether the unlawful conduct alleged was in fact the responsibility of a Community institution, the Court of Justice determined that in the present case, the applicants merely alleged that the Decision which allowed the Commission to fix the amounts recognized as chargeable to the EAGGF was unlawful. That Decision, however, was concerned solely with internal financial relations between the Commission and the French Republic, and was not intended to give, and could not have the effect of giving, instructions to the SIDO to adopt the decision giving rise to the alleged damage. The latter decision was adopted by the SIDO alone. As such, the damage that formed the basis of the applicants' claim was derived exclusively from the decision adopted by the SIDO, which was a national body, and consequently the Court of Justice had no jurisdiction to order compensation on the basis of Article 288 EC.[65] According to the Court's ruling, under the Community Regulation, the French national authority was granted a certain amount of discretion. While the general obligation to pay out subsidies to oil seed farmers derived from the Community

64. Joined Cases 89 and 91/86 *Étoile Commerciale and CNTA v. Commission* [1987] ECR 3005.
65. Ibid., paras 19-20.

measure, that Regulation did not instruct the national authorities to take a specific decision in respect of those farmers who had not applied for a certificate before processing the seeds. Consequently, this discretion meant that the national authorities could have taken a different decision. The Community could, therefore, not be regarded as being liable for the damage that arose.

The importance of the level of discretion available to national authorities in implementing Community law, when deciding which institution is liable for the damage caused, is further demonstrated when comparing the Court's decisions in *Sucrimex*[66] and *Krohn*.[67] The *Sucrimex* case concerned the sale of sugar pursuant to export licenses which fixed the rate of export refund. The licenses were lost in transit, and the applicants had to apply for new licenses. The licenses were replaced, and the sugar exported. When the applicant applied for the refunds, however, the French authorities paid only the refund applicable on the day that the replacement licenses were granted – the level of which was lower than under the original licenses. In granting the refunds on the basis of the rate applicable on the day that the replacement licenses were issued, the French authorities were relying on a non-binding opinion from the Commission that it had received by telex to the effect that replacement licenses could not be used to obtain refunds at a rate fixed in advance. The applicants sought to claim compensation from the Commission for the amount unpaid. In determining whether or not the injury could be attributed to the Commission by reason of its telex, the Court ruled:

> The telex message, like all the Commission's actions which are in dispute, is part of the internal co-operation between the Commission and the national bodies responsible for applying Community rules in this field; as a general rule this co-operation cannot make the Community liable to individuals.[68]

The Commission's opinion was not binding on the French authorities, and therefore, it was not the Commission, but the national authorities that were the authors of the decision to refuse the refunds.[69] As Oliver correctly comments,[70] this ruling appears harsh, since it is clear that upon receiving such a telex, a Member State will almost certainly follow it, despite its non-binding nature. The potential consequences of not complying with the Commission's instructions are too great for it to be able to disregard them.

By contrast, the Court was prepared to admit a claim against the Community in the *Krohn* case. The case concerned the importation of manioc pursuant to an agreement between the Community and Thailand. The relevant Community regulation required the national authorities to grant import licenses on request,

66. Case 133/79 *Sucrimex v. Commission* [1980] ECR 1299.
67. Case 175/84 *Krohn & Co Import-Export v. Commission* [1986] ECR 753.
68. Case 133/79 *Sucrimex v. Commission* [1980] ECR 1299, para. 22.
69. M. Brealey & M. Hoskins, *Remedies in EC Law*, 2nd edn (London: Sweet & Maxwell, 1998), 357.
70. P. Oliver, 'Joint Liability of the Community and the Member States', in *The Action for Damages in Community Law*, eds T. Heukels & A McDonnell (The Hague: Asser Institute, 1997), 306.

except 'where the Commission has informed the competent authorities of the Member States by telex that the conditions laid down in the Co-operation Agreement have not been fulfilled'. The national authorities were under an obligation to inform the Commission of all applications for import licenses. Upon application for an import license by Krohn, the Commission suspected that not all of the conditions of the cooperation agreement had been satisfied. It requested further information from the national authorities. Upon receipt of that information, the Commission sent a telex to the national authority informing it that the import license was to be refused. Unlike in its ruling in *Sucrimex*, the Court held that the damages caused could be attributed to the Community, on the basis of the telex sent to the national authorities by the Commission. The Court distinguished the two cases by reasoning that

> [t]he Commission's telex messages . . . were intended as an effective exercise of the power conferred upon it and their effect was to instruct the Bundesanstalt to refuse the import licences . . . It follows from the foregoing that the unlawful conduct alleged by the applicant . . . is to be attributed not to the Bundesanstalt, which was bound to comply with the Commission's instructions, but to the Commission itself. The Court therefore has jurisdiction to entertain the action brought by Krohn.[71]

In summation, a direct claim for damages in tort will be admitted by the Court under Article 288(2) EC, without the need to first bring a claim under national law. This is justified on the basis that the Community must make good the financial loss that can be said to flow from its institutions or its servants. In order to secure the admission of such a claim, however, the applicant must show that the injury suffered was indeed attributable to the Community, and not caused by the actions of the Member State. The question of attribution will be determined by the Court on the basis of the decision-making powers available to each of the institutions. Where the national authorities had the power to carry out the act claimed by the applicant, then liability will be attributed to them, and the case will not be admissible.[72] Where the national authorities did not have such power, then liability lies with the Community, and, as such, an action under Article 288(2) EC is admissible. Furthermore, where a national authority, which has a genuine discretion in implementing those Community provisions, has committed an infringement of Community law, the Community will not be liable, and a claim must be brought before the national courts. Only in the instances where the national authorities are under an obligation of mere instrumental application of an unlawful Community measure, and have no real discretion, will an action in damages lie against the Community.

71. Case 175/84 *Krohn & Co Import-Export v. Commission* [1986] ECR 753, paras 22-23.
72. Case 120/86 *J. Mulder v. Minister van Landbouw en Visserеij* [1988] ECR 2321.

5. ANCILLARY DAMAGE

The issue of ancillary damage arises in situations where the applicant has already secured a successful plea of damages, but, upon payment by the national authority, the award is not sufficient to fully compensate the applicant. The question is whether the applicant can then bring a claim against the Community to recover the balance so as to be fully compensated. This was the situation in *Vreugdenhil*,[73] where the applicant had tried to re-import a consignment of milk into the Netherlands which it had originally purchased in Dutch territory. Dutch customs refused an application from Vreugdenhil to import the goods free of customs duties on the basis that the milk did not fall within the meaning of 'returned goods' as prescribed by the Community customs regulations. Vreugdenhil commenced proceedings before the national courts and succeeded in having the Commission measure annulled by means of an Article 234 EC reference, on the basis that the Commission had exceeded its authority by failing to observe the balance of power between the institutions. The national courts, in implementing the Court of Justice's ruling, ordered the national authorities to reimburse the levy paid by Vreugdenhil. Some aspects of additional and related loss were not, however, recoverable under Dutch law. In seeking to receive full compensation, Vreugdenhil wrote to the Commission requesting compensation for additional losses such as the cost of obtaining a bank guarantee in the course of negotiating payment of the levy with customs authorities, interest lost on the sum paid that was not covered by the national order and various legal costs. The Commission denied responsibility for these claims, and so Vreugdenhil commenced a direct action against the Community under Article 288(2) EC. In addressing whether or not the applicant was entitled to recover such damage, Advocate General Darmon sought to identify and classify the damage:

> The admissibility of the claim for interest on the amount of the levy wrongly paid is unquestionably dependant on the prior exhaustion of the rights of action available under national law . . . The same is true, in my opinion, of the cost of obtaining a bank guarantee . . . The sole purpose of the bank guarantee was to enable Vreugdenhil not to pay the levy immediately and thus to retain the corresponding amount in its assets. Finally, as regards the cost of arguing its case to the Netherlands and German customs authorities, and then before the College van Beroep voor het Bedrijfsleven and the Court of Justice, it may be pointed out that in many Member States the remuneration of counsel or agents forms part of the costs of court proceedings . . . If the Court rules on the amount of damages, it will be necessary to determine whether at least partial compensation has not already been obtained in this regard. The expenditure involved in the discussions with the Netherlands and German customs authorities appears to be of the kind which an economic

73. Case C-282/90 *Industrie- en Handelsonderneming Vreugdenhil BV v. Commission* [1992] ECR 1937.

> operator carrying out frequent import and export transactions will incur as an integral part of his business activity and therefore cannot, in my opinion, be regarded as damage.[74]

In the Advocate General's view, therefore, both the cost of obtaining a bank guarantee and legal expenses comprised 'ancillary damage'. In the earlier case of *Roquette*, the Court had ruled that the payment of interest fell within the bounds of ancillary damage, and that a claim for such damage would be inadmissible under Article 288(2) EC. Recovery of such loss was therefore a question for the national court, to be decided in accordance with national law. As regards the costs of dealing with the national customs authorities, Advocate General Darmon considered that such costs were inherent in carrying on a trade that involved imports and exports. As such, this could not qualify as damage. However, earlier in his Opinion, the Advocate General had also stressed that 'the admissibility for non-contractual liability depends on whether or not the applicant could obtain full compensation for the damage in the national courts',[75] and concluded that 'the Community must "stand surety"' for any loss which was not recoverable under national law. The Advocate General justified this reasoning on the fundamental right to a forum, contained within the rulings of *Johnston*[76] and *Heylens*.[77] Therefore, while the damages sought may only be ancillary, and ought to be brought before the national court, this was not the case where such an action would be 'doomed to failure',[78] and the claim for damages should be admitted. Unfortunately, in its judgment, the Court of Justice offered only the bare minimum of guidance. No mention was made of the types of loss that might be recoverable under Article 288(2) EC, and the Court moved directly on to the substantive issues of the case.

A more comprehensive review of the possibility of claiming ancillary damage against the Community under Article 288(2) EC was offered by the CFI in *Nölle*.[79] In this case, the applicant sought damages for non-contractual liability against the Community in respect of a Council regulation imposing definitive anti-dumping duties on paintbrushes and similar products being imported from China. The applicant had already succeeded in having the Community measure declared invalid by means of an Article 234 EC reference, and had been awarded compensation by the German national court. The applicant was not satisfied, however, and felt that it had not been fully compensated for the loss. It therefore commenced proceedings under Article 288(2) EC before the CFI, claiming for legal expenses not covered by the order of the national court, and payment in respect of bank interest

74. Ibid., AG Darmon's Opinion, paras 20-22.
75. Ibid., para. 9.
76. Case 222/84 *Johnston v. Chief Constable of the RUC* [1986] ECR 1651.
77. Case 222/86 *UNECTEF v. Heylens* [1987] ECR 4097.
78. Case C-282/90 *Industrie- en Handelsonderneming Vreugdenhil BV v. Commission* [1992] ECR 1937, AG Darmon's Opinion, para. 31.
79. Case T-167/94 *Detlef Nölle v. Council and Commission* [1995] ECR II-2589, para. 42.

on the sums that it had borrowed for the purpose of paying the anti-dumping duty. With regard to the legal expenses, the CFI held that

> [i]n the case where an individual feels that he has been adversely affected by the application of a measure of Community law which he considers illegal, he has the possibility, when the implementation of the measure is entrusted to national authorities, to contest, at the time of such implementation, the validity of the measure before a national court in proceedings between himself and the national authority. Under the conditions set out in Article 177 [now Article 234 EC], that court may, or even must, refer to the Court of Justice a question on the validity of the Community measure in question. The existence of this action, however, will be able to ensure effective protection for individuals concerned only if it can lead to compensation for the damage alleged. It follows from the above-mentioned case-law that the question of the reimbursement of costs, which is an issue ancillary to the main dispute between the applicant and the Hauptzollamt . . . comes within the exclusive jurisdiction of the national court, which, in the absence of relevant harmonizing measures of Community law, must settle such a question, as indeed it has done in this case pursuant to the applicable national law.[80]

The CFI therefore refused to supplement the sum awarded by the national court with respect to legal costs. The Court also stated that the applicant had failed to demonstrate that recourse to remedies available under national law was not capable of providing them with effective protection of their rights. The Court then went further and declared that, even if the applicant had proved that its rights had not been effectively protected, it did not have jurisdiction under Article 288(2) EC to award compensation for the proportion of the costs that was not awarded by the national court in Article 234 EC proceedings.

As Ward comments,[81] the ruling by the CFI on the recovery of ancillary damage diverged from that of both the Court of Justice and the Advocate General in *Vreugdenhil*. While the Court did not rule on the issue of the types of loss that are recoverable under Article 288(2) EC, it did admit the claim and assess the substantive merits of the case. This implies that all losses that were not recoverable before the domestic court, including ancillary loss, could be claimed under Article 288(2) EC. Advocate General Darmon, while in agreement with the CFI in *Nölle* that legal costs amount to ancillary damages and should be recovered under national law, in his opinion argued that any shortfall in the sum awarded at the national level should be recoverable by means of Article 288(2) EC. This line of reasoning appears to represent most clearly the Court's judgment in *Unifrex*.[82] The CFI in *Nölle*, however, suggested that ancillary damage, whether or not it could be made good under national law, could not be supplemented by an action under

80. Ibid., paras 35-36.
81. A. Ward, *Judicial Review and the Rights of Private Parties*, 2nd edn (Oxford: OUP, 2007), 307.
82. Case 281/82 *Société à responsabilité limitée Unifrex v. Commission and Council* [1984] ECR 1969.

Article 288(2) EC against the relevant Community institution. As regards the claim to recover bank interest, the CFI ruled that since public authorities in the Federal Republic of Germany can incur liability only if fault is established on the part of the authority responsible, and since the declaration of the invalidity of Regulation 725/89 EC by the Court of Justice was attributable to the unlawful conduct of the Community institutions and not that of the public authorities in Germany, prior exhaustion of domestic remedies could not, in the present case, ensure effective protection for the subjective rights which the applicant derives from Community law.[83]

This conclusion is consistent with the ruling of the Court of Justice in *Vreugdenhil*, in that both Courts agreed that claims for bank interest would be admissible under Article 288(2) EC. It was not clear, however, whether both Courts considered that bank interest amounted to ancillary damage.[84] Given that the CFI accepted the claim for bank interest as admissible, whilst ruling that legal costs, by their nature as ancillary damage, were inadmissible, it can be inferred that bank interest did not constitute ancillary damage, whereas the Court of Justice in *Vreugdenhil* admitted to hear the plea on the recovery of bank interest, even though it appeared to constitute ancillary damage.

In conclusion, the Courts' rulings on the recovery of ancillary damage are far from clear. From the rulings in *Roquette*, *Vreugdenhil* and *Nölle*, it can be deduced that claims for legal costs will be classified as ancillary damages, and claims for such costs will not be admissible under Article 288(2) EC. Any actions in this respect must be brought before the national court. As regards supplementary charges such as bank interest, the rulings in *Vreugdenhil* and *Nölle* have left some doubt as to whether these constitute ancillary damages or not. It does appear, however, that the Court is prepared to hear the merits of such a claim, and these actions should be considered as admissible where it is not possible to recover these types of damage under national law.

6. FAILURE OF SUPERVISION

While the Court has consistently ruled that an effective remedy must be available against a Member State before it national courts in the event that it infringes a directly applicable rule of Community law,[85] a question mark remains as to whether the Commission can be held to account under Article 288(2) EC where it has failed to bring the Member State into line under Article 226 EC, which allows the European Commission to initiate an action against a Member State that has breached its Community obligations. Initially, it was not clear whether such

83. Case T-167/94 *Detlef Nölle v. Council and Commission* [1995] ECR II-2589, para. 41.
84. A. Ward, *Judicial Review and the Rights of Private Parties*, 2nd edn (Oxford: OUP, 2007), 380.
85. Case 46/93 *Brasserie du Pêcheur v. Bundesrepublik Deutschland and The Queen v. Secretary of State for Transport, ex parte Factortame and others* [1996] ECR I-1029.

liability could exist. In *Lütticke*,[86] for example, the Court did not rule as to whether or not such a claim against the Commission fell within the ambit of claimable damage under Article 288(2) EC, but rather decided that, on the facts of the case, the Commission had not failed in its duty of supervision. Where the Commission has failed to commence or pursue proceedings under Article 226 EC, it appears unlikely, however, that the Community will be liable in damages.[87] In its ruling in *Star Fruit*, the Court held that

> [i]t is clear from the scheme of Article 169 [now Article 226 EC] of the Treaty that the Commission is not bound to commence proceedings provided for in that provision but in this regard has a discretion which excludes the right for individuals to require that institution to adopt a specific position. It is only if it considers that the Member State in question has failed to fulfil one of its obligations that the Commission delivers a reasoned opinion. Furthermore, in the event that the State does not comply with the opinion within the period allowed, the institution has in any event the right, but not the duty, to apply to the Court of Justice for a declaration that the alleged breach of obligations has occurred.[88]

Given that the Court has specifically ruled that the powers granted to the Commission under Article 226 EC confer upon it a right to act, as opposed to a duty to act, it is hard to see how an applicant could claim damages resulting from a breach of duty on the part of the Commission. Furthermore, there exists the issue of causation. A good example of the causation problems that arise in attempting to pin liability on the Commission for a failure to adequately supervise a Member State is given by Advocate General Dutheillet de Lamothe in his opinion in *Lütticke*.[89] The applicant in that case brought an action against the Commission for its failure to address either a directive or decision to Germany under Article 97(2) EEC (now repealed) ordering it to abolish a tax on milk powder. Advocate General Dutheillet de Lamothe reasoned:

> The many hypotheses which can be made with regard to the scope and consequences which a directive or a decision of the Commission might have had suffice, in my opinion, to show that there is no causal link between the damage suffered and the failure to act for which the Commission is reproached.[90]

As Oliver, citing the Court's ruling in *Procureur de la République v. Waterkeyn*,[91] accurately concludes,[92] the failure of the Commission to bring such an action

86. Case 4/69 *Alfons Lütticke GmbH v. Commission* [1971] ECR 325.
87. P. Oliver, 'Joint Liability of the Community and the Member States', in *The Action for Damages in Community Law*, eds T. Heukels & A McDonnell (The Hague: Asser Institute, 1997), 299.
88. Case 247/87 *Star Fruit v. Commission* [1989] ECR 291, 301.
89. Case 4/69 *Alfons Lütticke GmbH v. Commission* [1971] ECR 325.
90. Ibid., AG Dutheillet de Lamothe's Opinion, 347.
91. Joined Cases 314-316/81 and 83/82 *Procureur de la République v. Waterkeyn* [1982] ECR 4337.
92. P. Oliver, 'Joint Liability of the Community and the Member States', in *The Action for Damages in Community Law*, eds T. Heukels & A McDonnell (The Hague: Asser Institute, 1997), 300.

cannot be said to have caused the Member State to continue its infringement. As such, no claim can be brought in damages against the Community for failure to act under Article 226 EC and thereby bring an end to an infringement of Community law by a Member State.

7. MEMBER STATE RECOVERY

From the above discussion, it is apparent that the general strategy of the Court is to require the applicant to recover damages from the national authorities wherever possible – regardless of whether or not, in fact, the Community is ultimately liable. The question arises, therefore, as to whether a Member State which feels that it was neither responsible for the breach, nor unjustly enriched by it, can seek to recover the sums paid out to the applicant from the Community. The first point to be made is that the Court has clearly held that no such claim may be brought by way of a preliminary reference. In *Granaria* the Court unequivocally ruled that 'a question relating to the application of the second paragraph of Article 215 [now Article 288 EC] cannot be determined in proceedings under Article 177 [now Article 234 EC] of the Treaty'.[93] The effect of this is that the national court cannot receive a ruling as to whether the Community is liable in whole or in part. The Court gave no justification for this, but Oliver concludes that the ruling is in line with the principle that the Court cannot decide questions of fact when answering a preliminary reference, nor can it guarantee an adequate right of defence to the Community institution concerned.[94] Where the applicant has successfully recovered repayment of a duty unduly paid, such as a customs duty or an agricultural levy, then the Member State will be reimbursing sums that will have already formed part of the Community's own resources. In this case, where the Member State is so entitled under the provisions of Council Regulation 1552/89 EC on the system of the Communities' own resources, it may deduct the amount that was repaid to the applicant from the declaration of own resources which Member States are obliged to send to the Commission. This deduction constitutes a correction of the earlier declaration, which included the duties unduly paid by the applicant. Where the unduly paid levy was made in the context of the CAP, but where the Member State does not satisfy the criteria necessary to be able to make a deduction pursuant to Council Regulation 1552/89 EC, then it may be possible for the Member State to receive a contribution (partial reimbursement of the payment) or an indemnity (full compensation for the sums paid) from the Community under Council Regulation 729/70 EEC on the financing of the CAP. Advocate General Mancini raised this possibility in his Opinion in *Krohn*.[95] As Oliver observes, as a safety net in the

93. Case 101/78 *Granaria v. Hoofdproduktschap voor Akkerrbouwprodukten* [1979] ECR 623, para. 10.
94. P. Oliver, 'Joint Liability of the Community and the Member States', in *The Action for Damages in Community Law*, eds T. Heukels & A McDonnell (The Hague: Asser Institute, 1997), 293.
95. Case 175/84 *Krohn & Co Import-Export v. Commission* [1986] ECR 753.

event that the Commission fails to reimburse the Member State when clearing the accounts, the Member State has the right to bring an action to recover the funds under Article 230 EC.[96]

8. CONCLUSION

The Court's original position for instances concerning concurrent liability in claims for non-contractual damage was that admissibility under Articles 235 and 288(2) EC will be conditional on the prior exhaustion of national remedies. The subsequent evolution of the case law has qualified this principle that national remedies need only be exhausted to the extent that those national remedies offer effective protection to the individuals concerned, and are capable of leading to compensation for the damage alleged. Under certain procedures, therefore, the Court will deem national law to vest the applicant with remedies that are sufficient to compensate for the injuries suffered, and with other procedures where this is not the case. It is only with regard to this first group of procedures that the applicant will be required to exhaust national remedies before embarking upon a claim against the Community. In the case of the latter procedures, the Court of Justice (and now the CFI) has been willing to admit direct claims against the Community without requiring that an action first be brought against the national authorities.

Where an applicant seeks to recover an amount paid under an allegedly unlawful Community measure which has been collected by the national authorities on behalf of the Community, then it must first bring an action against the national authorities in the national courts. Only if the applicant can prove, either directly, or after having received a declaration from the national court to the same effect, that national law does not provide sufficient redress to cover the applicant's loss, can a claim be brought before the Community courts under Article 288(2) EC.

Similarly, where the applicant is bringing a claim on the basis that it has not received payments that were due to it, the damage sought is a restitutionary claim for a liquidated sum – i.e., the amount that would have been paid to the applicant if the national authorities had not relied on the unlawful Community act – and a direct action before the CFI under Article 288(2) EC will not be admissible unless or until the applicant can prove that no further remedy exists under national law. This needs to be distinguished from the situation where the applicant is claiming against a Community measure, which unlawfully entitles *someone else* – i.e., the applicant's competitor – to a subsidy. In this instance, a direct action under Article 288(2) EC will exist.

A direct claim for damages in tort will, however, be admitted by the Court under Article 288(2) EC without the need to first bring a claim under national law. This is justified on the basis that the Community must make good the financial loss

96. See further P. Oliver, 'Joint Liability of the Community and the Member States', in *The Action for Damages in Community Law*, eds T. Heukels & A McDonnell (The Hague: Asser Institute, 1997), 293-295.

that can be said to flow from its institutions or its servants. In order to secure the admission of such a claim, however, the applicant must show that the injury suffered was indeed attributable to the Community, and not caused by the actions of the Member State. The question of attribution will be determined by the Court on the basis of the decision-making powers available to each of the institutions. Where the national authorities had the power to carry out the act claimed by the applicant, then liability will be attributed to them, and the case will not be admissible. Where the national authorities did not have such power – or, in the language of *Bergaderm*, had no discretion in how to act – then liability lies with the Community, and, as such, an action under Article 288(2) EC is admissible.

As Harding illustrates,[97] the problems with the *Kampffmeyer* ruling and the requirement to exhaust national remedies prior to seeking redress against the Community are predominantly twofold. First, the action before the national court, particularly where this action is subsequently appealed, may prove to be a long, complicated, and therefore expensive ordeal. While many applicants with meritorious claims will be able to recover full compensation, subject to national rules on recovery, others may not be so fortunate, and may be obliged to bring action before the Court of Justice, provided, that is, that such an application has not already been time-barred. Second, while it is likely that in such a situation the national court would, in any case, refer a question to the Court of Justice on the potential liability of the Community, that decision lies within the discretion of the national court. There is no guarantee that the national court will make such a reference.

Despite the amount of criticism that the Court's rulings in this area have attracted, even the most ardent critics cannot maintain that the Court's approach is wholly unjustifiable. Hartley raises two policy arguments in favour of the Court's approach.[98] The first concerns the question of liability as between the Community and the Member States. In some cases, liability may lie wholly or in part with national authorities. If the Community were to reimburse the applicant directly, then it may experience difficulties in obtaining reimbursement from the Member State. Such a situation arises only seldom, however, and the policy concerns should not be overstated. Furthermore, as has been seen above, more often than not it is the Community that ought to bear ultimate financial responsibility, and not the Member State. This is especially so in the case of duties and levies, which constitute Community resources. Second, justification can be found for the Court's approach in the need to limit access by private parties and thereby prevent a flood of cases descending upon an already overwhelmed Court. While this is not an uncommon argument in many areas, the danger here is once again overstated, as once one case has been decided, the Commission will be in a position to settle similar matters out of Court.

97. C. Harding, 'The Choice of Court Problem in Cases of Non-contractual Liability under EEC Law', *CMLRev.* 16 (1979): 403-404.
98. T.C. Hartley, 'Concurrent Liability in EEC Law: A Critical Review of the Cases', *ELRev.* 2 (1977): 263.

More plausible are the arguments raised against the restrictive position adopted by the Court. The first argument addresses the Court's insistence on assessing whether a remedy exists before the national court and whether this is, in fact, relevant to the question of admissibility. On the one hand, if the Court did not take account of the existence of national remedies, by declaring an action inadmissible, it would run the risk of denying the applicant access to justice, should there exist no remedy at national law. On the other hand, however, if the Court only applies inadmissibility in the instance where there exists a national remedy, then it is forced, in each case, to examine whether such a right actually exists. This is a precarious situation for the Court, as it does not have jurisdiction to rule on whether a remedy does in actuality exist at a national level, for this is a question for the national court, applying national law. Second, the Court's approach is likely to lead to a lack of uniformity. If the majority of cases are dealt with by the national courts, under national law, then the outcomes will differ depending upon the Member State in which proceedings are brought.[99]

The preceding paragraphs have sought to explore and explain, as clearly as possible, the Court's rulings in the area of concurrent liability – an area fraught with complication and contradiction. It is an area, however, which is also highly significant for applicants seeking to receive compensation from the Community. A mistake in choosing the court before which to bring an action can be fatal to a claim. While a limitation period of five years appears generous at first glance, that time can soon be up, and may not be sufficient where appeal proceedings are launched at a national level, resulting in a denial of justice for those genuinely entitled to redress.

99. Ibid., 264.

Selected Bibliography

Books

Beatson, A. & Tridimas, T. (eds). *New Directions in European Public Law.* Oxford: Hart, 1998.

Brearley, M. & Hoskins M. *Remedies in EC Law*, 2nd edn London: Sweet & Maxwell, 1998.

Claes, M. *The National Courts' Mandate in the European Constitution.* Hart: Oxford, 2006.

Craig, P. & de Búrca, G. (eds). *The Evolution of EU Law*. Oxford: OUP, 1999.

Craig, P. & de Burca, G. *EU Law*, 4th edn Oxford: OUP, 2007.

Dougan, M. *National Remedies before the Court of Justice*. Oxford: Hart, 2004.

Douglas Scott, S. *Constitutional Law of the European Union*. Pearson Longman, Harlow, 2002.

Eeckhout, P. *External Relations of the European Union. Legal and Constitutional Foundations*. Oxford: OUP, 2005.

Ehlermann, C.D. & Atanasiu, I. (eds). *European Competition Law Annual 2001: Effective Private Enforcement of EC Antitrust Law*. Oxford: EUI, Hart Publishing, 2003.

Fines, F. *Etude de la responsibilité extracontractuelle de la Communauté économique européenne*, in Bibliothèque de droit international, Librairie générale de droit et de jurisprudence, Paris, 1990, vol. 101.

Harlow, C. *State Liability: Tort Law and Beyond.* Oxford: OUP, 2004.

Hartley, T.C. *The Foundations of European Community Law.* 6th edn Oxford: OUP, 2007.

Heukels, T. & McDonnell, A. (eds). *The Action for Damages in Community Law.* The Hague: Asser Institute, 1997.

Kilpatrick, C. et al. (eds). *The Future of Remedies in Europe*. Oxford: Hart, 2000.

Lee, M. *EU Environmental Law*. Oxford: Hart, 2005.

Lenaerts, K. & Van Nuffel, P. *Constitutional Law of the European Union*. 2nd edn London: Sweet & Maxwell, 2005.

Lenaerts, K., Arts, D. & Maselis, I. *Procedural Law of the European Union*. 2nd edn London: Sweet & Maxwell, 2006.

Lonbay, J. & Biondi, A. (eds). *Remedies for Breach of EC Law*. Chichester: Wiley's, 1997.

Maduro, M.P. et al. (eds). *The Past and Future of EU Law, The Classics of EU Law Revisited on the 50th Anniversary of the Rome Treaty*. Oxford: Hart, 2009.

Prechal, S. *Directives in EC Law*. 2nd edn. Oxford: OUP, 2006.

Schermers, H.G., Heukels, T. & Mead, P. (eds). *Non-contractual Liability of the European Communities*. The Hague: Kluwer, 1988.

Schermers, H.G. & Waelbroeck, D.F. *Judicial Protection in the European Union*, 6th edn The Hague/London/New York: Kluwer International, 2001.

Stuyck, J. & Gilliams, H. *Modernisation of European Competition Law*. Antwerpen, Intersentia: Leuven CCLE series, 2002.

Tridimas, T. *The General Principles of EC Law*. 3rd edn Oxford: OUP, 2006.

Van Gerven, W. *Torts: Scope of Protection, Ius Commune Casebook for the Common Law of Europe*. Oxford: Hart, 1998.

Wakefield, J. *Judicial Protection through the Use of Article 288(2) EC*. The Hague: Kluwer, 2002.

Ward, A. *Judicial Review and the Rights of Private Parties*. 2nd edn Oxford: OUP, 2007.

Articles

Anagnostaras, G. 'State Liability and Alternative Courses of Action: How Independent Can an Autonomous Remedy Be?'. *YEL* (2002): 355.

Andenas, A. 'Liability for Supervisors and Depositors Rights: The BCCI and the Bank of England in the House of Lords'. *Company Law* 22(8) (2001): 226.

Arnull, A. 'Out with the Old'. *ELRev.* 31(1) (2006): 1.

Biondi, A. & Johnson, L. 'No Small Matter: The Right to Recovery of Charges Levied in Breach of Community Law'. *European Public Law* 4 (1998): 313.

Biondi, A. 'The European Court of Justice and Certain National Procedural Limitations: Not Such a Tough Relationship'. *CMLRev.* 36 (1999): 1271.

Bronckers, M. 'The Relationship of the EC Courts with Other International Tribunals: Non-committal, Respectful or Submissive?'. *CMLRev.* 44 (2007): 601-627, 611.

Caranta, R. 'Governmental Liability after Francovich'. *Camb. L.J.* 52 (1993): 272.

Convery, J. 'State Liability in the United Kingdom after "Brasserie du Pêcheur" ', CMLRev. 34 (1997): 603.

Craig, P. 'Francovich, Remedies and the Scope of Damages Liability'. *L.Q.R.* 109 (1993, Oct): 595.

Curtin, D. 'Directives: The Effectiveness of Judicial Protection of Individual Rights'. *CMLRev.* 27 (1990): 709.

Deards, E. '*Brasserie du Pecheur*: Snatching Defeat from the Jaws of Victory'. *ELRev*. 22(6) (1997).

Drake, S. 'Twenty Years after Von Colson: The Impact of "Indirect Effect" on the Protection of the Individual's Community Rights'. *ELR* 30 (2005): 329.

Dubouis, L. 'La responsabilité de l'État pour les dommages causés aux particuliers par la violation du droit communautaire'. *Rev. fr. dr. adm.* (1992): 1.

Eilmansberger, T. 'The Green Paper on Damages Actions for Breach of the EC Antitrust Rules and Beyond: Reflections on the Utility and Feasibility of Stimulating Private Enforcement through Legislative Action'. *CMLRev* 44 (2007): 431.

Granger, M.P.F. 'National Applications of Francovich and the Construction of a European Administrative Jus Commune'. *ELRev*. 32 (2007): 157.

Green, N. & Barav, A. 'Damages in the National Courts for Breach of Community Law'. *YEL* 55 (1986).

Groussot, X. & Minssen, T. 'Res Judicata in the Court of Justice Case-Law: Balancing Legal Certainty with Legality?'. *ECLRev*. 3 (2007): 385.

Harding, C. 'The Choice of Court Problem in Cases of Non-contractual Liability under EEC Law'. *CMLRev*. 16 (1979): 389.

Harlow, C. 'Francovich and the Problem of the Disobedient State'. *ELJ* 2 (1996): 199.

Hartley, T.C. 'Concurrent Liability in EEC Law: A Critical Review of the Cases'. *ELRev*. 2 (1977): 249.

Hilson, C. 'Role of Discretion in EC Law on Non-contractual Liability'. *CMLRev*. 42 (2005): 677.

Hoskins, M. 'Tilting the Balance: Supremacy and National Procedural Rules', 21 *ELRev*. (1996): 365.

Kakouris, J. 'Do Member States Possess Judicial Procedural Autonomy?'. *CMLRev*. 34 (1997): 1389.

Komninos, A.P. 'New Prospects for Private Enforcement of EC Competition Law: *Courage v. Crehan and the Community Right to Damages*'. *CMLRev*. 39 (2002): 447.

Lee, I.B. 'In Search of a Theory of State Liability in the European Union'. Jean Monnet Working Paper No. 9/99.

Martin Rodriguez, P. 'State Liability for Judicial Acts in European Community Law: The Conceptual Weaknesses of the Functional Approach'. *Columbia Journal of European Law* 11 (2005): 605.

Odudu, O. & Edelman, J. 'Compensatory Damages for Breach of Article 81'. *ELRev*. 27(3) (2002): 327.

Oliver, P. 'Brasserie/Factortame Case Note'. *CMLRev*. 34(3) (1997): 675.

Prechal, S. 'Community Law in National Courts: The Lessons from Van Schijndel'. *CMLRev*. 35 (1998): 681.

Reich, N. 'Horizontal Liability in EC Law: Hybridization of Remedies for Compensation in Case of Breaches of EC Rights'. *CMLRev*. 44 (2007): 707.

Ross, M. 'Effectiveness in the European Legal Order(s): Beyond Supremacy to Constitutional Proportionality?'. *ELRev*. 31 (2006): 474.

Rudden, C. & Bishop, W. 'Gritz and Quellmehl: Pass It On'. *ELRev.* 6 (1981): 243.

Schockweiler, F., Wivenes, G. & Godart, J.M. 'Le regime de la responsabilité extra-contractuelle du fait d'actes juridiques dans la Communauté européenne'. *Revue Trimestrielle de Droit Européen* (1990): 26.

Smith, F. 'Causation in Francovich: The Neglected Problem'. *I.C.L.Q.* 46 (1997): 925.

Stein, E., 'Lawyers, Judges and the Making of a Transnational Constitution', *American Journal of International Law* 75 (1981): 1.

Stein, E., 'Toward Supremacy of Treaty-Constitution by judicial fiat: on the margin of the Costa Case', *Michigan Law Review* 63 (1965): 491.

Steiner, J., 'From Direct Effects to Francovich: Shifting Means of Enforcement of Community Law', *ELRev.* 18, no. 1 (1993): 3.

Szyszczak, E., 'European Community Law: New Remedies, New Directions', *MLR* 55 (1992): 690.

Szyszczak, E., 'Making Europe More Relevant to Its Citizens', *ELR* 21 (1996): 35.

Tatham, A., 'Restitution of Charges and Duties Levied by the Public Administration in Breach of Community Law: A Comparative Analysis', *ELRev.* 19 (1994): 146.

Theodossiou, M., 'An Analysis of the Recent Response of the Community to Non-compliance with Court of Justice Judgments: Art. 288 (2) EC', *ELRev.* 27 (2002): 25.

Thies, A., 'Biret and Beyond: The Status of WTO Rulings in EC Law', *CMLRev.* 41 (2004): 1661-1682.

Tison, M., 'Do Not Attack the Watchdog! Banking Supervisors Liability after Peter Paul', *CMLRev.* 42 (2005): 639.

Tridimas, T., 'Liability for Breach of Community Law: Growing Up and Mellowing Down?', *CMLRev.* 38 (2001).

Tridimas, T., Black, 'White and Shades of Grey: Horizontality of Directives Revisited', *YEL* 21 (2001-2002).

Van Gerven, W., 'Non-contractual Liability of Member States, Community Institutions and Individuals for Breaches of Community Law with a View to a Common Law for Europe', *Maastricht Journal of European and Comparative Law* 1 (1994): 6.

Van Gerven, W., 'Bridging the Unbridgeable: Community and National Tort Laws After Francovich and Brasserie', *I.C.L.Q.* 45 (1996): 507.

Van Gerven, W., Of Rights, Remedies and Procedures, *CMLRev.* 37 (2000): 501.

Vasquez, C., What Is Eleventh Amendment Immunity?,' *Yale Law Journal* 106 (1996-1997): 1683.

Wattel, P.J., 'Köbler, Cilfit and Welthgrove: We Can't Go On Meeting Like This', *CMLRev.* 41 (2004): 177.

Wils, W., 'Concurrent Liability of the Community and a Member State', *ELRev.* 17 (1992): 191.

Zuckerman, A., 'Appeal to the High Court against House of Lords Decisions on the Interpretation of Community Law – Damages for Judicial Error', *CLJ* (2003): 177.

Index

Kluwer European Law Collection

GENERAL EDITIOR

Andrea Biondi

LIST OF PUBLICATIONS IN THIS SERIES

1. E. Guild: *The Legal Elements of European Identity: EU Citizenship and Migration Law*. 2004. ISBN: 9041123040
2. E. Spaventa: *Free Movement of Persons in the European Union: Barriers to Movement in their Constitutional Context*. 2007. ISBN: 9789041124708
3. M. van Empel: *Financial Services in Europe: An Introductory Overview*. 2007. ISBN: 9789041127013
4. A. F. Tatham: *Enlargement of the European Union*. 2009. ISBN: 9789041124630
5. A. Biondi and M. Farley: *The Right to Damages in European Law*. 2009. ISBN: 9789041124760

www.ingramcontent.com/pod-product-compliance
Lightning Source LLC
Chambersburg PA
CBHW071438230926
51846CB00001B/269
9789041124760